RUN LIKE A GIRL

RUN LIKE A GIRL

A Memoir of Ambition, Resilience
and Fighting for Change

CATHERINE McKENNA

Toronto, 2025

Sutherland House
416 Moore Ave., Suite 304
Toronto, ON M4G 1C9
Copyright © 2025 by Catherine McKenna

All rights reserved, including the right to reproduce this book or portions thereof in any form whatsoever. For information on rights and permissions or to request a special discount for bulk purchases, please contact Sutherland House at sutherlandhousebooks@gmail.com.

Sutherland House and logo are registered trademarks of The Sutherland House Inc.

First edition, September 2025

If you are interested in inviting one of our authors to a live event or media appearance, please contact sranasinghe@sutherlandhousebooks.com and visit our website at sutherlandhousebooks.com for more information.

We acknowledge the support of the Government of Canada.
Title: Run like a girl : a memoir of ambition, resilience, and fighting for change / Catherine McKenna.
Names: McKenna, Catherine, author.
Description: First edition. | Includes index.
Identifiers: Canadiana (print) 20250244926 | Canadiana (ebook) 20250244985 | ISBN 9781998365593 (softcover) | ISBN 9781998365876 (EPUB)
Subjects: LCSH: McKenna, Catherine. | LCSH: Cabinet officers–Canada–Biography. | LCSH: Environmental policy–Canada. | CSH: Cabinet ministers–Canada–Biography. | CSH: Canada–Politics and government–2015- | LCGFT: Autobiographies.
Classification: LCC FC656.M35 A3 2025 | DDC 971.07/4092–dc23

Manufactured in Canada
Book design by Kate Hall
Library and Archives Canada Cataloguing in Publication

ISBN 978-1-998365-59-3
eBook 978-1-998365-87-6

For my family

INTRODUCTION

INTRODUCTION

Life is messy.

At different points in my life, I actually thought I had things figured out.

When I was a teenager growing up in Hamilton, Ontario, a hardscrabble steel town, I thought I would be an Olympic swimmer. I made it to the Olympic trials, but that was as far as I got.

When I was in my twenties, I went to law school and thought I'd be a lawyer. I got married and moved to Indonesia, where I managed to get a job at a law firm. Then I moved to Timor-Leste, where I worked for a UN peacekeeping mission, which convinced me that working on things that mattered to me was critical to how I wanted to live my life. But then it was time to move back home to Canada.

When I was in my thirties, I had kids which was amazing, but also very hard. It totally changed my perspective. I quit practicing law to start a charity, thinking I could be a good mom and change the world. But we had a terrible government, so improving the things I cared about—like human rights and Indigenous reconciliation—was next to impossible.

In my forties, I decided to run for public office. We built an amazing team over two years with a hardcore grassroots campaign. Our motto was Run Like a Girl. And I won. I was appointed minister of the environment and climate change and worked hard to bring people together to do big things. While I did a lot that I'm proud of, such as securing a national climate plan, I wish I'd fought back more against the oil and gas industry and the Conservative politicians they sponsored. I was nicknamed Climate Barbie by my haters, a name I really hated. When my family and I received threats, I hated that way more.

Then one day, just over a month before I turned fifty, I decided to leave politics. Before an election in which I would easily have been re-elected, I just got on my bike, went to one of my favourite spots in the riding I represented, and announced I was done. I knew many people would be surprised and wouldn't understand my decision, while others would think I was chased out because of all the attacks. The truth is that while I loved most of my time in politics, I'd promised myself to leave when I'd done what I'd come to do. And it was time to focus on the two things that mattered most to me: my kids and tackling climate change.

Along the way, I got unmarried, then met an incredible guy who has an awesome daughter, and got remarried. And now we're a family of six. I started my own business, created a movement called Women Leading on Climate, and I only work on things I really care about with people I like.

So yes, life is messy. But honestly, I wouldn't have it any other way.

When I try to make sense of everything I've been through, including eight bonkers years in politics, I remember a ground-breaking 1990s Nike ad campaign (designed by women for women) that I cut out from a magazine and put on my dorm wall when I was twenty. I looked at it every single day for years–whenever I felt down, overwhelmed, or uninspired, or was just trying to get through the day. I'm a pack rat, so I went to my basement recently and found clippings of the ad in a box of random things from my life. I loved how it broke down assumptions about what it means to be a woman in sport. It resonated with me and many other female athletes. The lines that hit me the hardest were: "You became significant to yourself. Sooner or later, you start taking yourself seriously. You know when you need a break. You know when you need a rest. You know what to get worked up about and what to get rid of. And you know when it's time to take care of yourself, for yourself. To do something that makes you stronger, faster, more complete. Because you know it's never too late to have a life. And never too late to change one. Just do it."

I know it may seem cheesy or weird that a campaign by a big sports company had such an impact on me. But it did. When I first saw it, it spoke to me. Up to that point, I'd been trying to do everything that was expected of me: be good at school; be good at sports; be a good girl. That was definitely what my dad expected of me, although he also convinced me I could be as good as any boy at anything I wanted to be.

Unlike my mom's generation, girls my age grew up being told we could have it all, but we needed to do all the right things in a way that was acceptable to others. And God knows what having it all even meant. At that point, all I wanted to do was be myself. Whoever that was. Then, it was definitely a swimmer with bad chlorine-bleached hair, constantly falling asleep in class after morning workout. I was tough, fierce, a member of a great team, and not someone who was judged on stupid things I didn't care about, like how I looked or what I wore, but rather on my swim times in the pool.

It's exhausting to have people constantly making assumptions about you. I've talked to so many women and young people that I know I'm not alone in this.

INTRODUCTION

It's an annoying fact of life that much of our time is either living up to the expectations of others or fighting them. Existing in someone else's frame of who you should be, what you should do, and how you should do it. But what if what really matters is what the Nike ad says: the most important thing is "being significant to yourself."

I'm not saying it's easy. It means trying not to care about what others think, going against the grain, dyeing your hair blue or any other colour if that's what you want to do. But I've learned it's only when I focus on what matters to me, what I want to achieve or what I want to get rid of, that I feel strong and empowered, if not always happy. And I love that the ad was both realistic and optimistic, recognizing that some days you wouldn't feel like you could live life the way you wanted, but that didn't mean you were defeated: "Because you know it's never too late to have a life. And never too late to change one." Amen.

Let me be clear about what this book is and what it isn't. It's not about how to live your life. You won't find twelve rules. Nor is it a tidy memoir–I still have several decades to go. Instead, I've tried to represent different moments from my life alongside objects and images that capture what I thought or think. I'm someone who thinks about things much better visually than through writing. Maybe it makes more sense to think of this as a scrapbook you can read from beginning to end or just flip through.

While I think a lot of women my age will relate to my experiences, I really hope some of it will also make sense to young people trying to make a difference in the world. I know how frustrated many of you are because things can seem so screwed up. We are facing massive existential problems like climate change and inequality, and our leaders either don't seem up to the task or are committed to making things worse. You went through a global lockdown and were cheated out of critical years of your lives. And while social media allows you to connect with friends and people around the world with similar interests, brutal algorithms also feed you messages that increase feelings of anxiety and lower your self-esteem. And layered on top of all of that, there's the challenge of just getting through life's ups and downs with pressures from parents, teachers, partners, friends and siblings.

I meet a lot of young people, especially young women, who try to do what I did before I finally worked up the courage to do things my own way. We map out our careers and then figure out how we'll shoehorn our personal lives into that framework. The problem is that life has a way of upending your best-laid plans.

When I was following the career trajectory others had envisioned for me, I didn't

**YOU WERE BORN A DAUGHTER.
YOU LOOKED UP TO YOUR MOTHER.
YOU LOOKED UP TO YOUR FATHER.**

**YOU LOOKED UP AT EVERYONE.
YOU WANTED TO BE A PRINCESS.
YOU THOUGHT YOU WERE A PRINCESS.**

YOU WANTED TO OWN A HORSE.
YOU WANTED TO BE A HORSE.
YOU WANTED YOUR BROTHER TO BE A HORSE.
YOU WANTED TO WEAR PINK.
YOU NEVER WANTED TO WEAR PINK.

YOU WANTED TO BE A VETERINARIAN.
YOU WANTED TO BE PRESIDENT.
YOU WANTED TO BE THE PRESIDENT'S VETERINARIAN.
YOU WERE PICKED LAST FOR THE TEAM.
YOU WERE THE BEST ONE ON THE TEAM.
YOU REFUSED TO BE ON THE TEAM.

YOU WANTED TO BE GOOD IN ALGEBRA.
YOU HID DURING ALGEBRA.
YOU WANTED THE BOYS TO NOTICE YOU.
YOU WERE AFRAID THE BOYS WOULD NOTICE YOU.
YOU STARTED TO GET ACNE.
YOU STARTED TO GET BREASTS.
YOU STARTED TO GET ACNE THAT WAS BIGGER THAN YOUR BREASTS.
YOU WOULDN'T WEAR A BRA.
YOU COULDN'T WAIT TO WEAR A BRA.
YOU COULDN'T FIT INTO A BRA.

YOU DIDN'T LIKE THE WAY YOU LOOKED.
YOU DIDN'T LIKE THE WAY YOUR PARENTS LOOKED.
YOU DIDN'T WANT TO GROW UP.

YOU HAD YOUR FIRST BEST FRIEND.
YOU HAD YOUR FIRST DATE.
YOU HAD YOUR SECOND BEST FRIEND.
YOU HAD YOUR SECOND FIRST DATE.
YOU SPENT HOURS ON THE TELEPHONE.
YOU GOT KISSED.
YOU GOT TO KISS BACK.
YOU WENT TO THE PROM.

YOU DIDN'T GO TO THE PROM.
YOU WENT TO THE PROM WITH THE WRONG PERSON.
YOU SPENT HOURS ON THE TELEPHONE.
YOU FELL IN LOVE.
YOU FELL IN LOVE.
YOU FELL IN LOVE.
YOU LOST YOUR BEST FRIEND.
YOU LOST YOUR OTHER BEST FRIEND.
YOU REALLY FELL IN LOVE.
YOU BECAME A STEADY GIRLFRIEND.
YOU BECAME A SIGNIFICANT OTHER.

Sooner or later, you start taking yourself seriously.
You know when you need a break. You know
when you need a rest. You know what to get worked
up about, and what to get rid of.

And you know when it's time to take care
of yourself, for yourself. To do something that makes
you stronger, faster, more complete.
Because you know it's never too late to have a life.
And never too late to change one.

Just do it.

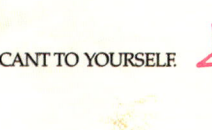

YOU BECAME SIGNIFICANT TO YOURSELF.

Nike print ad from the 90s that I ripped out of a magazine and taped to my dorm wall.

consider a lot of things that would have a huge impact on the course of my life. Things like the fact that I might define success differently at different stages of my life. That my perspective might shift after having kids. That I might have to move for a partner's job or make choices to be close to aging parents. It didn't occur to me that I might get sick or burn out or just want to take a break or do something totally different. Or that a connection from one part of my life would lead to a connection from another, and amazing opportunities I couldn't possibly have imagined would suddenly appear, and I'd have to throw out my carefully constructed playbook and jump. None of this meant I couldn't get where I wanted to go; it just meant my path would take a lot of unexpected twists and turns. Or I might decide to head in a different direction altogether.

Throughout this journey, I realized that things went way better—and I was way happier and accomplished a lot more of what mattered to me—when I did things my own way. No one can tell you how to do that. You need to figure it out yourself. Like my dad always said to me, "hard things are hard." But just keep going. And don't forget to live life and have fun with people you love while you're doing it. Otherwise, the hard days will seem impossible.

Deciding to run my own race wasn't easy. Far from it. I had to navigate a steep learning curve. First, I had to learn to stop holding myself to impossibly high standards (that they were usually someone else's didn't make casting them off any easier). I had to develop the confidence to be true to myself, which involved mustering the willingness and strength to confound other people's expectations. I had to learn when to follow the rules and when to toss them and write my own. Above all, I had to become comfortable with risk. When my inner voice was telling me I had to make a change, I had to listen, surrender to it, and seize the moment. I also had to remain flexible, practical and grounded in my decision-making. And when I couldn't see the path in front of me, I had to create one myself.

Running the race your own way isn't just hard and messy. It's also scary. Choosing to flout conventional wisdom and chart your own course in life is a risky choice for anyone to make. And still, we need to be real. Faking it and trying to meet the expectations of others is no way to live a life or make a difference. You need to have confidence in yourself, your voice and in whatever you believe matters. I haven't figured out much—only that this is the way to try to live your life and how we can start to live up to the challenges we face. Gord Downie of the Tragically Hip knew this when he sang: "No dress rehearsal. This is our life."

INTRODUCTION

If there is a message in this book, it is about running like a girl. It is about empowering women and girls around the world to speak up and step up even when—especially when—it's hard. We need our voices more than ever. To fight for women's rights and for human rights because they are under threat globally. To tackle the accelerating climate crisis, which is hurting the poorest and most vulnerable the most. While it can seem lonely, women are pushing for more ambitious climate action in cabinet rooms, in boardrooms, in our communities and in the streets. In this critical time, we need to raise our voices even more. We've seen the power of women. When we come together, we go further, faster.

So let's do it.

A LITTLE ABOUT ME

MY FATHER

My dad was a character. Larger than life, with a huge heart, a wicked sense of humour and Irish charm. But to really understand my dad, you need to know about his upbringing in Ireland.

My dad's father, Patrick Joseph "PJ" McKenna, was born in 1894 in Dungiven, a small town in the north of Ireland. He was the eldest of six children in an Irish Catholic family. Dungiven was a mixed community of Catholics and Protestants, and tension between the two groups always simmered just beneath the surface.

Patrick studied accountancy in Belfast before going on to work as a clerk and publican. In February 1921, at twenty-seven, Patrick joined the Irish Volunteers to fight for Ireland's independence. He felt it was time for him to step up. Patrick rarely spoke about this time in his life or the brutal and painful civil war that followed, but one thing he did share with his family was his pride in being part of the revolutionary movement led by Michael Collins, a brilliant strategist and leader of the armed resistance against the British forces. Patrick never applied for a military service pension from the Irish Volunteers, telling his family he hadn't fought for a reward and that he had not done enough to warrant one.

After Ireland's independence, Patrick joined the new Free State Army. Five years later, he was the officer in charge of the barracks in Athlone, a town in central Ireland. It was there he met my grandmother, Mary Dolan. Mary was the fourth of eight children from a modest but well-educated Catholic family from Athlone. She and two of her sisters were educated at the National University of Ireland, which was highly unusual for women at the time. Their family valued education for both their sons and daughters. She also had two sisters who were nuns and two brothers who were priests. Patrick and Mary married shortly after they met.

By the time my dad was born in 1938, my grandparents were living in Collins Army Barracks, Dublin, where my grandfather oversaw Arbour Hill Prison. My granny and grandfather already had a busy household with four boys running around: Dermot, Kieran, Pádraig and Gearóid. And when Granny got pregnant again, she was, understandably, hoping for a girl. But out came not one but two boys—my dad and his beloved twin, Tom, born one hour before him.

My Granny already had four boys and out came the twins, including my Dad. The poor woman!

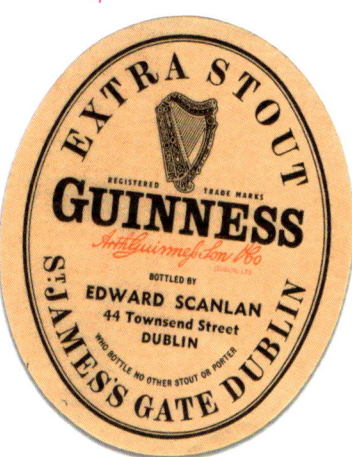

My Dad playing for the London Irish Rugby Club. He was a wing forward. He took rugby very seriously!

My grandfather retired from the army in 1946. With six sons in school, he needed to find new employment. So in his early fifties, he began his second career. He bought a pub on Townsend Street, a busy port area in Dublin. It was called McKennas. Pubs like this were known as "early houses," because they opened at 6:30 a.m. to dockers who had been unloading boats all night. They attracted all sorts. As one of my uncles said about his father, "He had balls!" The family lived on top of the pub, and my grandmother was notorious for saying, "We may be from Townsend Street, but we are not of it." She meant her children were going to study hard and work hard in order to find their way out to a better life. She loved her boys with all her might, but she was tough–she had to be with all those boys.

My dad and his brothers went to O'Connell School, where they were educated by the Congregation of Christian Brothers, known for its strict discipline. He spent his free time playing Gaelic football and hurling during the school year and swimming with his brother Tom in the summers at Blackrock Baths. He also helped out at the family pub where he and his brothers spent many hours hauling kegs of Guinness into the dank, cramped cellar where they bottled the beer.

Education was a top priority in the McKenna household. At the time, university was largely reserved for the wealthy, but my grandparents made sacrifices to send their eldest sons to university, with the expectation that they in turn would help to pay for their younger brothers' education. My father studied dentistry at University College Dublin, graduating at the top of his class (a fact he never let us forget). He also captained the university's rugby team. My granny once said, "John was an aggressive young man, though very good natured. I hated going to the rugby matches because John always seemed to be the fellow on the ground with ten over him getting their back on him."

In the early 1960s, my father moved to London to practise dentistry and play for the London Irish Rugby Club. He was a fearless wing forward and earned a reputation for playing both sides of the scrum with equal flair. After a few years, he left London for Canada to join his brother who had moved there and to further his dental studies at the University of Toronto. He, of course, also played rugby, including earning a cap for representing Canada in a match against England. It was then that he met my mom.

MY MOTHER

My mom was born in Val-d'Or, Quebec, in 1946, the eldest of three girls. Her father, Alan Hopper, was a quiet, reserved Protestant from Cookstown, Ontario. Her mother, Mary Cushing, came from a lively Catholic family in the Ottawa Valley.

My grandfather studied mining engineering at the University of Toronto and worked at mines in northern Ontario. Eventually, he moved to Val-d'Or, which means "valley of gold." Val-d'Or is in the Abitibi region of Quebec, one of the most important mining areas in Canada. There, he met my grandmother, who was teaching at a Catholic school, and they married in 1944. They started their life in a log cabin in Bourlamaque, a small mining townsite. My grandfather rose through the ranks and became the mine superintendent and later manager of Golden Manitou Mines. My mom and her sisters grew up in a small, close-knit and largely anglophone community located right beside the mine.

In 2024, my mom and I took a road trip to Val-d'Or. It was fascinating to hear her describe her childhood: picking blueberries in the summer, tobogganing and skating on the rink in winter. She recalled walking to the mine's canteen to buy sweets. When she was twelve, her father finally bought a TV, and she could watch shows like Bonanza. When she grew up there were many anglophones; when we visited, the town was almost entirely French.

Although my mom's family loved their life in Val-d'Or, the 1960s was a decade that brought change. The Quiet Revolution reshaped Quebec. Quebecers demanded more control over their affairs–to be "maîtres chez nous" (masters in our own house). This movement challenged the anglophone dominance in industries like mining, where most management positions were held by English speakers from outside Quebec.

My grandfather found himself at the heart of this cultural and political shift. Though his roots in the mining industry went back decades, he was at ground zero of what would become Quebec's Quiet Revolution. My mom remembers it being a difficult time. She recalls that the only time she ever saw her father smoke was after a tense meeting with René Lévesque, then-minister of natural resources and later premier of Quebec. Levesque would become the champion of Quebec sovereignty

My mother (far left) around age 18 with her parents, her younger sisters Margaret and Carole, and their dog, Skippy. Taken at their house in Nenagh, Ireland

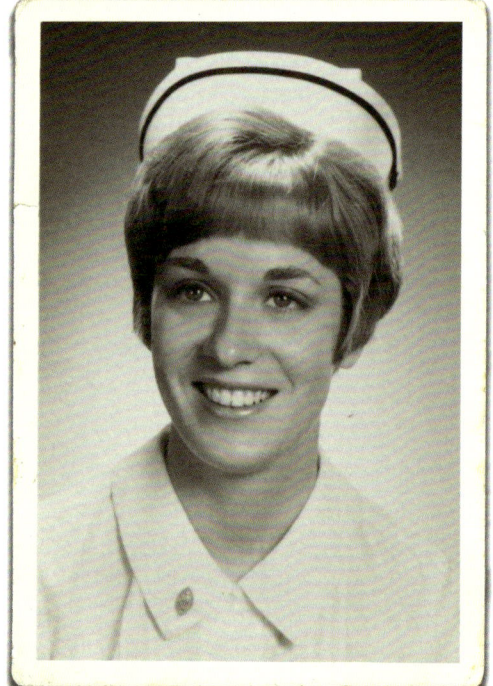

My mom with my grandmother at the Manitou townsite.

and he was determined to end English control of Quebec's resources. In 1964, after striking miners surrounded my grandmother's car, my grandfather decided it was time to leave. He took a job managing a Canadian-owned mine in Silvermines, County Tipperary (just outside of Nenagh in Ireland). He hoped the change would offer a fresh start.

When my mom and I visited Nenagh in 2023, we learned something unexpected. My grandfather had been the manager when the IRA bombed the Mogul mine in July 1971. The explosion was so powerful it was heard across the valley. Workers at the Mogul mine had been on strike for two and a half months. An IRA operative, sympathetic to the workers, took several hostages and planted explosives at the mine's electrical transformer. One worker was killed. It's hard to imagine what my grandfather must have felt having moved his family for the promise of a quieter life. He never spoke about it to my mother, who was eight months pregnant with me at the time.

My mom had just finished high school when her parents moved to Nenagh, so she helped them settle in and then moved to Dublin for a bit of an adventure, taking some courses at University College Dublin. She then returned to Canada to study nursing at the University of Toronto. She might look innocent in her nursing uniform, but as she tells it, she was secretly smoking in her dormitory room and sneaking in after curfew with her friends. Fortunately, she was no shrinking violet when she met my father.

IRISH-CANADIAN WEDDING

One day in 1967, my mom called her dentist's office to make an appointment. She was told: "Your dentist isn't around, but there's this young Irish guy filling in. Do you want to see him?" She said sure. It was my dad.

My mom says that it was clear right away that my dad took an interest in her. There was her Irish connection. He liked her sense of humour. And, as my dad tells it, "She was a looker." My mom had met his type before: handsome with a lot of swagger and tall tales, but what was different was the twinkle in his eye. And though he was very much one of the boys, she could also see he could be a real gentleman.

Dad did eventually ask her out, but strangely, never on weekends. She thought, "I guess he's got more important dates." In fact, Dad never went out Friday nights because he wanted to rest up for his rugby games on Saturday. On Saturday nights, after their matches, he didn't want her to see him and his rugby friends after a fair number of pints. Eventually, he decided that she was up for it and that he wanted to marry her. He always said that he was the luckiest man in the world to have found her.

They were married in Ireland in December 1969, a wedding that received prominent coverage in the local Guardian paper as an "Irish-Canadian wedding." By that time, my dad was working as a dentist in Hamilton, and my mom was a member of the teaching staff of St. Joseph's Hospital in Hamilton as well. Soon afterward, they bought a house nearby where my mother still lives over fifty years later. That's where they made their life and raised the four of us: me, the eldest, Sean, Maureen and David.

Right: My Mom and Dad were married in the Church of our Lady of Lourdes in Silvermines, County Tipperary, Ireland on December 30, 1969.

GROWING UP WILD

Growing up, we ran wild in the ravine and woods behind our house. There was no such thing as playdates—my parents would have found the idea hilarious. "Your whole day is a playdate," they'd have said. My friends and I built forts, played capture the flag and fished for weeds in the creek, leaving them in jars until they smelled awful—perfect for throwing at the older kids who wrecked our forts. It's ironic I was later called Climate Barbie because my mom never let me play with Barbies. I was busy doing other things, so I didn't care.

This disgusting jar of weeds from the creek was perfect for throwing at the older, bad kids.

Me in Madame Kelday's grade 2 class with not only an embarrassing bowl cut by my mom, she curled my bangs for picture day!

ÉCOLE NOTRE-DAME

We took a bus to our French Catholic grade school, École Notre-Dame. It was halfway across the city by Gage Park, and the ride took about forty-five minutes. We could have gone to the French immersion school around the corner, but my parents believed that being in a fully francophone school would mean we would speak better French. They both thought that was important. That Notre-Dame was also a Catholic school was the clincher.

I even had the "privilege" of being a bus patrol on the bus around Grade 6. That meant I wore an orange fluorescent belt that went around my waist and across my chest. I was tasked with trying to keep the other kids from misbehaving. Our bus, *autobus bleu*, had a lot of rowdy older boys who didn't pay any attention to me, which made it a challenge. I took the job seriously and meticulously wrote up offences for our principal, Jacques Girard. They ranged from throwing projectiles, pushing, standing, and the use of *language vulgaire*. I would even write down the actual words used! At least once a week, Monsieur Girard would announce on the school sound system that everyone on *autobus bleu* had to immediately come down to the gym. Everyone would file in quietly and the offences would be read out. We would be told the behaviour was unacceptable and would not be tolerated. But nothing changed. My siblings still tease me and call me the narc.

We spoke French all day long at school, even in the playground. We weren't even taught English until Grade 4. And while my friends in English school learned Louis Riel was a traitor, we were taught he was a hero.

me with our cat, Velvet.

My school wasn't fancy. It had no grass or play structures in the yard—just cement. Like thousands of other Canadian kids, we'd play physical games like dodgeball and British bulldog. I managed to break my arm when I slid on ice into the school wall to avoid being tagged. In winter, we would climb the huge mounds of snow piled in the parking lot and slide down.

I had a good group of friends, but I was especially close to my best friend, Joan. She was quiet and shy and the smartest person in our class. Her mother was from Quebec, so she was fluent in French when we started school. I was always trying to keep up with her perfect marks in French *orthographe et grammaire*. I would sleep over at Joan's all the time. I loved going to her house because it was so quiet and tidy compared to mine. We would hang out doing crazy art projects while her mom played Nana Mouskouri. We also read lots—everything from Comtesse de Ségur to Anne Hébert's *Les Fleurs du Mal*. We were pretty nerdy. We could not have cared less.

It was only when I was near graduating in Grade 8 that I recognized how tough life was for many of the kids who came to École Notre-Dame. One kid came to school with bruises all over and fought any kids that joked about it. Another showed up with dirty clothes and kids made fun of him. Other kids showed up with almost nothing in their lunchboxes, so we shared our food.

I'm glad my parents sent me to École Notre-Dame. I learned to speak French well with a decent accent, which came in handy later in life. But I also learned that not everyone had it as good as I did, or my comfortably middle-class neighbours. It wasn't their fault—life just wasn't fair.

 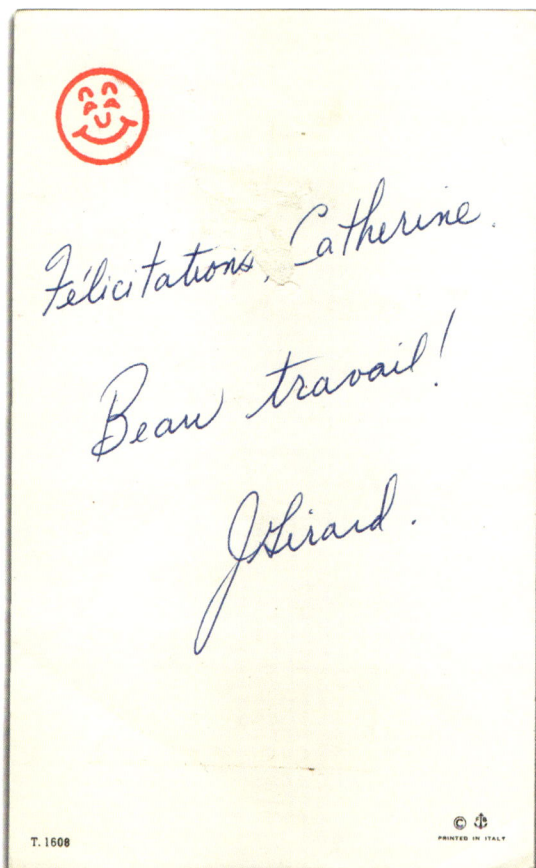

A religious card of the Virgin Mary that was given to me for doing well on an assignment by our principal at École Notre-Dame, Jacques Girard.

MY PRAYER CORNER

I have a complicated relationship with the Catholic Church. Although it didn't start off complicated. We were Irish Catholic, so we went to church on Sundays. That's just what you did. And there was no way out of it unless I had a swim meet. We'd often have the local priest over to the house for Sunday dinner. I think the priests loved it because they got a good roast beef dinner and a few glasses of red wine, and there was no discussion of God or sin or any expectation of advice.

École Notre-Dame had several Soeurs Grises as teachers, so that was where we got our heavy dose of Catholicism. I was even in the church choir for a while, though I was in the group of singers who they told to just mouth the words. I would go to confession there too. It was a big deal. You'd have to wait in a long line where you were supposed to be quiet but instead did your best to make your friends laugh. We also figured out what we should each say at confession. At age twelve, there really wasn't exactly a lot of variation. We would each go into the small confessional booth with a priest on the other side of the screen who you could barely make out and confess. "*Mon père, pardonnez-moi. J'étais méchante avec mon frère. J'ai menti. Je n'ai pas fait mes devoirs.*" Then we'd be told we were forgiven and to say a few Hail Marys or Our Fathers. We'd say them as fast as we could and then keep chatting with our friends until our teachers gave us the evil eye.

I even had a prayer corner in my room in Grade 3. That year I was taught by Soeur Monique. I really liked her even though she was very strict. When you did well in class, she would give you a religious card as a reward. I was expected to do well at school—in truth, my dad expected me to be better than that—so I worked hard to get a lot of cards. It was Soeur Monique's idea to make a prayer corner. I put my cards in my prayer corner with a rosary and a candle. Every once in a while, I would kneel and pray and, truthfully, it felt good. My relationship with the Catholic Church was uncomplicated then. But that couldn't last.

It was always a race to be the first in. I liked to win!

With my Dad at the beach.

CHASING WATER

My family is obsessed with water. As kids, we'd occasionally travel to the coast of Ireland in the summer to visit our Irish cousins and swim in the freezing Atlantic Ocean with my dad yelling, "Get in! It's tropical!" We took road trips to Florida, escaping our cramped car to dive into the ocean. At home, our backyard pool made us the cool house that other kids wanted to come to. Now, we swim together whenever we can—at cottages, backyard pools, even in the frigid Irish Sea at the historic "Forty Foot" swimming spot in Dublin. The water is where we can all be together and just have fun.

At Rossbeigh beach (on the Ring of Kerry, Ireland) with my Dad, my uncle Gearóid and my brother Sean. Water was freezing!

RUNNING LIKE A GIRL

> "My coach said I run like a girl, and I said if he could run a little faster, he could too."
>
> — Mia Hamm, American soccer player and two-time Olympic gold medallist

When I was nine, I played soccer for the Kirkendall soccer league at the reservoir near my house in Hamilton. It wasn't like organized soccer for kids nowadays. We wore our crappy, everyday running shoes, any shorts we could find, and an ugly Kirkendall T-shirt with a local sponsor's name on it. And it was co-ed. More boys than girls, but we all played together. My dad was the coach.

I loved it. I loved racing down the field after the soccer ball. I loved being in the middle of things when we all pushed each other over to get the ball. I loved trying to score. And of course, I loved scoring.

But the reality is the boys dominated. Not because they were better. They were just louder and travelled in a pack. And some of these boys didn't like girls like me—girls who didn't really think about the fact that they were girls. Girls who were just part of the team. Girls who loved the rush of the game. Girls who played hard to win.

One day, one of the boys on my team who seemed to really hate me hurled the ultimate insult—he told me I ran like a girl. I ran like a girl?! I knew what he was saying: I wasn't as good as the boys. I wasn't as tough as them. I didn't fit in. I should just get lost.

It's funny looking back on how that experience affected me. I decided from then on that to succeed, I needed to be just like the boys. I needed to be as hardcore. I needed to be part of the pack. I needed to fit in. I needed to run like a boy.

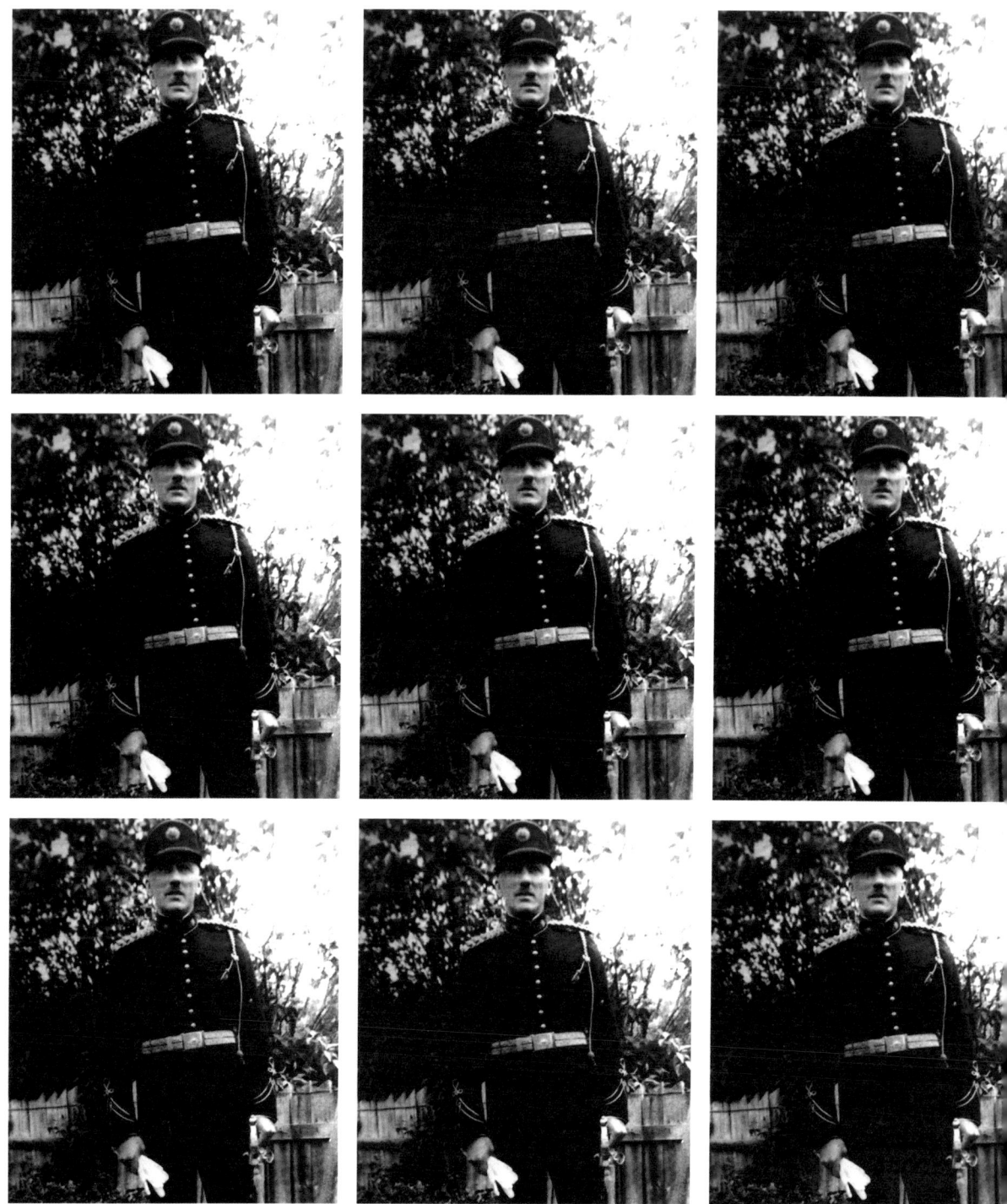

My grandfather, Commandant Patrick Joseph McKenna, Irish Army (2224), 1894-1969.

DAD'S VIEW OF POLITICS

When you're Irish, politics is never far from the surface of any conversation.

My dad could talk to anyone about anything—and usually did. In fact, he often waited until his patients' mouths were stuffed with cotton swabs or rubber dams and they were, therefore, powerless to respond, and then he'd impart his political views, of which he had many—all of them pointed, fiercely held, and shaped by his Irish upbringing and experience as an immigrant to Canada. He revered politics because he'd seen it serve as the source of so many profound changes in his homeland. Of course, the Irish had to fight for their freedom, but politicians played a crucial role in achieving independence, and my father never forgot that.

 As a result, political awareness, discussion and debate were just in the water when I was growing up. After emigrating to Canada, my father wasted no time informing himself about the political issues of the day and becoming a model citizen in his newly adopted country. He was forever emailing journalists to congratulate or castigate them for their takes on this or that issue. CBC Radio was on around the clock and piles of newspapers and magazines could be found throughout the house—not just The Globe and Mail, Hamilton Spectator and Maclean's, but also The Irish Times and many other newspapers and magazines, from Canada and abroad. Wednesday nights, after he picked us kids up from swimming, he stopped at a variety store on "the mountain" to load up with an armful of newspapers, while we each got to buy a Mars bar. (In Hamilton, "the mountain," where the Niagara Escarpment creates a natural 100-metre elevation above the lower city, is a defining feature of the landscape.)

 Politically, my dad was an old-school Pierre Elliott Trudeau Liberal. Trudeau became the prime minister soon after my father arrived in Canada, and my father embraced him and his politics fully. Having grown up in a country where the Irish had been oppressed for centuries, where religion divided families and communities and language was critical to their identity, Dad was a staunch supporter of Trudeau's views on multiculturalism. He enthusiastically endorsed the need for different cultures to find ways to coexist peacefully.

As deeply as he loved Ireland, he was an enormously proud Canadian. He appreciated the country in a way that sometimes only immigrants truly can. Canada welcomed him and provided opportunities when it was challenging to find a good job in his homeland despite many years of education and training. But he also worried that Canadians didn't realize how fortunate they were to live in a bilingual country that welcomed immigrants, whatever their background, and protected individual rights and freedoms.

He talked often about Ireland to all of his kids and grandkids. He told them stories about Irish independence and the importance of fighting for your rights, of course. But he also spoke about the potato famine, when the British cruelly starved the Irish people. And about the sad scene at the airport when he left Dublin, which was packed with tearful parents saying goodbye to their kids, who had to leave the country because there was no future for them there.

That experience indelibly marked him, and not just because it made him forever aware that politics matter. It gave him a lifelong empathy for the underdog. He knew firsthand what could happen to people who lacked political power. Anti-elitist to the core, he always stood up for the little guy, explaining that the Irish are deeply sympathetic to underdogs because they had been one for so long when the English occupied their country. I think that's one of the reasons he loved Hamilton so much. It was the underdog compared to Toronto, maybe a bit run-down, but with a fierce and proud spirit. Dad was constantly taking friends that were visiting for walks along Hamilton's waterfront or in the Royal Botanical Gardens to show off the best sides of the city.

He also constantly reminded us that the steel mills and the large smokestacks that Torontonians often made fun of for spewing pollution into the air (thankfully now being cleaned up) meant jobs, more houses and full bellies. If the steel industry packed up and left, Hamilton would have even less. And he reminded us that without the unions that represented steelworkers and fought for their rights, many of his patients wouldn't have dental benefits. We got it. Dental benefits not only supported the ability of workers to afford dental care, we as a family also depended on those mills too.

Dad hated economic inequality. Since I was a kid, I remember him always railing about how unfair it was that CEOs made so much more money than their employees. He often sent long emails to journalists at The Globe and Mail and other media outlets either deriding them or congratulating them for their stance on CEO compensation. When he died, I found an email he wrote to Steve Paikin, a famous Canadian journalist from Hamilton: "Another good topic for you is the excessive compensation of CEOs in this day and age. EXECUTIVE PAY HAS GOT TOTALLY OUT OF HAND. The CEO of an average large public company earned about 20 times as much as a front line worker in 1965–today that figure is 275 times higher. WHY?"

We also followed Canadian politics closely. In 1985, when I was in my early teens, I vividly remember watching TV with my dad when Canadian Prime Minister Mulroney and US President Ronald Reagan met in Quebec City. The meeting, which began on St. Patrick's Day, was dubbed "The Shamrock Summit" because the two leaders boasted Irish heritage and sang "When Irish Eyes Are Smiling" for the cameras.

My dad and I thought the whole thing was hilarious. First, we weren't fans of Mulroney or his politics. Second, we didn't really consider him Irish, since he came from Baie-Comeau, Quebec which in my dad's eyes didn't count. But, in a way, I think my dad also loved that cheesy moment because whether or not Mulroney had enough Irish street cred in his eyes, Mulroney was celebrating Ireland and its heritage, a country my Dad loved and missed.

A few years later, in November 1988, we watched the free trade debate between Mulroney and Liberal leader, John Turner. It was the mother of all election debates. My entire family was glued to the TV. Mulroney had been against free trade in the 1984 election, but at the Shamrock Summit, he and Reagan agreed to begin negotiations on a comprehensive trade agreement, which eventually led to the Canada-U.S. Free Trade Agreement of 1988. It ultimately laid the groundwork for the North American Free Trade Agreement (NAFTA) that also included Mexico.

My dad was vehemently opposed to free trade because he thought Canadian workers would wind up losing their jobs to Americans or Mexicans. During an intense, impassioned exchange during the debate, we cheered when Turner famously said, "I happen to believe that you sold us out!"

Unlike many dentists, he loved his job. As for his patients, I'm not sure how many people really like their dentists, but they sure liked my Dad. He was kind, funny and could talk about anything. I worked at his office for a few summers and would often find him singing Irish ballads or reciting Yeats to his patients or pointing at the globe in his office saying, "Where's Bosnia?" (or whatever country was being mentioned on the CBC News playing in the background).

I'll never forget my high school friends telling me that when they went to the dentist to see my Dad, he'd inevitably point to a picture of me and say: "That's my daughter. She's not that smart or attractive but if you find her a date to prom, I'll give you 100 bucks and throw in a limo." They thought it was hilarious but I could also tell by the looks on their faces when they retold the story to me that they were thinking: "What kind of father says that about his daughter?" That was his sense of humour. And we learned to take it. (He also screamed "Don't do it" out of the window of our station wagon whenever we drove by a wedding party outside of church. We kids would all duck.)

When my Dad passed away in 2023, I read over the many messages he received when he retired. They're classic:

"Thanks for calling me handsome even when I wasn't. Also thanks for fixing my front teeth like 20 times. It helped me when trying to meet my wife."

"How to replace you? Can't be done. I am going to miss your raising a controversial subject matter only once my mouth went numb."

MY FAMILY

When you come from a big family, especially an Irish Catholic one, you can't really get away from it. As my Mom said, "family first" but she might as well have said "family always." And while some of the stereotypes about sibling birth order ring true, when you're just one of the kids, the most relevant thing is the age gap.

So there is me, the eldest, definitely bossy, organizing and setting the rules for most of the games we played, but also the first to defend my siblings against my parents, our teachers and other kids. My brother Sean, the easy-going middle child, who never rushes but is always around to hang out and have fun. My sister, Maureen, the angelic-looking but subversive middle child with an independent streak (who adamantly refused to smile for any family or school picture or eat our breakfast porridge) who cracks the funniest jokes and has a heart of gold. And then my brother, David, the youngest who is smart, sensitive, always game to join in and who remembers the details that no one else notices.

Some of my favourite memories are from our Sunday family dinners which, to be clear, were never optional (except when those "bloody swim meets" happened). My dad held court and liked to stir things up. He'd pick a topic, and no matter which side he took, we were expected to argue the opposite. He expected us to have views. There were always multiple conversations going on at dinnertime. It was noisy, messy and practically pandemonium. He loved it. My mom was the peacemaker, laughing or rolling her eyes. No wonder Question Period in the House of Commons felt so familiar.

My tenth birthday celebrated with the family

My Dad with my Granny and her friend (visiting from Ireland) with my siblings.

Band Aid, 'Do they Know It's Christmas' LP Record, 1984.

WHAT KEPT ME UP AT NIGHT

I've always been a worrier—something I get from my mom. When I was babysitting my siblings, I'd stare through the screen in my bedroom window, desperately waiting for our parents' wood-panelled white Chevrolet Caprice station wagon (with the awesome third row of seats facing rearward) to pull into the driveway. I'd convince myself they'd been in a crash and we'd have to move to Ireland to live with our Irish cousins. Inevitably, they'd come home fine and I'd be absolutely relieved, but furious at them for being late.

I also worried about big things. When the hit song "Do They Know It's Christmas?" came out in 1984, the video with images of starving children floored me. I couldn't understand why governments weren't stopping the Ethiopian famine. Surely we had enough food in the world for all these children and their families. I was starting to realize that I cared about what happened in other parts of the world and that I wanted to help. Like a lot of people, I had absolutely no idea how.

SWIMMING

I loved swimming, but it wasn't until I was around eleven that I started swimming competitively with the Hamilton-Wentworth Aquatic Club. I loved it. All the practices. But especially the thrill of competing. I loved getting onto the blocks and racing for ribbons. I kept all my ribbons with my times listed in a photo album. Before I knew it, I went from swimming a few times a week to nine or ten practices at pools all across Hamilton, early in the morning and again after school. It took up most of my free time, but I thought it was great.

Many of my friends quit swimming because their parents put a lot of pressure on them to excel at it. My parents were the absolute opposite. My dad only came to swim meets if there was no other way for me to get there, and then he would hide in the back and read his newspapers. I would find him and say hi. "Great swim!" he'd say. "I haven't swum yet!" I'd say. "You all look the same in your swimming togs," he would answer and go back to reading the Irish Times. The only thing my parents insisted on was that swimming not get in the way of schoolwork. When I first qualified for nationals my dad said I couldn't go because I would miss school, which was infuriating since I had straight As. Eventually, though, he relented.

In high school, I trained at the McMaster University swimming pool. My school, St. Mary's, was on the university campus, so I'd swim in the morning at 6 a.m., go to school, then walk back and train with the McMaster swim team after school. Then I'd go home, eat dinner, do my homework and go to bed.

Swimming left me exhausted. I'd fall asleep in class, so my notes would have these places where the pen trailed off because my hand had just dropped. But it also kept me out of trouble. You don't have a lot of free time, and you're always tired from training, so you don't party a lot. But I would sometimes go out with my friends on a Saturday night because there was no practice until Sunday afternoon. I'd be with my best friend Kelly and a group of other St. Mary's girls that I hung out with. We'd often catch up with the boys from Westdale High School. We'd tell our parents we were going to the local church dance–technically true–but what they didn't know was that we'd first go to a park where we'd gulp down whatever alcohol we'd dug up from our houses then cram into a dark church basement and dance the night away to the Smiths, New Order, Violent Femmes and the English Beat.

But most of the time, I was in my own little bubble with other swimmers. We all had silvery hair from the chlorine in the water. And even though there were faint smells of Finesse shampoo for the girls and some cheap cologne for the boys, we mostly smelled like chlorine.

We also had weird rituals, like shaving down our bodies before a big meet–legs, arms, even the invisible hair on our backs. We wore bathing suits that were five sizes too small to be as hydrodynamic as possible. But we were part of this group, and our identities were tied to swimming, so it all seemed normal.

The one thing about swimming that thankfully has changed was the focus on weight and body fat. All of us were weighed on deck in front of everyone else, and then someone took your fat measurements with a caliper. The results were posted on the bulletin board for everyone to see. Our coach would tell some girls they were too fat to be good swimmers and had to lose weight. Not only was it demoralizing and humiliating, it actually motivated many to quit.

Everything about swimming was hardcore: our practices were so intense I'd often feel like vomiting after. I'd always be asking myself if I was working out hard enough, if I was committed enough, if I was doing everything I needed to do.

And the reality is that sometimes doubt would creep in. Deep down you would think maybe you hadn't trained hard enough or that you'd put on too much weight or some other girl was faster than you.

You had to fight against it. Doubting yourself is fatal. When you get up on the blocks before a race, you have to believe. You have to trust your training and believe you're about to swim your best race ever.

To prepare for races, I would lie on my bed surrounded by motivational pictures and posters, and I would write down the times I wanted to achieve and picture myself beating them. Using a stopwatch, I'd go over my entire race in my head–swinging my arms before getting on the blocks, splashing water on my face, adjusting my goggles, launching into the water, executing every stroke and turn. I'd see myself feeling strong in the final lap, touching the wall, winning.

One of the benefits of having a routine like that is that it's calming. You're stressed before a race. The first time I was at Nationals, the stress was excruciating. My heart was beating fast. I went to the washroom at least five times, and I would already be wondering if I needed to go again. Having a routine helps you calm down and know what you need to do next. You've done it so many times before, so if you just focus on doing that next thing at a deliberate pace, you'll be fine.

The practice of visualization was also helpful when I started in politics. Sometimes I had to give high-profile speeches or go out in front of a whole bunch of cameras and talk about something I'd rather not have to talk about. I'd picture myself walking out, being calm, and I'd imagine exactly what I'd say and how it was going to go. And then I'd just do it.

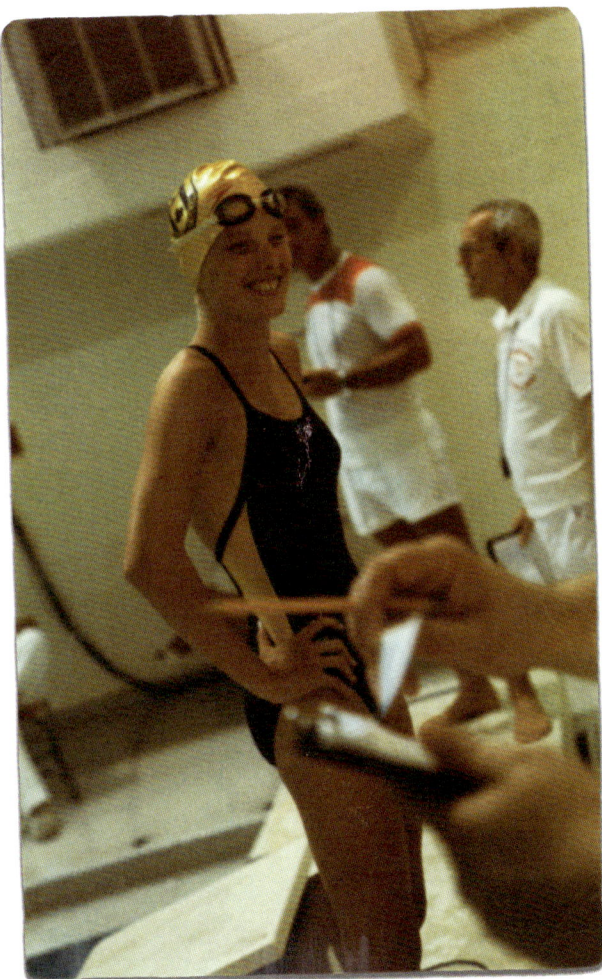

Wearing Hamilton Wentworth Aquatic Club colours and cap (HWAC).

DREAMING BIG

My heroes! I wanted to be just like these olympic swimmers — Victor Davis, Mark Tewksbury, Sandy Goss, Tom Ponting who won silver at 1988 Olympic games in Seoul. (This was also taped to my wall.)

People always ask me, "Did you want to be a politician when you were growing up?" No, "I wanted to go to the Olympics." That's all I wanted to do when I was young. And what I worked for every single day.

I vividly remember watching the 1984 Summer Olympics in Los Angeles: Alex Baumann breaking world records while winning golds in the 200- and 400-metre individual medley races, and Victor Davis and Anne Ottenbrite winning gold medals in their 200-metre breaststroke races. I cheered at the TV screen, jumped up and down, and sang "O Canada" at the top of my lungs during the award ceremonies. I especially admired those three because they proved that Canadian swimmers could be the best in the world. They didn't think making the Olympics was good enough. They were in it to win. I loved that spirit.

That's when I made up my mind I wanted to go to the Olympics. I was only twelve (almost thirteen) and hadn't even made the time standards to compete in any event at the National championships yet. The next Olympics were four years out, but I was all in. I had a crazy goal, and I knew I would have to train super hard every day to get there.

I was fourteen when I first made Nationals—in the 200-metre breaststroke. But then my breaststroke fell apart when I grew and my body changed, and for some reason, I just couldn't go faster. It was devastating. Going through puberty and having it destroy your goal sucked but what are you going to do? So I became a backstroker. I ended up competing in the 200-metre backstroke and the 400-metre individual medley.

Times are everything in swimming. And while it's true you're racing against other people hoping to be the first to touch the wall and win, when you're far from reaching the top swimmers, you're really competing against yourself. Your goal is to beat your best time. It took me a while to learn that.

Sometimes, despite all the training, six to seven kilometres per practice, you don't race well. Maybe you didn't train hard enough, maybe your taper before the swim meet didn't work as intended, or maybe your head wasn't in the game. One year at Nationals, I made the finals but came last in the race. I was crying, and my coach said to me, "What more could you want? You did your best time. You swam as hard as you could, and there were some girls who were faster than you." It felt a little harsh, and I was still disappointed, but then I realized, "He's kind of right."

Bottom line: while I swam at the 1988 Olympic trials, I just wasn't good enough to make the Olympic team. That was hard. But I had no regrets. I went far faster than I ever imagined I could when I was twelve, I learned to be disciplined, work hard and pull myself up when I was down—key life lessons—and I had a lot of fun doing it.

Competitive swimming taught me that hard work isn't just about pushing yourself through physical limits—it's about consistency, resilience and the discipline to keep showing up even when progress feels slow. Every lap in the pool and every early morning practice were reminders that success doesn't come overnight. It's built day-by-day, stroke-by-stroke. That mentality of perseverance and dedication has stuck with me. It's about being committed to the process, not just the result.

Looking up at my time after a race. I don't look impressed.

U2's third album, War. It came out in 1983. This is my copy. It was the first record I bought.

WAR

When I was eleven or twelve, U2's *War* came out. It was the first album I owned. The music was incredibly powerful, but it was the lyrics that stuck with me. My dad had told me stories about Ireland and the message of fighting for freedom and justice felt deeply personal. The song, "Sunday Bloody Sunday" hit hard, especially "And the battle's just begun / There's many lost, but tell me who has won." When I asked about Bloody Sunday, he explained how British soldiers opened fire on unarmed civil rights protesters in Derry, mostly Catholics, killing fourteen people in 1972. He explained that the shooting showed to the world the injustices faced by the Irish Catholic community in Northern Ireland. They had no voice, no protection and no power. Bono later said the song was a protest against the never-ending cycle of violence and bloodshed in Northern Ireland that hurt regular people and tore families apart, and the need to end violence by bringing people together and listening to each other. The album *War* still reminds me that the fight for justice is about all of us standing up against violence, hate and division, wherever it exists.

NEVER FORGET WHERE YOU'RE FROM

I loved growing up in Hamilton, aka Steeltown or "the Hammer." Going to the reservoir park by our house at night and hanging out with my friends. Running along the nearby Bruce Trail or in Cootes Paradise behind McMaster University. Shopping at Jackson Square and buying shiny pink lipstick from Faces. Going to Hutch's by the harbour for fish and chips or Stoney Creek Dairy for tiger stripe ice cream. Getting army pants from the Army Surplus store on James Street North or cool sunglasses from Deja Vu on King Street. Turning on the TV or going to a movie and seeing two Hamilton boys, Eugene Levy and Martin Short, cracking people up. Wandering around the Festival of Friends at Gage Park, listening to local bands and buying silver anklets. Sitting in a car at the top of the Hamilton "mountain" with a boy you were waiting to kiss, awkwardly gazing down at the city lit up by the Stelco and Dofasco smokestacks. Going to Tim Hortons (founded in Hamilton, of course) for coffee and a donut.

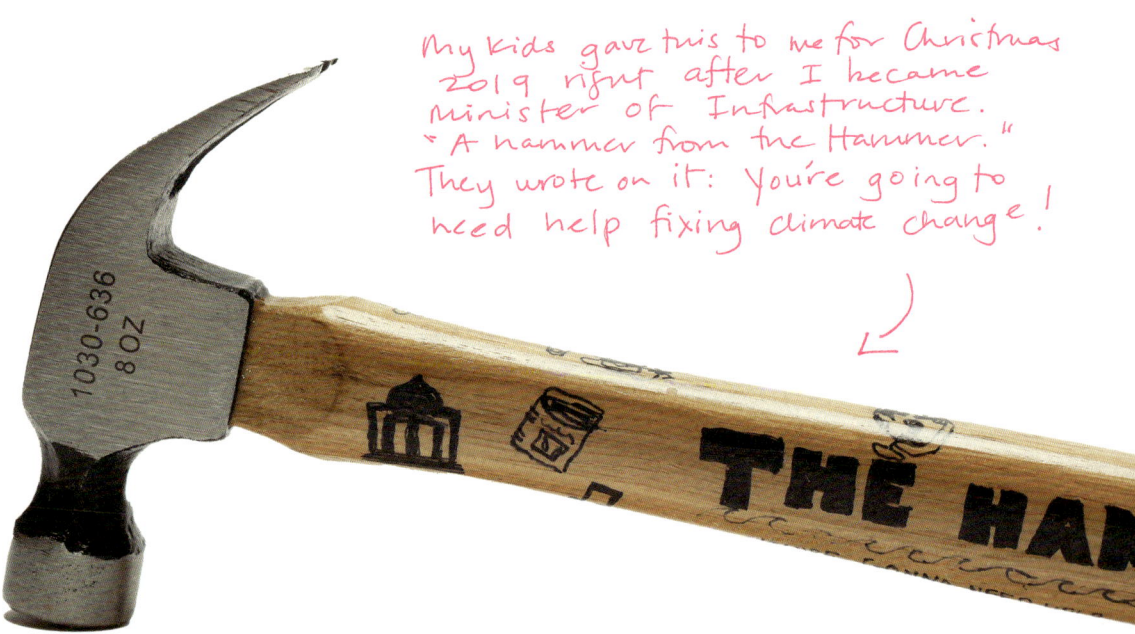

My kids gave this to me for Christmas 2019 right after I became Minister of Infrastructure. "A hammer from the Hammer." They wrote on it: You're going to need help fixing climate change!

I loved that Hamilton was scrappy and had grit. A city that was proud of its steel-town roots and the community that was built around it. Where your friends and neighbours were as important as anyone else. A place where everyone cheered on our beloved Tiger-Cats ("Oskee wee wee…Eat 'em raw!") against the hated Toronto Argos.

And there was the Copps family. Victor Copps was the beloved mayor of Hamilton in the '60s for more than a decade. Back in the day, you'd go see concerts at the Copps Coliseum (and hope for an NHL team to play there one day). Victor's daughter, Sheila Copps, was elected as the federal member of Parliament for Hamilton East in 1984. She was a prominent minister in the Jean Chrétien government and served as minister of environment, like me. And she was the first woman to be named deputy prime minister. But more than that, she was a model in a lot of ways for women in politics—for being the first sitting MP to give birth while in office but also for calling out the sexist treatment of women in politics.

John Crosbie liked to taunt her when he was minister of justice in the Mulroney government. He thought he was hilarious when he told her in a debate in Parliament in 1985, "Just quiet down, baby." But she wasn't having it. She stood up and famously retorted: "I am a member of Parliament, thirty-two years old, elected to represent the people of my area, and I resent the comments of the minister who is responsible for equality of women in this country. I resent his remarks in the House . . . I'm not his baby, and I'm nobody's baby." He later apologized to her but it was not easy being a female politician in the '80s and '90s. Sheila was from Hamilton, and she was also "of Hamilton," as my grandmother might have said. She was proud, tough and up for a fight. She had the Hamilton spirit.

I was shocked when I figured out that not everyone loved Hamilton. I still remember going to a frat party in Toronto when I was about eighteen. My friends and I were getting chatted up by some private school guys, and one of them asked where I was from. I told him Hamilton. He thought that was the funniest thing ever. "Do you have to wear a gas mask when you go around town?" I wasn't prepared, so I came up with some lame reply about how I'd far rather hang around Hamilton than with a loser like him. I never forgot it. And I never forgot where I was from.

FIGURING OUT LIFE

FINDING YOUR PEOPLE

I was excited to go off to university. I mean, like a lot of kids I loved my family, but they can be a lot. But the decision about where I should go to school wasn't without drama. I originally accepted McGill University. It was far away in cool Montreal, where I could use my French, and Kelly, my best friend from high school, was going there. But in the end, the University of Toronto just made sense. It was not only a great school but it also had the best swim team in the country. The only problem was I'd missed the deadline to apply for residence. But in came Byron MacDonald, the fantastic head coach of the varsity swim team and a good fixer for his recruits. He sorted me out. Someone on the team had an aunt who was a nun, and that connection helped get me into St. Joseph's College—the Catholic all-women's residence on Wellesley Street that was part of St. Michael's College.

But let's just say I wasn't a perfect fit for St. Joe's and my days as a bus narc were long behind me. When I was dropped off at the residence, a number of things stood out. First, it was run by nuns. Second, there were no phones in our rooms. If someone called or came by the front desk and you were out, a private note was left with your name on the message board. This created much hilarity as my swimming friends constantly dropped by to leave bizarre notes that my friends in residence would read out loud. Third, they took the condoms out of the frosh kits—because that would stop St. Mike's kids from having sex. But the real kicker was "man hours": Men (even younger brothers) could only come to your room in the afternoons on the weekend. It's not like I had anyone I really wanted to visit me, but it just seemed weird. At the men's residences, women could come anytime but couldn't sleep over (at least officially). When I learned that, I was livid at the disparity. I even started a petition but quickly realized there was zero chance of changing things.

I met some really great people at St. Joe's—my people. I figured out who many of my friends would be on the first night. We were all invited by the nuns to the residence basement. When we got downstairs, they did a little performance. At the end, they set up a sundae bar with bananas, cherries and whipped cream. It was a nice gesture but all I wanted to do was join my swim team friends who were busy drinking nearby at the legendary Brunswick House. My roommate Jen looked at me and we started laughing uncontrollably. My next-door neighbour Hillary joined in. Then a few other girls came over—Michelle, Katie, Melanie, Bernadette and Tina. We built the biggest, most over-the-top sundaes imaginable. Then we scarfed them down and got the heck out to meet up with my swimming friends.

Lying on the floor at St. Joe's College with my good friends, Hillary and Jen — friends to this day.

We won the women's and men's university swimming championships in 1993. Our coach Byron is soaked because we chucked him in the pool!

WHAT A TEAM CAN BE

The most important lesson I learned about what it means to be part of a team—any team—came from swimming at university. Being on the University of Toronto Varsity Blues Swim Team, and my final years as a captain, taught me how powerful it is to come together with others who might be very different from you but are committed to a shared goal—a goal that is way bigger than your own success.

Swimming was a huge part of my life at UofT. I got up early almost every weekday morning, put on my ugly, bright blue swim parka if it was cold, and biked to the pool on Harbord Street. We all traipsed in, changed largely in silence, and jumped into the pool to swim our guts out. Then we all went off to class—though I'm not sure I always retained much, given the many jagged lines trailing all down my notebook pages. Then in the afternoon, it was back to the pool. But by then, we were all laughing and chatting until Byron cut it off with the first set "starting on the red top" (of the clock). After practice, we'd often grab a slice or two at Cora Pizza across the street and on more than a few Thursday nights, we'd end up at a nearby pub drinking a few too many beers.

At Christmas break, Byron ran a team training camp in Florida or Barbados where we trained even more—swimming five hours a day or about thirteen or fourteen kilometres. This time spent training with no distractions was key to getting into top shape and bonding as a team, especially as we were jammed four to room at a cheap hotel. My friend Mike wrote in the *Varsity* student newspaper about his "supreme winter weight loss program," intense swimming and a daily diet of pasta, a pint of rum, dancing and less than six hours of sleep. If you followed the program, he wrote, "you too can lose fourteen pounds in two weeks."

On many weekends during the school year, we'd have swim meets at UofT or another university. And these were totally different than when I swam as a kid, where you were focused largely on your own race. This was about the team. We cheered everyone on. Not just because every point counted toward a team win—though they did, and Byron was obsessed with figuring out the best configuration of racers and races so everyone would get points to help us win—but because we were a team.

We'd been through so much—fun times, sure, but we were often exhausted, injured, or just struggling with life or school—and we were there to lift each other's spirits and cheer everyone on.

In my third and fourth year, I was chosen by my teammates to be one of the captains of the women's team. It was an honour and I took the role seriously. I may not have been the fastest in the pool, but I was among the most committed to team building and team spirit. I remember Byron even asked me to figure out how to buy a cat for one of our team members because he thought she was lonely. In fourth year, when the team seemed to need a pick-me-up, my co-captain and roommate, Rebecca Glennie, and I would host team parties at the Brunswick Street apartment we shared with our awesome roommate, Deirdre, who was always up for it and became an honorary member of the team.

There's no doubt our massive team spirit contributed to our success. Our women's team won the university national championships three times when I was there, and the men won twice. And it was pretty sweet that both our teams won in Toronto in 1993 when I was one of the captains. I love the picture of all of us with the banners, and Byron soaking wet because, naturally, we threw him in the pool to celebrate.

Some of my best friends to this day were on the swim team—Rebecca, Mike, Steve and Leanne. I love that we still hang out when we can and even swim together occasionally—though we're a fair bit slower now.

I recently asked Byron, one of the most successful university coaches in North America, what he believes are the key attributes of a winning team. His answer applies far beyond the sports world, including winning in politics. He said it starts with leadership at the top—the person whose entire job is about leading the team (often with the help of a strong and respected right-hand person—in his case, Linda Kiefer, the very talented assistant swim coach). The leader is compassionate and principled. They are knowledgeable about the work and outcomes that need to be accomplished to be in a position to win. This requires the ability to plan a long way out while setting short-term targets along the way and adjusting on the fly when things aren't working. That person also understands what motivates each member of the team (maybe even better than they understand it for themselves) and is willing to put in the time to get the best out of each person.

You also need to ensure internal leadership with strong team captains—people who are respected by their teammates and can help motivate them to perform their best.

You need to attract, recruit and nurture talent. No amount of planning will enable you to win if you don't have the talent to make it happen. But inevitably, once you attract stars, you will need to stroke egos when needed and ensure they understand their success is also critical to the team's success.

You need to instill pride in the organization, making sure everyone on the team feels like they belong, are proud to be part of it, and see themselves as contributing to something bigger than themselves. This takes a lot of work—not just building the team as a whole but also working with individuals to foster that spirit. You need to ensure everyone understands the long-term commitment that's required of them and that they step up and do the hard work in the pool every day and then compete as part of the team with pride and enthusiasm.

Byron concluded that when you have all these ingredients, you have put yourself in the best position to win. I've applied the lessons I learned from Byron and the Varsity Blues swim team to every team I've built.

HARD — I DESERVE IT!

Although I didn't win any medals, I overcame my biggest obstacle — myself. Next year I will train harder, eat better, sleep more, organize things better. I can only improve from here! I never thought that I'd ever be able to match my old best times. I did! ~~alleen~~ Next year I'll get the medals. Now, I'm happy.

I love being on the blocks. Knowing that this is the moment I've waited for and dreaded for so long! You can never know what it's like until you're there. People cheering, yelling your name — knowing they really care, they want you to do well. Looking up at the clock in amazement at your time. That's when everything — the mornings, the bad meets, the practice-after-meets, the pain, the sacrifices all <u>are</u> worth it. I wouldn't stop swimming for anything !!!!!!!

It's a part of me and I love it!

I OVERCAME MY BIGGEST OBSTACLE: MYSELF

When I was young, I wrote letters to myself—not diary entries, just moments I wanted to capture. I found one from the day I finally beat my best time in backstroke after a year of struggle. "I overcame my biggest obstacle—myself," I wrote. Competitive swimming taught me perseverance. Progress isn't linear, but persistence, hard work, and self-belief make personal victories more meaningful.

> *This note is cringe to read now. But I often lacked confidence so it was impatant that I could write this (in or around 1995). This was probably the first time I recognized that winning doesn't always mean winning medals.*

THE KIDS ARE ALRIGHT

The first time I really thought about the environment and climate change was in June 1992, watching coverage of the first international Earth Summit. Nearly 180 world leaders had gathered in Rio de Janeiro to address a wide range of environmental and development issues and come up with a new framework for international cooperation. I was fascinated.

Al Gore–then a US senator and an influential advocate on environmental issues–was there, as was Maurice Strong, the Canadian diplomat and environmentalist who served as the summit's secretary-general. It was at this summit that the United Nations Framework Convention on Climate Change (UNFCCC) was established to curb greenhouse gas emissions. This was over thirty years ago–when the world officially acknowledged climate change was a global problem!

But what struck me wasn't just the urgency of climate change–it was seeing so many young people, especially young women, fighting to protect the planet. I was so impressed when I watched the then-twelve-year-old Canadian, Severn Suzuki, daughter of beloved environmentalist David Suzuki, deliver an incredible speech calling out world leaders: "At school, even in kindergarten, you teach us how to behave in the world. You teach us to not fight with others, to work things out, to respect others, to clean up our mess, not to hurt other creatures, to share, not be greedy. Then, why do you go out and do–do the things you tell us not to do? Do not forget why you are attending these conferences–who you are doing this for. We are your own children. You are deciding what kind of world we are growing up in."

I remember thinking, "My God, she's just a kid, but she's taking world leaders to task for their failure to lead." Her willingness to fight fearlessly for a cause she passionately believed in made a huge impression on me. It was when I really became aware of the perils of climate change.

Right: Collage of cover of LIFE Magazine, November 1988.

INTERNATIONAL RELATIONS

While much of my undergrad was spent in or around the pool, I did love my classes (even the ones I sometimes fell asleep in) because they opened my mind to a much bigger world than Canada. I chose to major in international relations even though I didn't really understand what international relations was about. In high school, I started to develop an interest in events that were going on in the world. In a way it was inevitable, as my dad always insisted we pay attention to what was going on globally. We had a map in our kitchen where he'd make us find whatever foreign hotspot was on CBC News. I remember when I was in Grade 10 and a civil war broke out in South Yemen. None of us knew where it was so he made us find it on the map hanging in our kitchen.

I also didn't have any real idea about where a degree in international relations would lead, but it seemed a long way off before I had to figure out my career.

Although I loved watching politics and debating political issues, I wasn't involved in party politics. What I learned in my introductory political science course was that the reality of politics for women was depressing and unappealing. I wrote a paper, "Women in Elite-Level Political Activities." It was full of depressing examples of women being virtually excluded from the party elite, fielded in "lost cause" ridings or rarely appearing in Cabinet. The only positive story I highlighted was the federal NDP leader, Audrey McLaughlin, the first female leader of a Canadian political party. That fact didn't make politics any more appealing to my younger self.

My other courses highlighted what was then Canada's ability to play an outsized role in the world, from the important role of our military in both world wars to the founding of the United Nations, to Lester B. Pearson's role in solving the Suez Crisis and establishing the UN's first peacekeeping operation, to the Canada-US Free Trade Agreement.

Left: Pictures provided to media of G7 leaders and their spouses at the G7 Summit held in 1996 in Lyon, France.

I studied under incredible professors including the indomitable Janice Stein. It seemed like she was everywhere. After her class, I would turn on the TV or radio only to find her speaking about the latest global conflict in the Middle East. Another professor, John Kirton, taught an entire course about how Canada emerged as a principal power in the world, including through the role it played at G7 summits. I was part of his G7 research group, which focused on Canada's role in influencing global politics. Through this group, I was able to attend the G7 Leaders' Summit in Lyon, France, as a student journalist in June 1996. I remember the agenda of the summit being derailed by a terrorist attack in Saudi Arabia right before the start, all the leaders being men (including Bill Clinton, Jean Chrétien and Jacques Chirac), and Hillary Clinton wearing a pink dress suit when she went out with the spouses of the leaders (the "first ladies"), including Aline Chrétien. And the food was delicious—especially the cheese.

By the time I finished my final year at U of T, I was ready to stop reading about the world and start experiencing it. After four years of studying the idea that Canada could and, in many cases, had played an important role in the world, I decided what I wanted to do with my life. I wanted to work for the United Nations and be a Canadian who was making a difference in the world. To be clear, I had zero idea how to do that.

FIGURING OUT LIFE

WHAT I WOULD TELL MY 20-YEAR-OLD SELF

Catherine McKenna
@cathmckenna

Me at #Age20 without a care in the world....What I would tell my 20 yr old me: Live life. Have fun. Make mistakes. Fall in love. Fall out of love. Work hard. Take risks. Don't take yourself too seriously. Be kind. Care. Never give up. Repeat.

227   148   3,036

Dear Catherine,

I hope that you can use this book to write down all the wild adventures that you have during your travels around the world, as well as any earth-shattering discoveries that you make along the way! Remember to send me postcards since my year in Kingston will be considerably less exciting than yours in Spain, or Asia, or wherever you may be. Happy birthday!

LUV,
Deirdre ☺

February
S M T W R F S
          1 2 3 4
5 6 7 8 9 10 (11) Manila
12 13 14 15 16 17 18
19 20 21 22 23 24 25
26 27 28

April
S M T W R F S
            Bali Jakarta
      2 3 4 5 (6) (7) 8
      9 10 11 12 13 14 15
austin (16) 17 18 19 20 21 22
23 24 25 26 (27) 28 29
30   Sean
                  home

June
S M T W R F S
              1 2 3
4 (5)(6) 7 8 9 10
11 12 13 14 15 16 17
18 19 20 21 22 23 24
25 26 27 28 29 (30)
                  home?

August
S M T W R F S
      1 2 3 4 5
6 7 8 9 10 11 12
13 14 15 16 17 18 19
20 21 22 23 24 25 26
27 28 29 31

SEARCHING FOR KOMODO DRAGONS

After I graduated, I worked for six months at a small law firm doing clerical work. I was hell bent on saving enough money to go backpacking in Southeast Asia. As it happened, my swimming pal and housemate at the time, Steve, was keen to set off to film a documentary about Komodo dragons, found only on a few Indonesian islands. He didn't seem worried that he had no experience making documentaries or that Komodo dragons were the largest living lizards, with poisonous venom that could kill you. We compromised. We'd travel to several countries in the region first and end up in Indonesia to film the documentary.

We left Canada in February 1995 with the requisite Canadian flags stitched on our backpacks. The first part of the trip was eye-opening. On one hand, the locals' daily lives and culture couldn't be more different from what I knew, but at the same time, everywhere we went, there were familiar Western touchstones—Céline Dion's "The Power of Love" blaring in every cab or bus, *Forrest Gump* and *Pulp Fiction* playing at every hostel we stayed at. Like many travellers, I carried Pico Iyer's brilliant book *Video Night in Kathmandu* while living it. We visited temples, partied in Roppongi in Tokyo, hiked the Annapurna Circuit in Nepal, danced all night at the full moon party on Koh Phangan, and ate nasi lemak in Kuala Lumpur. I also got dysentery in Kathmandu, dengue in Bangkok, and chipped my front tooth somewhere along the way. My dad didn't find my smile very funny.

My good friend and roommate, Deirdre, gave me this diary to use on my trip to Southeast Asia.

Then we reached Bali, Indonesia, and it was time to get to work. We were a hilarious crew: Steve; two of his friends from university, Bill and Greg; and me. We learned we could only spend a day on Komodo Island, which made filming a documentary about the dragons nearly impossible. So instead of focusing on Komodo, we decided to document our travels through East Nusa Tenggara, the southeast islands of Indonesia, aiming to capture the essence of this incredible, diverse place and pitch it as a potential series. Steve always dreamed big.

We had a sixty-day visa, so the documentary's name became *60 Days in Indonesia*. Steve was the team leader. Bill was the coproducer. Greg was the videographer. I found myself in the de facto role of amateur diplomat. Though I preferred organized plans, the rest of the group was more interested in letting life unfold. I did consider ditching the operation more than once, especially during the tough hike to Mount Rinjani's crater—we were unprepared, and Bill drank all our water. Bill and Greg wound up in a fight. But we survived, and the sunrise over the crater rim was one of the most astonishing things I'd ever seen.

There were so many amazing experiences: staying with a family in Lombok that invited us to join in a Hindu ceremony; chartering a fishing boat for a five-day voyage from Gili Trawangan to Timor; stopping at remote villages; and, of course, visiting Komodo Island. The dragons were large, smelly and lazy that day (thankfully—they can run fast and climb trees). We climbed Kelimutu in Flores and saw its stunning multicoloured volcanic crater lakes. Meanwhile, our plans to explore West Timor were foiled for security reasons that would only really make sense to me later.

The experiences we had were amazing but getting around was often a slog. Mainly we took local buses crammed with people, live animals and fish for sale. The return trip to Bali was a seventy-two-hour bus ride across four islands. When we arrived at a bus depot in Mataram, Bill's backpack containing most of our footage had vanished. A heated confrontation followed, but I intervened with my broken Bahasa Indonesia, asking the driver if he could help us out. Miraculously, the next morning, the driver returned with the bag.

The documentary, edited by Steve, eventually aired on the Outdoor Life Network in Canada and the Travel Channel in the US, more often than not playing in the middle of the night. That trip was hard and hilarious at the same time, but it locked in my love of travel and meeting new people. I'd visited just five islands but now I knew there were at least seventeen thousand more to explore.

Me, Steve and Greg (who knows where Bill was!) standing at the top of Kelimutu volcano in Flores, Indonesia in our official Wide Eyed Productions t-shirts.

COOL BRITANNIA

Backpacking through Asia was sweet, but it was time to face reality. After returning to Canada, I was back at the small law firm for a few months to save money. I'd been accepted to the London School of Economics (LSE) which was a top school, but expensive, especially in Canadian dollars. I'd started dreaming of studying international relations and having an international career, and LSE seemed like the perfect place to start thinking about the world from a different perspective.

London in the mid-1990s was alive with energy. "Cool Britannia," a name for the UK's cultural resurgence at the time, was everywhere, and the hottest bands—Oasis,

After the Aldwych bus bombing I never looked at double decker buses the same way.

Blur and the Spice Girls—were all from the UK. I didn't realize it, but my roommates and I were living in the heart of the city's transformation. I shared a cheap, small, run-down apartment close to LSE with two Canadians, Yasmin and Paul. It was in a converted industrial building in the diamond district of Hatton Garden on a gritty lane called Lily Place, one of the smallest streets in London, about twenty feet long (yet every cabby knew it). Late one Saturday night every month, school buses would drop people off for a rave in our building.

LSE was buzzing with politics. It was clear the Conservative government, after nearly two decades of rule, was about to be replaced by Tony Blair's New Labour. Every professor seemed to be working with the Labour Party in some way, doing research, preparing policy platforms or helping with speeches. It felt like the political centre of the English-speaking universe. And, maybe not surprisingly, many of the students from Canada, the US and UK who went there ended up in politics.

Swimming was still a part of my life, though not as central as before. I joined the London University Swim Team (yes, we wore shirts that said "LUST"), but the focus was less on the sport and, as the name suggested, more on going for drinks after practice. To make extra money, I started teaching swimming at a public pool near LSE. Incredibly, one of Tony Blair's kids happened to be in my class. I would look up and see Blair, then the opposition leader, sitting in the stands reading the Sunday papers just like my dad had done. I even found the courage to speak to Cherie Blair once. I mentioned how much I admired the Labour Party, much like I admired the Liberal Party in Canada. She quickly corrected me: "Labour has nothing in common with Canadian Liberals," and walked off. Okay, then.

At the same time, Canada seemed distant, both geographically and politically. In October 1995, the second Quebec sovereignty referendum was on everyone's minds. The Canadians at LSE were glued to the news, waiting to hear whether Quebec would separate from Canada. There was no live coverage in London, so I called the Canadian High Commission to see if it could host a viewing. I was nervous but decided to ask for "Royce" instead of the high commissioner, thinking it would give me a better chance of being put through to him. I'm sure he was surprised to be put on the line with a grad student. I politely asked that he show the TV feed of the results to students, and he graciously agreed. Watching the results unfold with my friends was painful. Early returns showed a strong "Yes" vote for separation.

I remember feeling both sadness and frustration. Quebec, a place I loved, might break away from Canada. I had spent a few months one summer studying Quebec literature and film at Laval University and, combined with my mother's childhood in Val-d'Or, my francophone education and family trips to la *Belle Province*, I felt a pretty strong connection to Quebec. When the results came in–50.58 per cent "No" to 49.42 per cent "Yes"–we breathed a sigh of relief, but the margin was still terrifyingly close.

Things weren't perfect in the UK either. The Provisional IRA ended its ceasefire, and shortly after bombings resumed. The first occurred in the Docklands in February 1996, followed by another attack just a week later in Aldwych, near The Strand, where my friends and I happened to be celebrating a birthday. My friend Mike was still at the pub when the bomb went off on a London double-decker bus going by outside. I'd left earlier and came home to a frantic answering machine message from Mike recounting what had happened. Luckily, he was fine. He was a lifeguard and helped the injured.

The bombing in Aldwych really shook me. It felt surreal. I remembered the lyrics from "Sunday Bloody Sunday": "How long must we sing this song?" It was a stark reminder of how fragile peace can be, and how quickly things can change. Around the same time, General John de Chastelain, a Canadian, was playing a leading role in the Northern Ireland peace process, overseeing the decommissioning of weapons as part of the Good Friday Agreement. This was a hopeful sign that even the most entrenched conflicts could, eventually, find a path to resolution.

My year at LSE was incredible. I studied under brilliant professors such as Fred Halliday, and I saw a new kind of politics taking shape, one that engaged people and inspired hope. But Canada, despite the referendum, rarely came up in discussions. I realized my country was not quite as important on the global stage as I had thought, and maybe, hoped.

YOU GO TO LAW SCHOOL TO BE A LAWYER?

I decided that if I really wanted to make a difference in the world, I needed a foundation in international and human rights law. This led me to McGill Law in September 1996. It was a strange experience. The Quebec referendum was still very raw for many students. Most of my Quebec francophone friends were ardent separatists who were strong supporters of the "Yes" side while my Quebec anglophone friends and the students from the "rest of Canada" were generally federalists, many of whom had been involved in organizing rallies at McGill in favour of the "No" side. It made for an often explosive first year, both in class and out. In my first-year constitutional law class, you could see the passion and flashes of anger from students who railed against the repatriation of the Constitution without Quebec. Even at the weekly coffee parties sponsored by law firms ("coffee" was a misnomer as the free drink of choice was beer), my separatist friends—who were also the most fun—absolutely refused to drink a Molson Canadian.

I found law school suffocating. I'm not sure what I expected, but even at my fairly open-minded school, there was something about law that made me feel trapped. The dry and rigid curriculum, the structured way of thinking, and the competitive nature of many of the students drove me bonkers. I couldn't believe it when it came out during my first year that a secret study group existed that was made up of the students who had declared themselves the smartest. I was delighted when my unassuming friend Awi, who was always ready to party and definitely not a part of this group ended up at the top of our class that year. So much of law school seemed self-important and disconnected from the real-life issues that I wanted to work on. I think that's why my friend Simon was able to convince me to stop trying to look like a young lawyer and chop off my hair and bleach it white (instead it turned kind of yellow) for our trip to law games at Dalhousie University. The kinder of my friends thought it gave me a Brigitte Nielsen vibe. I wasn't so sure.

Fortunately, McGill didn't require you to take tax law or wills and estates (areas I knew I would never practise in), but you did have to take business law. In that class, I was taught that a CEO and board are legally obliged to maximize net present value for shareholders. It seemed absurd to me. The law was requiring profits at the

NOVELTY IN COIFFURES

Suitable for ladies called to the bar (as they soon will be, of course).

expense of everything else. For one thing, protecting the planet for the long term has little to do with maximizing profits and share price in the short term. I didn't buy it.

While I didn't always love my law courses—who can love the rule against perpetuities in common law property?—I did love the atmosphere at McGill Law and made many friends there. Some luminaries would turn up later on in life, including the esteemed Irwin Cotler, who taught a course on human rights law and would later serve as minister of justice and attorney general. I also met people who would become my future cabinet colleagues, David Lametti and Marc Miller. David Johnston, the future governor general of Canada, was also teaching at McGill Law. He hired me to help prepare his securities law course, which involved a lot of photocopying. Fortunately, I was able to take classes in international law and Islamic law and even did an independent writing course on humanitarian law with our exceptional dean, Stephen Toope.

There is a lot of pressure at law school to get hired at a big firm. Like most of my class, I went through the horrific weeklong summer job search. You run around doing interviews all day and then at night are vetted during fancy firm cocktail parties. After second year, I landed a summer job at Stikeman Elliott in Toronto, I think largely because I was a competitive swimmer and the firm motto, at least unofficially, was Work Hard, Play Hard.

I asked a friend working in corporate law what area of law at the firm had at least some focus on public policy. He told me to look at competition law and talk to the partner in charge, Lawson Hunter. My timing was good, as the largest banks in Canada were looking to merge in two separate deals. I spent much of the summer with a huge team of students reviewing massive boxes of documents, including secret PowerPoint presentations prepared by consulting firms like McKinsey. These made the case that the mergers were going to mean lower prices and more innovation (and fewer jobs, of course).

Not that it mattered what I thought as a summer student, but I certainly didn't think that going from five major national banks to three was going to be a win for competition or consumers. I figured it would mean everyone would pay more in banking charges and have less choice, while a lot of employees would lose their jobs when the companies merged. Liberal Finance Minister Paul Martin wasn't convinced either, and he ultimately rejected the mergers. After that summer, I was pretty sure I was not meant to be a corporate lawyer.

Left: I picked this print up when I lived in Jakarta. It reminded me that so much of being a lawyer is slightly ridiculous.

Jumat Hitam (Black Friday) on November 13, 1998 in Jakarta, Indonesia where a number of student protesters at Atma Jaya University fighting for a more democratic future were injured and killed by Indonesian security forces. Scott and I were on the streets that day and this is what we witnessed.

JUMAT HITAM (BLACK FRIDAY)

I was in my last year of law school at McGill, and frankly pretty bored, when my boyfriend, soon-to-be husband, Scott, was posted by the Canadian foreign service to Indonesia. Scott and I had met during our first month at LSE. Although we didn't date then, we became good friends. He was earning a master's degree in international history and would start working in Ottawa that September. That was the same time I was starting law school. We started dating not long after.

Politically, I was now a card-carrying Liberal and he was a Progressive Conservative (at least at the time). This wasn't a big deal because we actually shared similar views. Scott was from Alberta, and his politics leaned fiscally conservative and socially liberal. That was pretty close to where I was, too. We shared many similar interests. Like me, Scott was up for crazy adventures and loved the outdoors and travel. We both knew pretty early on that the relationship was going to be serious.

When he started looking at postings abroad, I made a strong case for Indonesia. I really wanted to go back. As luck would have it, Scott was chosen for a posting in Jakarta. The only downside was that it was a year before I finished law school. The summer before the posting started, we went on a canoe trip together in Algonquin Park. One night, we were in our canoe for a sunset paddle on Shirley Lake. It was spectacularly beautiful, with the sun glinting off the lake. I asked Scott to marry me. He said yes.

It was quite a time to be in Jakarta. In 1998, almost on the same day Scott accepted the posting, Suharto resigned after being president for thirty-two years. Anti-Suharto protests led by students were rocking the country. Suharto no longer had allies or support. On May 21, he stepped down. Although Suharto was credited with transforming Indonesia into a modern, relatively prosperous Muslim state of 200 million people, his regime was marked by massive corruption and the violent suppression of human rights.

Scott and I moved to Jakarta that September (I missed the first month of my third year and travelled back a few times during the year) and I planned to join him full-time after graduation. It was worth it to be back in a country I loved.

Among Scott's responsibilities as a junior diplomat at the Canadian embassy was reporting on the student demonstrations. On a visit in November, I arrived in Jakarta on a rainy night. Scott had sent our driver, Opi, in our awesome (though not always reliable) 1974 lime green Mercedes to pick me up at the airport. He told Opi to bring me to the Semanggi Overpass in Jakarta, where he was with other diplomats and foreign correspondents covering the protests underway. I was shocked to see thousands of students bravely lined up against the Indonesian police and military. The students wanted Suharto brought to justice and stronger democratic reforms. The protests fizzled in the rain that night. But the next day the students were back on the streets near Atma Jaya University and faced off against the military on the normally jammed road. I joined Scott again. It was very tense. Scott told me to move towards the university campus. For the first time, I noticed snipers on the top of high-rise buildings. Many of the students were chanting and wearing masks and scarves to protect against tear gas. Suddenly, the police and military started firing. I ran with everyone else toward the university. Students fell. It was mayhem.

We hid behind a wall of the university and could see students lying on the grounds in front of us, bleeding. Other students were rushing out to gather them in. I called Scott on a cell phone. He asked if I was okay and could I get to the hospital to find out how many students had been injured or killed so he and the journalists with him could report it. I went with protesters to the university hospital and found the morgue in the basement. I heard students sobbing over a friend who had been killed. The Jakarta Post estimated that twelve died that day, Black Friday, many of them students.

It was surreal. I'd come from McGill, living my nice life and studying law with a focus on human rights–but in a completely academic and abstract way. And here were students putting their lives on the line. That's when I realized what fighting for rights is about and what standing up for democracy really means. I understood, in a way I hadn't before, what my father had been trying to teach us about how precious freedom and democracy are and how you can never take them for granted. After Black Friday I did everything I could to finish law school and return as quickly as possible to Indonesia. That's where I wanted to be.

A YEAR OF LIVING DANGEROUSLY

I finally moved to Jakarta in fall 1999, at the height of the Asian economic crisis. There weren't a lot of jobs. I had decided not to spend another year in Canada doing my articles. I studied hard and wrote the New York Bar that summer immediately before getting married. I hadn't yet found out if I'd passed, so I wasn't qualified yet as a lawyer, and I got nowhere with the UN. The Department of Foreign Affairs and International Trade told me Canada and Indonesia didn't have a treaty that allowed diplomatic spouses to work. But I needed a job and was determined to find one.

Me as a new lawyer in Jakarta. The learning curve was steep!

Indonesian puppets used in Wayang Golek (traditional puppet theatre).

I scoured the Martindale-Hubbell global index of lawyers and started cold-calling any with connections to Canada, looking for leads. Amazingly, it worked. I had two offers and started my legal career with Soewito, Suhardiman, Eddymurthy & Kardono—a respected corporate law firm run by four Indonesian women who employed two smart and supportive Canadian-born lawyers. I worked on my Irish passport to get around the Canadian spousal issue. (Thank you, Ireland!)

Despite being only 28, the firm had many associates who were younger than me. I worked on a range of issues, from oil-and-gas law to new regional autonomy laws, where I tried to draw parallels with Canadian federalism. It was a massive learning curve. I was trying to figure out how to be a lawyer in a new country, with different laws and where politics and law often seemed to merge. I was pretty lost but thankfully my colleagues were understanding and helped me out. I took Indonesian language classes early in the morning so I could hopefully one day carry on a real conversation with Indonesians in their language. At the same time, I was immersed in Indonesian culture, attending traditional Javanese weddings with colleagues. Each were incredible experiences that left me with many beautiful hand-printed silk batik sarongs and shawls.

The years after Suharto were tumultuous: Indonesia saw a succession of presidents, ongoing antigovernment demonstrations, riots and random episodes of mass violence. This kept Scott extremely busy. Many moments during our time in Jakarta, we felt like the characters in the film The Year of Living Dangerously.

To relieve the stress, Scott and I hosted dinner parties for foreign correspondents and diplomats (or at least, the fun ones). At one, cell phones started buzzing with news that a bomb had gone off somewhere in the city. Everyone except me jumped up from the table and headed out to the streets. Scott wanted to witness what was happening firsthand before writing a report about the incident. I turned on CNN and BBC and watched as people who only minutes before were eating dinner with us were on the streets providing live reports.

Every once in a while, we'd throw parties with friends upstairs at Café Batavia, located in Kota Tua, the old town in Jakarta. Café Batavia was in a 1830s building constructed during Dutch colonial rule, with gorgeous teak wood and large, shuttered windows. It looked exactly like Rick's Café from the movie Casablanca.

It was a great place to bring together our Indonesian friends and colleagues, as well as foreign journalists and diplomats, to blow off steam.

One young diplomat we befriended was Rory Stewart, the third secretary at the British High Commission. He would later walk across Central Asia and Afghanistan in the months after 9/11 (a plan he first announced at one of our dinner parties) and write a bestselling book about the experience. And then he became a member of parliament for Britain's Conservative Party, served in a number of portfolios, ran for party leader, and wrote a bestselling book, *How Not to Be a Politician*. He and I would later talk about how absurd politics can be. He was always entertaining. In Jakarta he would recite long poems he'd learned by heart and regale us with stories about the long walks he took throughout Indonesia. More than once, he called me a half hour before a dinner party he was hosting, announced he was going to be late, and asked me to entertain the guests at his party until he arrived. He showed up later with no explanation and joined in the fun.

We also came to know Maria Ressa when we lived there, the extraordinary Filipino-American journalist who spent nearly two decades as CNN's lead investigative reporter in Southeast Asia. At the time, Maria was running CNN's Jakarta bureau. I often watched her bravely covering the latest bombing, political scandal, student demonstration or riot. Later, she became the cofounder and CEO of the media company Rappler which exposed the murderous, autocratic regime of President Rodrigo Duterte of the Philippines, and called out social media companies for their complicity in fuelling hate, disinformation and authoritarianism. In 2021, Ressa won the Nobel Peace Prize for "her efforts to safeguard freedom of expression, a precondition for democracy and lasting peace." She is one of my heroes.

UNDERWATER AWAKENING

One of the best parts of being in Indonesia was snorkelling and learning to scuba dive. Over the course of our years in Southeast Asia, Scott and I did about 200 dives, escaping the chaos of daily life. It opened my eyes to the vibrant underwater world—eagle rays and stingrays, lionfish, octopus, stone fish, seahorses, shrimps, parrotfish, moray eels, giant barracuda, cuttlefish, reef sharks—and the most amazing, vibrant coral reefs, teeming with life. Sadly, I also saw the human impact on the ocean—bleached coral, collapsing ecosytems and plastic pollution.

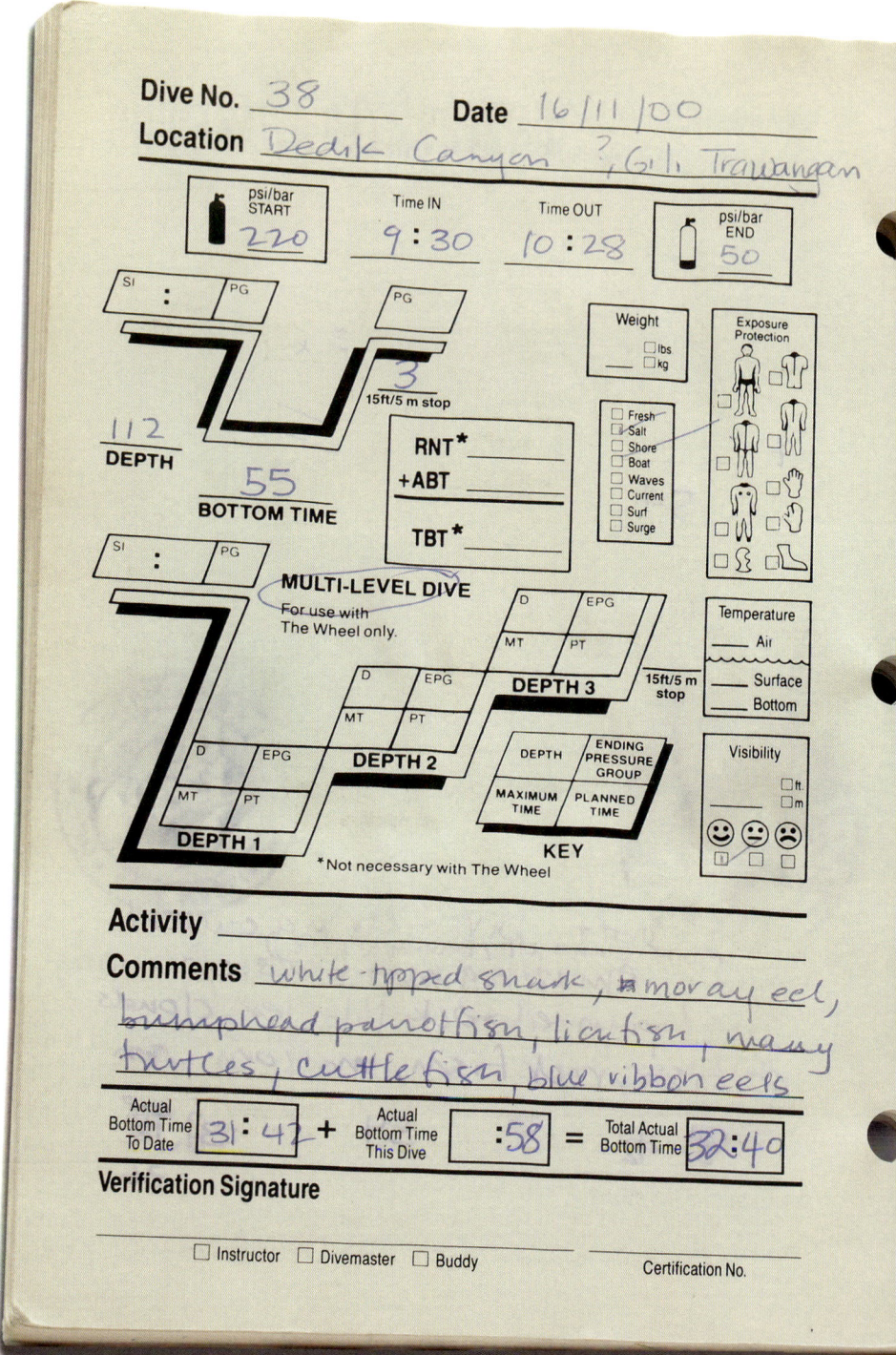

My dive book from my time in Jakarta. I loved writing down what I saw during my dives.

Dive No. 39 Date 18/11/00
Location Nusa Penida (near Pandang Bai), Bali

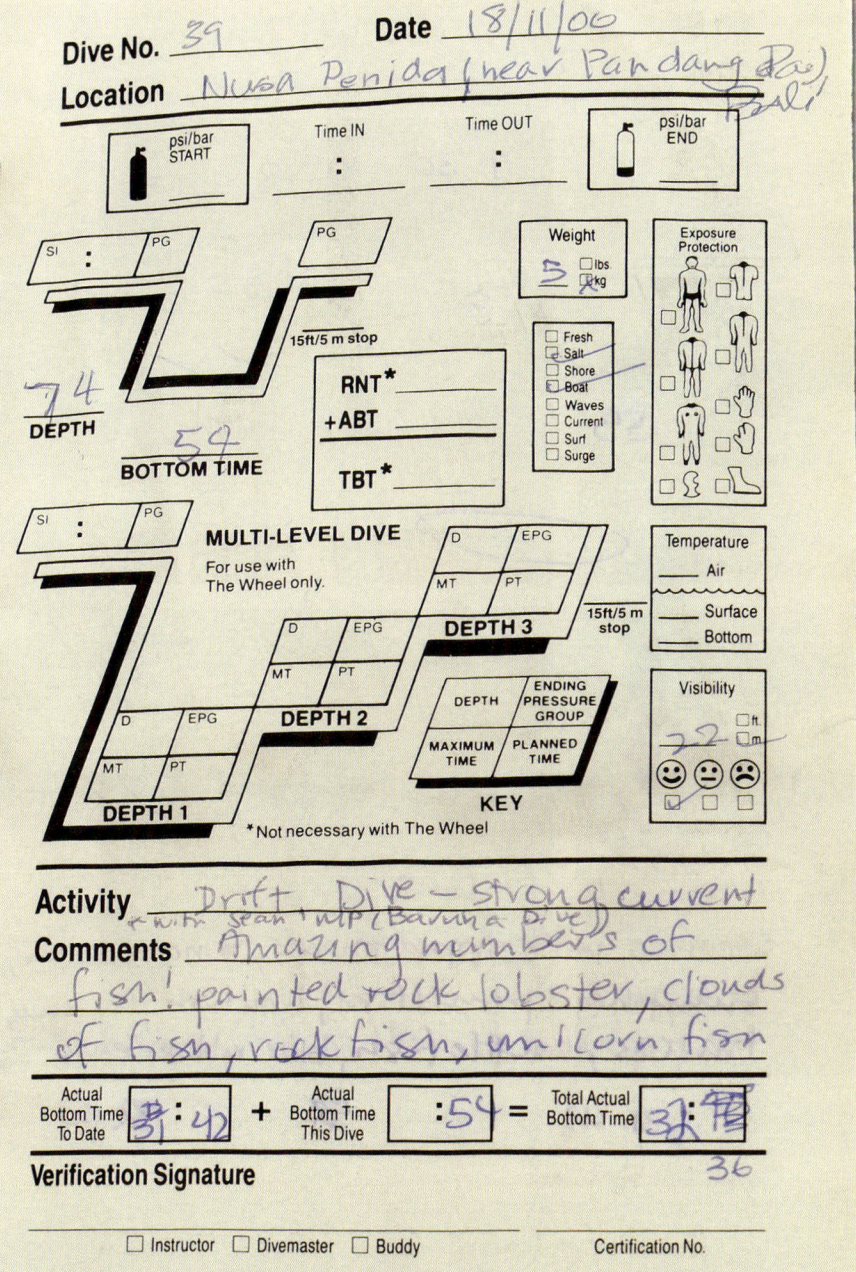

DEPTH 74
BOTTOM TIME 54

Weight 5 kg

Visibility 22 m

Activity: Drift Dive — strong current * with Sean + NP (Barina Dive)
Comments: Amazing numbers of fish! painted rock lobster, clouds of fish, rockfish, unicorn fish

Actual Bottom Time To Date 31:42 + Actual Bottom Time This Dive :54 = Total Actual Bottom Time 32:42 36

Clockwise from top left: Canadian peacekeepers in Timor-Leste. Timorese line up to vote in the 1999 independence referendum. Timorese farmer. Catherine with colleagues including with UN Transitional Administrator in East Timor, Sergio Vieira de Mello.

FINDING PURPOSE IN TIMOR-LESTE

Scott spent a lot of time visiting and reporting on the terrible human rights violations committed by the Indonesian military or their proxies in East Timor (the official name was changed to Timor-Leste after the country gained independence in 2002), which had been brutally and illegally occupied by Indonesia since 1976. It is estimated that a quarter of Timor-Leste's population died from violence, hunger or illness.

In 1999, Indonesian President Habibie, responding to international pressure, announced that the Timorese could choose between special autonomy and independence. He was convinced they would choose special autonomy. He was wrong. On August 30, 1999, almost 99 per cent of Timorese bravely voted in a referendum overseen by the UN. Almost 80 per cent chose independence from Indonesia despite intimidation by anti-integration forces.

Scott and I were on our honeymoon and watched with horror when all hell broke loose after the vote. Pro-integration militias, furious with the loss, and supported by the Indonesian military, looted and burned homes and killed many Timorese. In early September, Scott flew to the capital of Dili to help with the evacuation of Canadians, many of whom had been bravely supporting the independence movement. It was a very dangerous time. We were devasted when one of our friends, Dutch journalist Sander Thoenes of the Financial Times, was killed by the militias.

International pressure, including from Portuguese Prime Minister António Guterres, brought a UN-backed intervention in Timor-Leste. An international force led by Australia helped re-establish order and the United Nations Transitional Authority in East Timor (UNTAET) helped secure the path to Timor-Leste's formal independence in 2002.

At the end of Scott's posting in Indonesia, he and I decided to look for work in Timor-Leste so we could help the Timorese build their new country. I headed to Dili to hopefully find a new job with the United Nations peacekeeping mission. I was now oddly qualified due to my experience working as a lawyer in Indonesia and my Indonesian language skills, however limited.

Peter Galbraith, head of UN Political Affairs, needed a lawyer to help renegotiate the Timor Gap Treaty between Australia and Indonesia. It governed maritime boundaries and offshore petroleum development in the Timor Sea off Timor-Leste. Signed during Indonesia's illegal occupation of Timor-Leste, it was highly advantageous to Australia. It now had to be renegotiated to enforce Timor-Leste's rights to its waters and resources. For a young lawyer, the job presented a fascinating and extremely challenging opportunity, and I jumped at it.

It was an incredible experience. I was acutely aware of how much was at stake. Timor-Leste, one of the poorest places in the world, needed money for health care,

Me working on a Garuda Indonesia plane to East Timor, listening to my yellow Sony Walkman.

education, infrastructure and a lot more. The negotiations were fraught. Galbraith, working with the Timor-Leste chief minister Mari Alkatiri (later the prime minister), led the negotiations for the UN. Galbraith and Alexander Downer, the Australian foreign minister, loathed one another. They spent meetings yelling at each other across an apparently unbridgeable divide. Downer was a condescending bully, insisting that Timor-Leste was lucky Australia was renegotiating the treaty at all.

Somehow, we managed to achieve an interim agreement. The Timor Sea Treaty was signed on Timor-Leste's independence, May 20, 2002. While there were still issues to resolve, I was hopeful that the revenues that would flow from the Timor Sea Treaty would make a real difference in improving the lives of the Timorese. There was a massive celebration where world leaders including former US President Bill Clinton flew in to show solidarity with the incredibly brave and resilient people of Timor-Leste.

My time in Timor-Leste changed me. I saw first-hand the incredible resilience of the Timorese in their long struggle for independence. I also saw what the United Nations could do at its best. Before Timor-Leste gained its independence, the UN had never rebuilt a nation. In just a few years, despite many challenges and setbacks, and with a lot of improvisation and pragmatism, the UN mission, led by the highly skilled diplomat Sergio Vieira de Mello, supported Timor-Leste's journey to formal independence. Multilateralism, for all its faults, had worked. (Tragically, Sergio and twenty-one of his UN colleagues were killed in a suicide bombing in Iraq just two years later where he was serving as special representative of the UN secretary general.)

My time in Timor-Leste also gave me an idea I would later act on. During negotiations, Timor-Leste was greatly outnumbered by the Australian diplomatic team and the big oil and gas companies who threw their weight around. We had only one Timorese lawyer, Niny Borges, and a few public servants, so we scrambled to get expert advice. It occurred to me there were many lawyers working in Canada who had relevant experience and would have been excited to volunteer and help the Timorese. It was a simple supply-and-demand problem: the Timorese needed relevant legal help, and I knew where to find that help. It was the seed of something important. All I had to do was figure out how to connect lawyers who had the relevant expertise with the governments and organizations in developing countries that needed it.

SISTER PAOLA

I first met Sister Paola on a visit to Timor-Leste in 2000. A tiny but fierce Italian nun, she helped set up orphanages and a vocational school for young women. During the occupation of Timor-Leste, she and other sisters hid resistance members, and later sheltered over one hundred women and children, refusing to leave them when the pro-Indonesian militias were on a rampage. After my visit, she gave me a needlepoint with the words, "Timor Leste." Sister Paola was tenacious and she taught me that true power doesn't always come from might.

She also showed the side of the Catholic Church I was still drawn to: the social justice side, focused on improving the lives of the most vulnerable and marginalized rather than the side that wanted to lecture about abortion and gay marriage. This better side I knew from my uncle Dermot, a Jesuit priest, and that I would later appreciate most about Pope Francis.

Left: A needlepoint given to me by Sister Paola, made by one of the young women at the Sisters of Mercy Vocational School in Timor-Leste.

BEING A MOM

DOING SOMETHING THAT MATTERS

Scott and I returned to Ottawa in the fall of 2002. It was time to come home to be closer to our parents and we wanted to start a family. Scott was back working at the Department of Foreign Affairs and International Trade. I reluctantly joined the Ottawa office of Stikeman Elliott as an associate in competition and trade law.

I'd never really planned to become a corporate lawyer, and I found most of my day-to-day work unbelievably dull especially after my UN job. I was working with smart people and appreciated the intellectual aspect of competition and trade law, but it never excited me. I was always very happy when merger deals were put on hold or died because it meant I would get a weekend off.

At that point in my life, working at a top Canadian corporate law firm was the safe choice. Scott and I had just bought a house and we now had a big mortgage. I was back to doing what I thought was expected of me.

When you work at a high-priced law firm, you're pretty much expected to be on-call around the clock. One Friday afternoon, I had to leave early to drive to Hamilton for my grandfather's ninetieth birthday party. I'd given the partner that I was working for a heads-up weeks before. But as I was getting ready to go, he called me and said, "Wait, I need you to do this one thing." I replied, "I'm really sorry. I have to leave now but I'd be happy to look it over in the car." He didn't miss a beat. "You know, when I was a junior lawyer, I would never have said that to a senior lawyer." I wasn't having it. "If it was your grandfather's birthday, I hope you would have said it was important and you needed to go." Then I left.

I did luck out in one important way at Stikeman Elliott. I met Antonio Lamer, the former chief justice of the Supreme Court of Canada, who joined the firm after spending twenty years on the bench. He was basically doing his own thing at the office and working mostly on public policy files. To me, this was far more interesting. Every day when I walked by his office, I'd say hello and ask if he had any interesting files I could help with. He always said he'd keep me in mind. Sometimes, in the late afternoon, Mr. Lamer, as we called him, would ask me and my friend and colleague Lynn to go for a drink to Hy's Steakhouse to talk about some legal issue that had come up. Hy's was then the go-to haunt for power brokers in town.

BEING A MOM

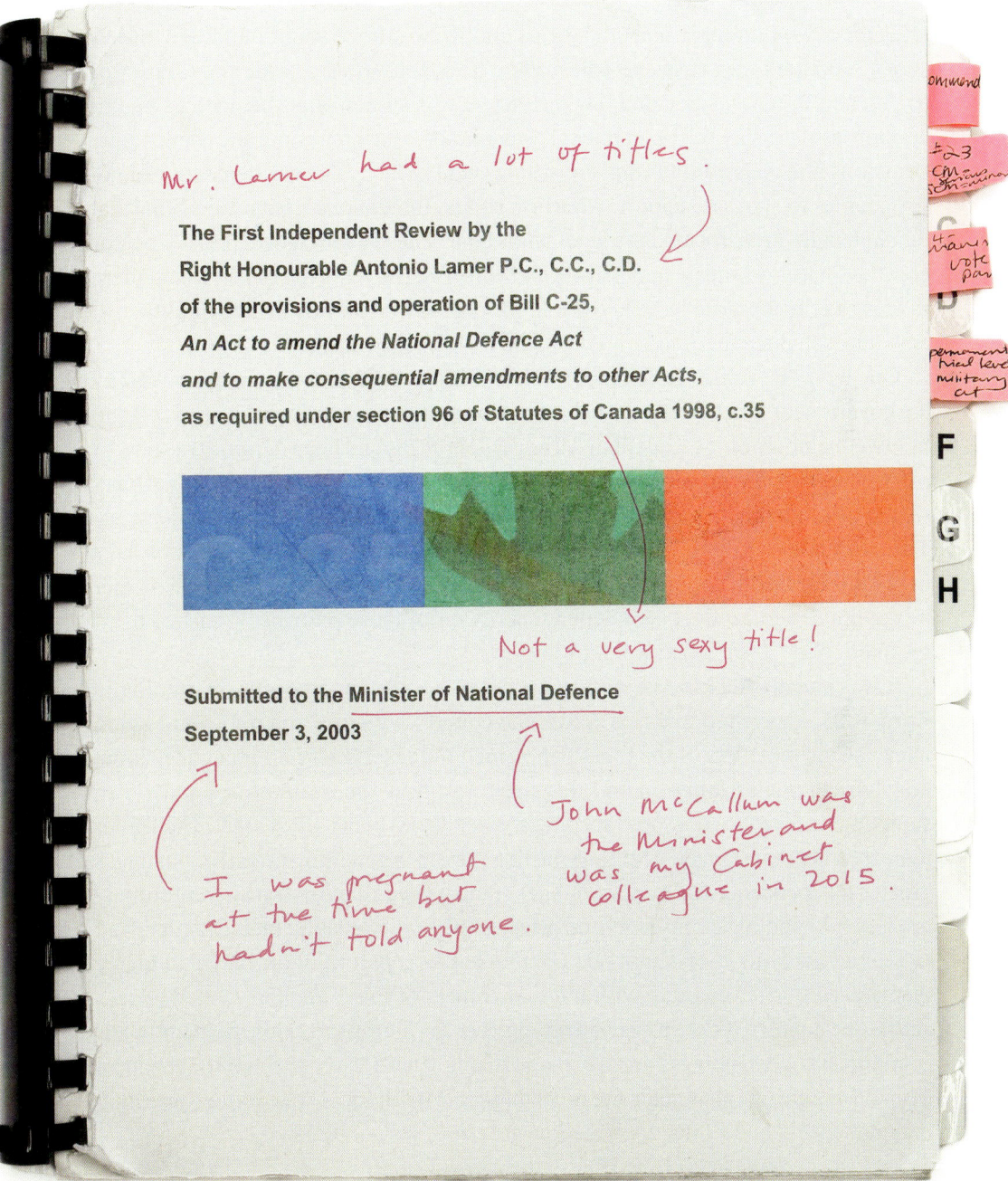

Mr. Lamer would regale us with stories and we would be spellbound. He told us about Supreme Court cases he'd heard and how, for ten years after the Charter of Rights and Freedoms became law in 1982, it was so new that the justices had to develop legal principles from scratch. It was extraordinarily stressful and challenging. Decisions like determining what constitutes hate speech. The entitlement of same-sex couples to spousal support. Abortion rights. Indigenous rights. Decisions that fundamentally transformed the legal landscape. These were critical precedents for how the Charter would be understood and enforced for years to come. I found these stories riveting because he talked about the part of the law that I cared about most: how it affected real people.

One day, Mr. Lamer called me into his office and said he'd been appointed by the government to conduct a six-month review of Canada's military justice system. In 1993, members of the Canadian Airborne Regiment had been deployed as part of a UN peacekeeping mission in Somalia. The mission became a source of national shame after members of the regiment tortured and murdered a Somali teenager. The subsequent investigation and court-martials exposed serious shortcomings in the military justice system. Reforms were subsequently brought in. Mr. Lamer was appointed to conduct an independent review of these reforms. He asked me if I wanted to join his team as a senior lawyer.

It was exactly the kind of work I longed to do. For six months, beginning in April 2003, I travelled to bases across the country with him and my friend Lynn, interviewing members of the Canadian Armed Forces. I learned a great deal about how bureaucracies function and, in particular, how the chain of command can sometimes prevent real issues faced by soldiers from being addressed. The Lamer Report found that Canada's military justice system is generally effective but needs greater independence for military judges. It also needs a more transparent, timely process for handling complaints and grievances. (Unbelievably, many soliders had to wait a year or more to simply be reimbursed for a pair of boots they had to buy themselves.) After meeting with many members of the Canadian Armed Forces across the country, I developed a deep respect for their professionalism and their commitment to defending Canada and Canadians. That blessed six-month sabbatical from corporate law also made me much happier. It felt like I was doing something that mattered. I knew I had to somehow get out of corporate law.

LEARNING WHAT LOVE IS

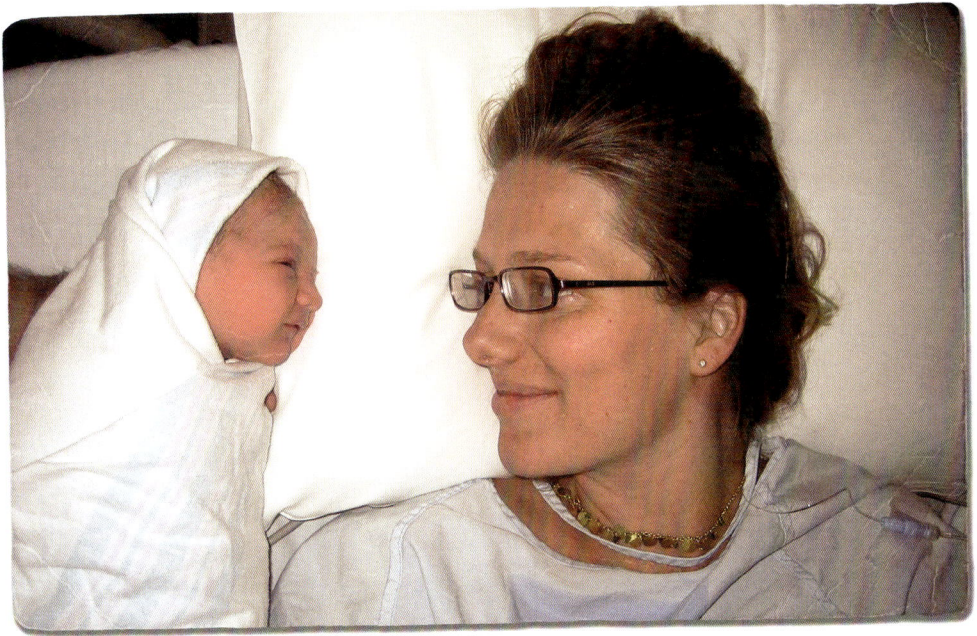

You can't really prepare yourself before you have a baby. I mean, people will tell you to read books like *What to Expect When You're Expecting*. But they're always focused on stuff, not emotions. What should you eat when you're pregnant, should you have an epidural or not, or how much maternity leave should you take? No one tells you how you're going to feel along the way. You know you're going to love your baby, but what does that feel like?

I remember after my first child, Matt, was born in 2004, I looked down at this tiny baby and felt the most overwhelming sense of love. On one hand, it is miraculous, but on the other, hundreds of thousands of other women also gave birth that same day. Still, I was filled with a surprising sense of joy that felt all my own.

Of course, nothing prepares you for the reality of having a baby either. Scott and I got home from the hospital, and Matt, still in his car seat, was on the table. I remember thinking, "It's harder to get a driver's license than to have a child. Who put us in charge of this new life? What do we do now?" It's such a consequential thing to take care of a baby, and no one really tells you how to do it no matter how many books you've read.

It wasn't always easy. I'd often be up at night exhausted, breastfeeding in the same rocking chair my mom had used when she was nursing her kids. I would often think about all the other women in the world who were doing the exact same thing at the exact same time. All of us sharing this incredible bond. That sense of kinship gave me huge comfort and kept me going.

RETHINKING MOM

My dad took up so much oxygen in our house that it was easy to overlook my mom, Pat. But she's a force in her own right. She's the rock of the family. The peacemaker. The healer. The organizer. And she never stops working. I took her for granted while I was a teenager. It's terrible to admit. But I stopped making that mistake long ago.

My mom gave up nursing when we were born in order to care for us, although she did teach prenatal classes at night to expecting moms. When we were older and had left the house, she went back to school to get a second degree. While she loved being a mom, she definitely enjoyed going back to work after we were gone. It's interesting to think about the path she might have taken in a different time.

When I was growing up, I didn't understand why she didn't work outside the house. At the time, I thought that success meant having kids and a career. Forget that my mom had had four kids in very quick succession not long after graduating from school, had very little outside help, or that my dad could barely change a diaper or load the dishwasher.

At the time, I never fully appreciated that my mom was always working and was always around for us. Driving us to dozens of swim practices a week (including the godawful 6am practices), making sure our homework was done, making meals, doing laundry, volunteering in the community. And family really was the most important thing to her. For her, it was always family first.

Amazingly, my mom never seemed resentful of the never-ending job of caring for four kids and managing the house, as well as taking care of my dad (who was a handful). I even remember her joking about the story of my dad going to play in a Golden Oldies rugby tournament not long after my youngest brother, David, was born. She was left with a baby and three other young kids while Dad was away for ten days! And then he came back injured. My mom is a saint.

My mom with the four of us. She is a hero!

It was only when I became a mom myself that I really appreciated how strong she is and how much sheer work she did to keep our family going. It's easy to have your strengths overlooked when you're a mom and you're just quietly getting things done. Beyond keeping our family going, there are other traits that I appreciate including that she is completely unflappable and totally practical. You can throw anything at her. She doesn't get overwhelmed. She deals with whatever the issue is and gets on with life. I love that about her. No matter what chaos was happening around her, she wouldn't make a fuss. I learned from her to figure out how to cope and get on with it. You don't dwell on it.

She is also frugal. She hates wasting money. She basically only shopped for our clothes at BiWay or at else Eaton's when there was a sale. Every one of the snowsuits she bought for me as a child came in a dark colour so it could be passed on to my brothers. If I wanted something cool to wear, I knew I had to hit up my dad.

She was also very practical while my dad was often clueless. One year, we drove to Florida and spent a day at Disneyland. My dad took me and my brother Sean while my Mom took the two younger kids. It started to pour. When we caught up again, Sean and I were drenched because my Dad had bought us terrycloth towels (in theory to keep us dry) while my Mom bought plastic ponchos.

To this day, when any of my kids get sick, the first thing they say is, "let's call Granny." They love that she was a nurse and they know they're going to get good advice, even if it's just some tender words and they're told to put a Band-Aid on it.

As a mother, I learned how difficult it was to work every day and leave the kids. There's no clear line between work and home. Some days, I wrote out my long to-do lists for home during my workday or quietly slipped out for doctor appointments. My work seemed a lot less important and I resented having to work late instead of being at home with our growing family, even if that was required to get ahead. I finally understood my mom's ethos of family first and why she made the choices she did.

BEING MORE AMBITIOUS AFTER HAVING KIDS

After Matt's birth, I took a six-month maternity leave. To my surprise, I had no time and all the time in the world (but boy, does that change when you have your second child!). While Matt slept, between his feedings, and often during them, I started developing the idea I'd hatched in Timor-Leste—launching a charitable organization to match Canadian lawyers and law students with governments and organizations in less developed countries needing legal expertise. I took inspiration from established organizations like Engineers Without Borders Canada. It was a big idea, but I thought it could work.

Fortunately, my good friend Yasmin Shaker, also a lawyer and my flatmate at LSE and McGill, was interested in starting it with me. We wanted to create a space for members of the Canadian legal community to help build a world where human rights were respected and the rule of law upheld. Governments and organizations in developing countries needed all kinds of legal advice, from human rights to corporate law. On the flip side, I knew many lawyers in the corporate world, in government or at not-for-profits would love to use their training to make a difference internationally.

Yasmin and I believed Canadians were uniquely placed to help level the playing field for less developed countries: we practise in both common law and civil law; we believe in the rule of law and human rights; we have strong institutions; and we have lawyers who come from all over the world. We decided to go with a straightforward name: Canadian Lawyers Abroad.

Starting something isn't easy. We needed to raise money. We reached out to lawyer friends and contacts at law firms and in the corporate world. An initial $5,000 cheque from Stikeman Elliot was a much needed boost. It helped get the idea out of our heads and into the world. We used it to get charitable status and set up a website. Once we had our website, we felt real.

Right after Matt was born, Scott had left the foreign service and established his own start-up, Peace Dividend Trust, which promoted economic development in post-conflict countries. Soon he was travelling over 100 days a year. Often, I was the only parent on call. Still, after six months, I went back to work at my law firm, doing what was expected of me—or maybe what I expected of myself. I was making

MESSAGE FROM EXECUTIVE DIRECTORS

It's hard to believe that 2006 was only our second year of operations at CLA-ACE. This past year we've made great progress towards our goal of providing opportunities for the Canadian legal community to actively engage in some of the most pressing legal issues in the developing world, and in Canada's north.

In 2006, we took a number of critical steps that will help build a more effective and sustainable organization.

We are very pleased to have established a partnership between CLA-ACE and the Faculty of Law at the University of Ottawa. Having a home base as well as institutional links to a law school that puts a great deal of emphasis on international law and social justice, offers common and civil law programs and is located in the nation's capital, is an excellent fit for CLA-ACE. We hope to build further on this partnership.

Catherine McKenna and Yasmin Shaker, Executive Directors of CLA-ACE.

Photo Courtesy of Paul Lawrence Photography

Last year we received charitable status. This will assist our fundraising efforts so that we can continue to expand and develop our Student Chapters, internships and pro bono projects. By donating to CLA-ACE, you are supporting programs that raise the level of awareness of pressing international issues at home, while providing legal assistance to groups abroad and in Canada's north, in the areas of rule of law, good governance and human rights.

We are also in the process of creating an Advisory Board composed of Canadians who represent the values of CLA-ACE, and because of their unique and distinguished backgrounds, can provide us with valuable guidance and advice. As you will

Continued on pg 2...

IN THIS ISSUE :

Message from Executive Directors	...pg 1
Essay Competition Winner	...pg 2
Pro Bono Program	...pg 3
2007 Summer Internships	...pg 3
Second Annual Conference	...pg 4
Student Chapter Update	...pg 5
CLA-ACE Advisory Board	...pg 6
Interview with Carolyn McCool	...pg 7
Dispatch from Ghana	...pg 9
Contact Information	...pg 10

CLA-ACE IS NOW A CHARITY!

We are pleased to announce that CLA-ACE is now officially a charity and we are therefore able to accept donations and issue tax receipts. Corporations and individuals are now able to donate on-line through Canadahelps.org using a link available on the main page of our website (www.cla-ace.ca). We rely on your donations to maintain and further develop and expand our programs.

CLA-ACE Newsletter, Vol. 2, February 2007

good money at a top firm—I could probably be a partner one day. I didn't find the job rewarding, but that was life. I could find meaning outside of work.

In reality, things were getting crazy. Scott was travelling much of the time, Matt wasn't sleeping well, and quite reasonably our caregiver had to leave by 5:30 p.m. After a hectic day, I would sneak out of the office hoping no partners saw me, rush home to feed Matt, have some playtime, give him a bath, and put him to sleep. I would eat quickly and get back to work. Well past dark, I'd turn my attention to Canadian Lawyers Abroad because it was important to me.

It's weird how kids can make you focus. Having Matt and living this way for a while cemented for me that I didn't want to waste time on anything that wasn't meaningful to me. I wanted to do something to make the world better, and that's what Canadian Lawyers Abroad was doing. I also wanted to be able to sometimes take Matt to a drop-in playgroup or the park during the day. I recognized that my career goals had changed.

So, I made what seemed at the time a hugely consequential decision: I decided to quit the law firm. I knew many of my colleagues probably thought that with a new baby I couldn't handle the hours and the work. While I certainly wasn't going to miss the ten-hour days, the reality is that I wanted more out of life than becoming a partner at a law firm.

Because we needed the money, I wasn't able to do Canadian Lawyers Abroad full-time yet. I initially worked as in-house counsel which gave me more time and energy to build Canadian Lawyers Abroad. While it was a bit of a curve in my career path, I realized it was great to be working in a much more relaxed environment with nice people.

Not long after, I had my second child, Isabelle. At this point, we had moved from a nanny share to hiring a full-time caregiver for our kids. Although it was a big expense, we were lucky that we could afford it. Having someone we trusted and who would stay with us as our family grew was such a gift. Lyn is absolutely wonderful with our kids and they love her dearly. She quickly became an indispensable part of our family.

Left: Canadian Lawyers Abroad newsletter, February 2007. We'd just become a charity. Best of desktop publishing!

Canadian Lawyers Abroad soon started to grow in ways we never expected. After we were approached by a number of awesome students from law schools across Canada, we launched a program to bring together students passionate about using their law degrees to improve people's lives. That wasn't exactly our plan (and still we had no money to pay ourselves), but we thought it was important and we remembered how keen we'd been in law school to meet with like-minded students and discuss international law, human rights and social justice in a way that went beyond the dry legal concepts taught in class.

We also created a student internship program to give students practical opportunities. Yasmin and I combed through our contacts and made new ones and placed students with ECPAT in Bangkok, an organization that works to end the sexual exploitation of children, and the Federation of Women Lawyers (FIDA) in Nairobi, a women's rights organization that works to advance gender equity and end gender-based violence by offering free legal aid to women who couldn't afford representation.

Two years later, after I had my third child, Cormac, we had raised enough money for me to finally work full-time for Canadian Lawyers Abroad. I took a substantial pay cut and had no benefits, and, like most charities, the funding was precarious, but I couldn't have been happier.

As I told Reva Seth for her book, *The MomShift*, "I actually became more ambitious after my children were born. I was less willing to settle for work that had little meaning to me, work that was just a way to pay our bills."

GETTING OUTSIDE MY COMFORT ZONE

In our early days, Yasmin and I created an advisory board of senior lawyers and other leaders with human rights and rule of law experience to lend credibility to the organization. I asked Antonio Lamer to join our board, and he accepted.

One day, he asked me to meet him in his office. "I wanted to ask you," he said using his serious judge voice, "Why are you sending lawyers overseas when we have Third World living conditions here? You could be working with Indigenous people here in Canada to improve their lives."

He knew what he was talking about. During his time on the Supreme Court, he wrote the *Delgamuukw* decision, a landmark 1997 ruling that confirmed the existence of Aboriginal title as a right beyond the right to hunt, fish or gather, but to the land itself. The decision underscored the need for the government to meaningfully consult and accommodate Indigenous people regarding their lands, and respect their historical and cultural practices.

Many students from the First Nations School of Toronto swore their oath during the mock trial using a ceremonial eagle feather belonging to Justice Harry LaForme. This is a feather I found while camping out with the Łutsël K'é Dene in Thaidene Nëné National Park Reserve.

I had to confront an uncomfortable truth. While I was aware of some of the injustices faced by Indigenous peoples in Canada—from the legacy of residential schools to the crisis of missing and murdered Indigenous women and girls, and the disproportionate incarceration rates—I could only guess at how limited my understanding truly was. I felt self-conscious about asking someone Indigenous to explain what I should have already known. I felt that if Canadian Lawyers Abroad focused on supporting Indigenous peoples and communities, we'd screw up and look like fools—or worse, we'd be seen as another outsider group with their own agenda.

But Mr. Lamer was right. We needed to look at ways we could work with Indigenous peoples where they wanted the help of the Canadian legal community and we could be useful. I started by reaching out to Indigenous leaders I knew. I asked Madeleine Redfern, then the Inuk mayor of Iqaluit, who also chaired the the Legal Services Board of Nunavut, to join our board and help us get our bearings. We created new student internships with organizations like the Mikisew Cree First Nation, the Yukon River Inter-Tribal Watershed Council, and the Legal Services Board of Nunavut where students supported their work.

A few years before I had met Phil Fontaine, the former national chief of the Assembly of First Nations, so I called him up and asked him what we could usefully do. He suggested we focus on supporting Indigenous youth. Justice Harry LaForme, an Ontario Court of Appeal judge from the Mississaugas of the Credit First Nation (and the first Indigenous person to sit on any appellate court in Canada) was a legend. I reached out to him and, in our meeting, he pointed out that most Indigenous youth have only negative experiences with the law. They don't have role models, so they don't dream of becoming lawyers.

In 2012, with the incredible help of Indigenous lawyers and law students including Karen Restoule from the Dokis First Nation, we developed a program called Dare to Dream. It was designed to inspire and empower Indigenous youth by connecting them with Indigenous lawyers, judges and law students who would provide them with mentorship, education and opportunities to explore careers in law and justice.

We started with a pilot project with the First Nations School of Toronto. Their Grade 7 and 8 students were part of a mock trial and sentencing circle presided over by Justice LaForme. It was amazing to see Justice LaForme swear in witnesses with a foot-long ceremonial eagle feather. The students did an incredible job playing their various roles, ranging from the victim (beaten and robbed of his shoes) to the accused to the jury. Sharla Niroopan, their amazing teacher, spoke afterward about how the students changed from being skeptical about the program to being inspired by it: "They were like, 'Screw law, screw the cops.' Now, they have created so many bonds with the lawyers …. They have connected with mentors."

I often thought that the non-Indigenous lawyers who were part of Dare To Dream learned as much as the Indigenous students. As part of our training, they learned about the systemic issues facing Indigenous people and were taught by Indigenous leaders about Indigenous culture and traditions. And through the program, they participated in what was often their first smudge ceremony and sentencing circle.

I will never forget a school trip to the Court of Appeal of Ontario where one of the students saw a framed copy of the apology on behalf of Canadians for the Indian residential school system in Justice LaForme's office. He said loudly to our group: "Too little, too late." He was absolutely right. I felt angry that it had taken so long for an apology to come from Canada but also hopeful that in a small way, Dare to Dream was helping to advance reconciliation.

Through my humbling experience with Dare to Dream, I learned that sometimes you need to push yourself to do things you feel nervous or completely unprepared to do.

FINDING YOUR MOM FRIENDS

There's this idea that I bought into that when you become a mom, you're automatically going to become friends with the other moms in your neighbourhood. After I had Matt, I went to the local community centre's mom and baby activities group to make some friends. I met some really nice people, but I felt like I didn't have much in common with many of them. And while I loved Matt, I wanted to talk about things other than kids.

That's when I got the idea to start a book club. The first meeting was at my house—I remember we ate pasta with two sauces (I was proud of myself because I'm really not a cook) and discussed Joan Didion's new book, *The Year of Magical Thinking*.

While a number of book-club members have come and gone, we now have a committed group. When we started, Patricia had just moved to Ottawa from England. I met her at the community centre drop-in with her daughter, Isabel. She became a diplomat and we both talked about everything going on in the world. My friend Stephanie, who I knew from university and was also a lawyer, had a little boy, Charlie. She introduced me to her childhood friend from Brockville, Sarah, who was working on environmental issues and loved everything to do with the British royal family. I met Caroline with her husband, Matt, at a "Bring an Interesting Stranger Party" that Scott and I threw. She was a lawyer from a family steeped in public service and politics, which meant that she had a great perspective on Ottawa. She introduced us to her friend Jane, a long-time environmentalist and was the first person I knew I needed to hire when I became Minister of Environment and Climate Change. Rachel, a doctor, was Jane's friend from Winnipeg and the first to bring homemade chicken noodle soup when you're sick. I invited Kate, who I knew from the neighbourhood. She was born in Reading, UK, was no BS, a punk rocker at heart, and a total hoot. And there was Meg, who loved the outdoors and was always hiking or cross-country skiing, who was the mother of one of Matt's good friends.

Our book club is not really about the books, although we all love reading including amazing books like Heather O'Neill's *Lullabies for Little Criminals,* Tanya Talaga's *Seven Fallen Feathers* and *Station Eleven* by Emily St. John Mandel. It's about our friendship, and getting away from our kids for a bit. The joy comes from just being together. And there's nothing more comforting than knowing that when I send out a group SOS text saying I've had a terrible day, whoever can make it shows up at my place that night for a chat and a laugh (or cry) over a glass of wine and some chips. I always feel a lot better.

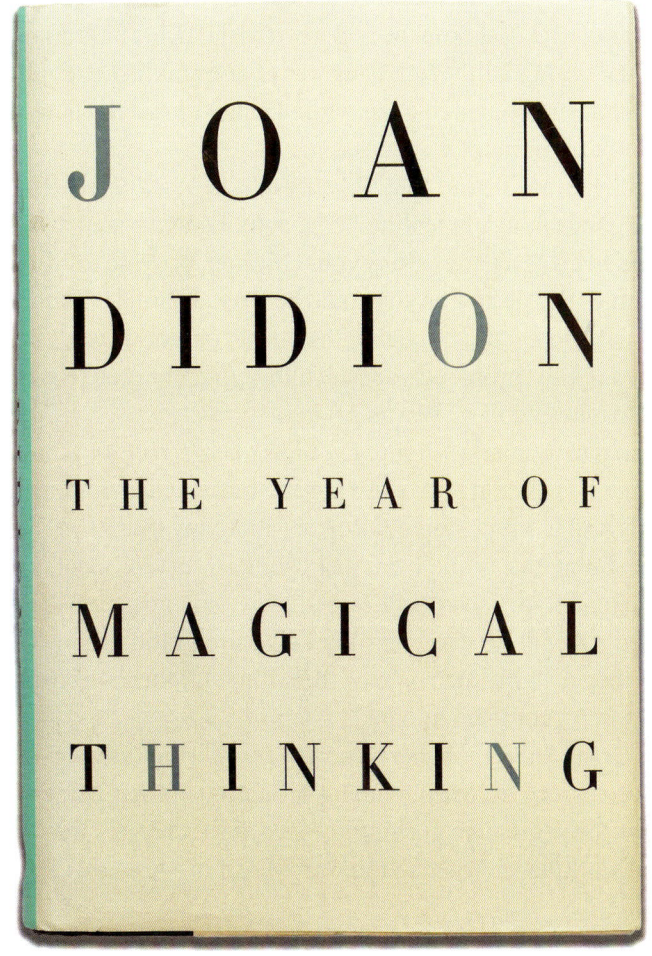

JUST HANG IN THERE

I often felt I wasn't a good enough mom. I was fortunate to have found our amazing caregiver, Lyn, who was with the kids during the day. But after a long day working, I was pretty exhausted and often on my own with the kids. I still feel guilty saying this, but on many nights, making it through the dinner, bath time and bed-time routines was a grind. And weekends seemed unbearably long. I'd take the kids to the pool at the local Y to play sharks and minnows. Or to IKEA, my favourite Sunday morning parenting hack. I'd drop the older two to the IKEA ballroom while Cormac and I went to the dining hall. We'd hang out over breakfast. He'd play with a toy car in the white plastic Ikea high chair while I tried to read the newspaper and feel normal. Those thirty minutes were heaven.

In our book club, we'd read *The Blessing of a Skinned Knee*, which included a chapter about "good enough parenting." The author emphasized that there are some things you need to do as a parent: love your children, provide food and shelter, and be mostly reliable. Her point was you could be a good parent without being perfect. You can, and will, screw up, but being the "best" parent—always being there and solving all of your kids' problems—doesn't allow your children to grow and become resilient. It also takes a toll on you as a parent.

What she said resonated with me. I couldn't be perfect, but that didn't mean I stopped feeling like I should be a better parent: more understanding, more patient, more engaged. And it didn't stop my worries about my kids.

It's (almost) funny that while I was just trying to survive, Scott was winning all sorts of "top 40 under 40" awards. It's not that he didn't deserve them. It's just that I felt I deserved a medal for every day my kids weren't too dirty when they left for school, when they actually ate some of their dinner, when we spent some time at the park, and when I got them into bed by 8 p.m.

Years later, I read Sheryl Sandberg's book *Lean In* which advised working women to become more assertive, confident and proactive in their careers (and to smile more), while at the same time pushing for structural changes that support gender equality in the workplace. My reaction was: "Lean in? Are you kidding me? More like hang in."

FINDING TIME FOR MYSELF

I have a drawer full of caps!

It took me a while to realize it was okay to do something just for myself. When I turned forty (and my kids were two, four and six) I found my way back to the pool, joining the YMCA National Capital Region Masters Swim Team. Those hours in the pool were my escape—time alone to recharge. Even though I felt a little guilty, I knew that doing something I loved made me a better mom and I started to feel more like myself.

Catherine McKenna

YOU CAN'T MAP OUT YOUR LIFE

I laugh when people look at my CV and think my career was a careful path to becoming a cabinet minister. As if. From where I stood, it felt like my journey was full of twists, turns and unexpected detours. Young people often try to map out their careers and personal lives early on, but real life doesn't work that way. That doesn't mean you won't get to where you want to go. It's easy to say, but don't let other people make you second-guess your choices because you think you'll disappoint them. It's your life.

A WINNING CAMPAIGN

POLITICS AND GUNS

The first time I thought about running in politics was in September 2010 when I took Matt (age six) and Isabelle (age four) to Question Period. I wanted to hear the debate about the long-gun registry, which the Conservatives, under Prime Minister Stephen Harper, wanted to abolish.

This was a personal issue. I was eighteen when the Montreal massacre happened in 1989. Like most Canadians, especially women of my generation, I was horrified by it: women in an engineering class at École Polytechnique in Montreal were gunned down by a madman who shouted: "You're all a bunch of feminists, and I hate feminists." Fourteen women were killed. Twelve were engineering students, one was a nursing student, and one was an employee of the university. Women not much older than me had been separated from the men and executed because they were women. It felt like an attack on all of us.

Later, the long-gun registry was brought in by the Liberal government, requiring all non-restricted guns including rifles and shotguns, and the military-style long gun used in the Montreal shooting, to be registered. And now the Conservatives were working to eliminate it. I was outraged and wanted to hear them explain why. And I wanted my two older kids to be there to listen to such an important debate.

We got passes to Question Period and climbed high into the middle balcony looking over both benches. The debate was terrible. It was hardly a debate at all. Just a lot of screaming. Over the noise, a Liberal member of Parliament would ask a serious question about why the Conservatives were abolishing the registry: "The chiefs of police are supporting it. Why wasn't the government?" Prime Minister Harper or a Conservative minister would never bother to answer the question and instead repeated talking points about how regular hunters and farmers were being targeted for their guns. It was noticeable that there were very few women MPs and almost none involved in the debate, even though the registry was created because women had been killed.

My kids couldn't believe what they were watching. Isabelle said: "Who likes guns?" Matt asked: "Why aren't there more women? And why are they all shouting?" Great questions.

In 1989, a police tactical squad enters the École Polytechnique de Montréal where 14 women were murdered. Their names are: Geneviève Bergeron, Hélène Colgan, Nathalie Croteau, Barbara Daigneault, Anne-Marie Edward, Maud Haviernick, Barbara Klucznik-Widajewicz, Maryse Laganière, Maryse Leclair, Anne-Marie Lemay, Sonia Pelletier, Michèle Richard, Annie St-Arneault and Annie Turcotte.

Credit: Ottawa Citizen

I left the gallery that day feeling angry and embarrassed for exposing my kids to such a pathetic scene. I felt ashamed as a citizen. Canadians deserved so much better. I remember thinking I could have done a better job holding those Conservatives to account. I imagined myself on my feet, demanding they explain how a law requiring gun owners to register a weapon—that might have prevented an angry, deranged young man from selectively murdering young, smart, hopeful women—could possibly be seen as targeting hunters and farmers. In what universe could concerns about mildly inconveniencing hunters and farmers be more important than giving police a tool to protect women from misogynist violence? Who was representing the voices of those women who were killed in Montreal or the far too many women who would be killed by their partners in the future? I remember thinking that there needed to be more women in that chamber holding the government to account. And that maybe one of them should be me.

My interest in party politics began four years earlier—in January 2006, to be exact—when the Conservatives won a minority government with Stephen Harper as prime minister. I loathed everything he and the Conservative Party stood for: an economy tilted in favour of big business rather than workers; a move away from Canada's role in the world being focused on multilateralism and peacekeeping to one much more aligned with President George W. Bush, the war on terror and climate denial. If I have anyone to thank for convincing me to enter politics, it's Stephen Harper.

It was clear after the Conservative win that the Liberal Party was in serious disarray. Paul Martin stepped down as leader and a leadership convention was set for December 2006 in Montreal. I decided to attend. When the convention rolled around, my second child, Isabelle, was five months old, and I was still breastfeeding her. I attended the sessions, policy discussions and candidates' events with her strapped to my body in a baby carrier. I can still see her fuzzy green slippers on her little feet sticking out from under the straps as I toted her from session to session.

I found my people at the convention: Liberals who shared my political views and cared as passionately as I did about the need for real change. I supported Stéphane Dion for his focus on climate action and strong federalist views. He won the party leadership.

It was my first foray into party politics and I was hooked: the carnival atmosphere, the like-minded people, the fascinating policy discussions. The experience energized me and whet my appetite for more.

At the 2006 Liberal convention with Isabelle in my indispensable baby carrier and Eddie Goldenberg, Jean Chrétien's former right-hand man. We were supporting Stéphane Dion for leadership, hence all the green.

Isabelle's fun green slippers.

In July 2008, when I was five months pregnant with Cormac, I was standing on my parents' street in Hamilton when a member of the local riding association drove by. He asked if I'd consider running in Hamilton Centre for the next election. They didn't have a candidate yet.

I started to think about it. But there were challenges. First, I may have been from Hamilton, but I hadn't lived there since my teens. Second, I was pregnant! I called up some of my politically minded friends. Most of them thought I was bonkers. "Well," said my good friend Alex, "being pregnant, the good news is no one will expect you to knock on a lot of doors."

I passed. And, unfortunately, Stéphane Dion lost the election that October to Stephen Harper. But now the idea was in my head. The invitation to run led me to take the idea of running more seriously. I knew that studies showed that women had to be asked to run many times in politics before they agreed to do it. Now I'd been asked.

DECIDING TO RUN

On April 14, 2013, Justin Trudeau won the leadership of the Liberal Party in a landslide victory. We'd already been through a series of leaders at this point. Stéphane Dion had resigned in the wake of the 2008 election, as had the subsequent leader, Michael Ignatieff, who led the party to an even greater defeat that gave Stephen Harper his majority government in 2011.

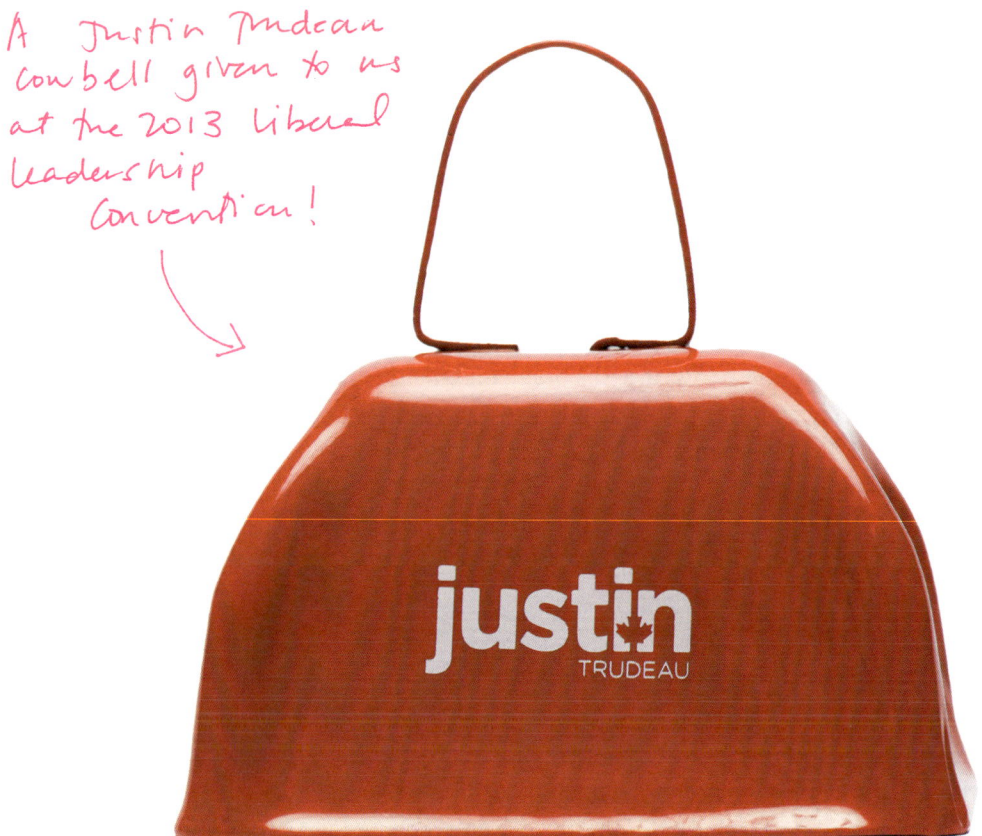

A Justin Trudeau cowbell given to us at the 2013 Liberal Leadership Convention!

For me, and many of my friends in the party and the country-at-large, Trudeau's win was inspiring. It meant generational change. In my case, it also marked a turning point. I saw a lot of similarities between Trudeau's hopeful vision and the ideas and values I cherished like tackling climate change, advancing Indigenous reconciliation, engaging young people in the political process, protecting the rights of all Canadians and supporting a more positive role for Canada in the world.

By then, I was running an organization called the Banff Forum, a public policy organization that brought together leaders from across Canada to discuss and debate the most pressing issues facing Canada. It was packed with people who were passionate about the country, like the journalist and author Andrew Cohen. Some were already in politics, like Conservative MP Michael Chong and Liberal MP Scott Brison, and others, like my friend François-Philippe Champagne, had decided to run in the 2015 election. I knew that as interesting as our debates were, simply talking about policy wasn't going to change things in Canada.

If I wanted to help reverse the Harper policies that I disagreed with, I needed to help get a new government elected. A Liberal government. Why Liberal? I've always believed in Liberal values—individual rights and freedoms, the rule of law and democracy, the free market while keeping the power of big business in check and protecting workers' rights. And while Liberals are idealistic, at our best, we're pragmatic and get big things done.

Still, despite my enthusiasm, I initially had some reservations about Justin Trudeau. I had never met him and I wasn't sure he had enough experience. And I certainly didn't think he deserved to be leader just because his father was Pierre Elliott Trudeau—which really did give him a huge advantage. However, he seemed to have a smart political team behind him, including Gerald Butts, the former principal secretary to the Ontario premier.

I knew Trudeau would need to find good candidates to step forward under the Liberal banner. That's when I decided this might be the right time to run.

YOU CAN DO IT!

Before I entered politics, I attended events for women in politics. They all focused on the barriers that women faced. How hard it is to find any work/life balance. How women in politics are attacked more frequently than men. How politics still favours certain kinds of men. How it's hard for women to raise money. How women are often dropped into unwinnable ridings.

I'm sure that for too many women, these meetings had the unintended consequence of making it seem like it was impossible for them to run. I thought to myself, "Okay, sure it's hard, but women need to step up, or we're never going to get more women in politics." Of course, it's also true that I had no idea what I was getting into, really. But let's agree on one thing: if you show up at a meeting because you're considering running, you don't want to hear all the reasons you're doomed to fail. You also want to hear the reasons you can succeed.

Once again, I thought back to my time in competitive swimming. You set a long-term goal to get elected, and then you figure out all the steps you need to follow to get there. I had no illusions about the challenge ahead of me, including the fact that the Liberal Party was polling in third place. But I certainly wasn't going to allow myself to be defeated before I even entered the race.

I thought about my situation and decided that while I didn't know a lot about winning a nomination to be a Liberal candidate, I figured I had at least some relevant skills and experience. I knew about fundraising, organizing and building a team.

Let's be clear: too many women talk themselves out of running because they don't tick all the boxes. We're less confident and, for a bunch of reasons, often all we can see are our shortcomings, often in microscopic detail. We tell ourselves we don't have deep experience, or the right skills, or a grasp of all the issues, so we write ourselves off and never step up to the blocks. We have to stop disqualifying ourselves. We don't need to have all the skills of an experienced politician to run for office. In fact, it can be an advantage. And trust me, you'll also learn as you go.

Because here's the thing: most women have more skills than they know. We've been involved in our communities. We've organized people and events. We understand issues, often from a very practical perspective gained from spending a lot of time with teachers, doctors, nurses and many other people and systems as we support

My daughter Isabelle was all in. She didn't understand why some people wouldn't want more women in politics.

our kids and aging parents. We have our own networks of friends, neighbours and family. And women know how to work hard. If you're nodding your head, then you already have a lot of the skills needed to be a great candidate.

The truth is that all politicians begin as amateurs. There are no job requirements. If you're eligible to vote, you're eligible to run. The process is open to anyone. And the system works best when we elect a diversity of people with a wide range of skill sets. The reality is we're only going to get more women elected if more women decide to run.

When I told Scott I was planning to run for a Liberal nomination, he supported my decision. He was also trying to make a difference in the world, so he understood why I wanted to be elected. We were fortunate that we could afford it. I had to leave the Banff Forum but I was able do some legal work to help pay the bills. Thankfully, Lyn was a constant in our kids' lives. Plus, Parliament was close to my home. If I won a seat, I could hop on my bike and be there in ten minutes. We'd find a way to make it work.

When I told the kids about my plans, they gave me the thumbs-up. My dad was thrilled. My mom, not so much. Her advice: "Don't do it." It wasn't what I wanted to hear, but I knew it came from a good place. She saw the unrelenting abuse that women in politics, including Sheila Copps, faced. And managing a family on top of a 24/7 job wouldn't be easy. But my heart and gut were telling me, loudly and clearly, that I should run.

I decided to seek my nomination in Ottawa Centre. It's where I lived and where my kids attended school. Truly, this was my community. Plus, our riding had never sent a female MP to Parliament. It was time to change that.

It would be a tough fight. The New Democratic Party had held Ottawa Centre for almost a decade. Paul Dewar, the incumbent, was popular and had won with more than fifty per cent of the vote in the previous election. But the riding had switched between the Liberals and NDP in the past. And when I looked at the polling, I thought I had a shot. I thought that if I put together a good team, and if we worked hard, and if the leader, Justin Trudeau, ran a truly great campaign, we could win. A lot of ifs, but doable. I figured I needed two years to win the nomination and that, most importantly, I needed to knock on doors and talk to people. So what if I was the underdog? I'm part Irish. Being the underdog is what we do.

YOU DON'T NEED PERMISSION

Weirdly, instead of announcing right away that I was going to run for the Liberal nomination for Ottawa Centre, I felt I needed to get the blessing of some of the local Liberal establishment, almost all men, to run. I spent (wasted, really) a few months trying to get their approval. I was naive. I figured if they saw me as a decent candidate, they would support me and help me get nominated.

It was a rough start. Again and again, I was told, directly or implicitly, that Ottawa Centre was a prestigious riding and needed a star Liberal candidate. Clearly, they didn't think they were looking at one. I never found a satisfying description of what a "star" candidate was in their minds, but I'm pretty sure it meant being a long-time Liberal loyalist, and also, a man.

While the Liberals saw the riding as prestigious, many also considered it unwinnable. "Why would you ever run in Ottawa Centre?" I was asked. "You're a smart woman. You'd be a good candidate, but you're going to lose there." Several former MPs and even a few Cabinet ministers suggested that I should run in a riding somewhere else that the party picked for me. Something, perhaps, in Hamilton. I said, "I don't live in Hamilton. I haven't lived in Hamilton since I was nineteen. And I don't need someone to give me a nomination."

"Well," many sighed, "you'll never win here." I had these conversations for weeks. The last one happened at a coffee shop where I met yet another so-called important Liberal. I listened to him talk for a long time about a road trip he'd taken. I was polite but a little impatient. I cut to the chase: "I just want to get your advice about running for the nomination in Ottawa Centre." And then he said it. "Do you know who I am?" he asked. I responded with gritted teeth: "Yes, I know who you are. I know you're important to the Liberal party which is why I've come to you for advice." Then he said, his voice dripping with condescension, "When you come talk to people, you really need to know who they are." I could see right then I wasn't going to get anywhere with him. He wasn't there to help me. He was there for me to stroke his ego.

I went home and pulled out another Nike ad I'd taped to my university dorm-room wall and read the last two lines out loud: "They will tell you no. And you will tell them yes."

That was the end of my conversations with so-called "Important Liberals." I decided I didn't need their permission to run. It didn't matter what they thought. It didn't even matter what my mom thought. In the end, it was up to me and my family. And we were in.

Somehow, I'd figure out my own way to make it happen.

> ALL YOUR LIFE YOU ARE TOLD THE THINGS YOU CANNOT DO. ALL YOUR LIFE THEY WILL SAY YOU'RE NOT GOOD ENOUGH OR STRONG ENOUGH OR TALENTED ENOUGH, THEY'LL SAY YOU'RE THE WRONG HEIGHT OR THE WRONG WEIGHT OR THE WRONG TYPE TO PLAY THIS OR BE THIS OR ACHIEVE THIS. **THEY WILL TELL YOU NO,** A THOUSAND TIMES NO UNTIL ALL THE NO'S BECOME MEANINGLESS. ALL YOUR LIFE THEY WILL TELL YOU NO, QUITE FIRMLY AND VERY QUICKLY. THEY WILL TELL YOU NO. AND **YOU WILL TELL THEM YES.**

Nike print ad from the 90s that I taped to my dorm wall.

THE NEW GIRLS CLUB

"Okay," I said to myself, thinking practically, "So what do I need to get this nomination?" Luckily, I had found an experienced campaign manager, Christine, who explained the deal to me. In a way, it's simple: whoever gets the most votes from registered Liberals in the riding on the day of the nomination wins. That means I had to convince existing Liberals to support me and sell new party memberships to bring new Liberals who would vote for me.

I wasn't sure if I could necessarily win over existing Liberal members, most of whom I didn't know, so I decided I was just going to sign up a ton of new people. This would be a lot of work. The nomination wasn't going to be handed to me. My plan was to be the first one out, sign up a lot of new members, and build up such a big lead that no one could catch up or maybe even want to run against me. But how do you do that?

Unhelpfully, the first thing I learned was that a lot of people don't want to join a party. They just don't. Maybe their parents or grandparents did, but today, most people aren't interested. So I would meet with people who were political types or at least loved talking about politics. I'd sit through long discussions with them telling me what they thought, which was interesting, but at the end of our meeting, when I'd ask them to buy a membership, they'd say, "I'm going to think about it." I'd go home thinking, "This is not going to work. All this time meeting up with people, and I've got next to nothing to show for it."

I decided I needed to be much more focused on outcomes: what would get me the most memberships in the shortest time? Then someone suggested that I start by writing down all of my networks. I thought that was interesting. But what were my networks? Did I even have any? "Well, you coach your son's soccer team," this person said. "That's a network."

A light went on. I was thinking about politics the wrong way. I thought I needed to find political people. But I just needed to find regular people who supported the idea of me going into politics even if they themselves weren't very political. I thought some more about it. I coached my four-year-old son's soccer team, and the players' parents were at every game. We all got along, so I thought I might be able to sign some of them up. And I did.

That felt good. I started making lists of other networks. There were my neighbours. There were people I knew from church. There were a bunch I knew from Canadian Lawyers Abroad. My book club. The local community association whose board I was on. Those were all networks. I had way more connections than I thought. They just weren't buddies from the golf course, a private club or a business network.

Once I started thinking in terms of networks, I quickly realized that the most valuable one I had was made up of the mothers of my kids' friends. I wasn't close with all of them. Some I didn't know by name. I only knew their kids' names—they were Charlie's mom or Sophie's mom. They didn't know me well either, but I figured they knew and hopefully liked my kids and that would be enough. It didn't matter that they weren't especially political or that most had never been involved in politics. That probably helped because while they weren't going to run in politics, many of them also wanted someone they liked who would.

When I told them what I was doing most said "That's great, how can I help?" That's the power of a network: the people in it will believe in you and support you because that's what they do. Families with kids are always helping each other out, whether it's buying tickets or giving rides. I asked these moms to sign up and to think of other moms they could sign up, and I learned I could count on them.

Before long, we had an event run by my friend Christine at a local pub. A bunch of neighbourhood moms came out, and all of them spent ten dollars to become a party member, and a lot signed up as volunteers. I remember thinking, "Okay, wait a minute, this isn't politics as usual. This isn't how they tell you to get memberships." But that's when things started to take off.

We didn't talk much about the government or policies. I had a simple form we used to recruit volunteers and fundraise. It said, "Be the change." That was the unofficial slogan of my campaign. It was broad, obviously, but it meant something to people. When they filled it out, they were saying, "Okay, I'm going to step up and be part of this." That was important to them. It meant they were engaged. It wasn't really about me. It was the opportunity to be a part of a movement that was trying to build something better in Ottawa Centre and maybe across Canada. I'd tell them, "Let's own this. We can't take democracy for granted."

I was also fortunate to be taken under the wing of Penny Collenette, a lawyer, professor and long-time Liberal who had run as the Liberal candidate in the 2008 election. She knew first-hand how tough the riding would be to win, but I think she liked my spunk and determination. She lined up three other women from different parts of the riding with political experience who unofficially joined my team—Lynne, Lynn and Joan. They were an awesome trio.

They showed me the ropes starting with "coffee parties." I'd never been to a coffee party or knew that coffee, thankfully, could be a euphemism for wine. The idea is to ask someone who supports you to invite a few friends to their house to meet you. They'd say something nice about you, and then you pitch everyone on becoming a member and voting for you for the nomination. The trio threw an awesome coffee party where about forty women from all over the riding came, found out more about me, and many signed up. I decided to do coffee parties hosted by friends, or friends of friends, or my friends' moms. I did them night after night after night.

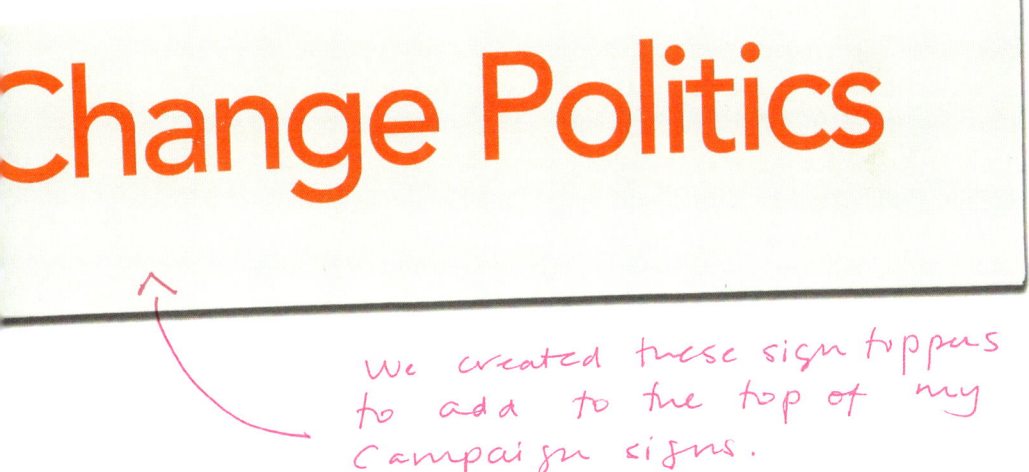

We created these sign toppers to add to the top of my campaign signs.

Eventually, I not only had lots of memberships, but I also had dozens of supporters and volunteers—moms, kids, teenagers, seniors—and for many of them, their first step was filling out that form. Some hosted events. Some organized fundraisers. Some concentrated on selling memberships.

My nomination campaign lasted nine months. It was tough juggling the nomination with kids and work. And I was always hoping I'd get a call saying a nomination date had been set. But it felt like the party establishment was sitting back, waiting to see if some "star candidate" would step forward. It was infuriating. We'd built a super strong team from the ground up. But this was like chasing ghosts. I'd hear a rumour that this person or that person was going to run. Some of them were very well known, and one or two had deep connections in Liberal circles. Almost all the names were men. It seemed there was always this unspoken assumption that sooner or later the right guy would come along and throw his hat in the ring.

In fairness to the party, it's true that it's almost always better if there's a nomination race because nominations are dress rehearsals for the campaign. You have to do the work. And you have to build a team. I was happy to have a race if someone else would finally jump in, but it seemed like we were just wasting time.

Finally, in May 2014, the nomination was held and I was acclaimed. I think all of our hard work scared folks off. To be honest, that was my plan. Run so hard and do so much work that others would realize they couldn't catch up. And by the time the riding association declared me the winner, we had our own unconventional but incredible team entirely built from scratch.

The meeting making me the official candidate was held at my kids' school. I had a few people speak, including an inspiring young volunteer on my campaign, Fritz. He spoke about how our campaign was a bridge between young people and the better future they wanted. Afterward, we went out to a local restaurant and celebrated. My dad came with my mom to Ottawa for it and had the time of his life. He talked to every single person. He was as excited that I was involved in politics as I was. And I was really proud of the team we'd built. I may not have won over most of the old boys club, but I had built a new girls club.

I remember walking home and thinking about all the hard work ahead. The election was still almost a year and a half away.

RUN LIKE A GIRL (FOR REAL)

When you start in politics, lots of people tell you how you "have to" do things—how to campaign, how to build your team, even what to wear (lots of Liberal red). And when you ask "why," the answer is always, "Because that's the way it's done." But I've never believed that you have to do things in a particular way. Following rules blindly has never been my style.

And anyways, I knew I was going to have to run the best campaign ever if I was going to have a shot at winning in the election. So from the start of my time as the official Liberal candidate, I made a promise to myself that I was going to do it my way. I was going to run like a girl.

I made up a list of 10 core campaign rules:

1. We are in it to win.
2. We will run a positive campaign.
3. Everyone is welcome—but no jerks!
4. I'm a mom first, candidate second (I won't be at my best if I can't get home to my kids).
5. It won't just be kid-friendly but we will engage kids and their parents.
6. Knock on doors, doors and more doors.
7. We will have a clear plan, track everything and meet or exceed all our goals—doors, calls, money, volunteers.
8. We will reach out and engage as many people as possible.
9. We will run a local campaign with issues that matter to residents.
10. We will have fun.

And one more that I didn't list with the others, but I knew was critical:

I will be true to myself!

That last one was the most important. I knew that while we would do everything in our power to win, we couldn't control everything. Justin Trudeau was going to have to run an awesome campaign, and Canadians would have to believe in the Liberals if we were going to have a real shot at winning. But running a campaign by staying true to myself was as important to me as winning—and it was something I could control. I wasn't going to change who I was for the campaign. I wasn't going to change how I looked, how I spoke, what I believed in or what was important to me. And I was going to do everything to engage as many people as possible, in all the ways I could think of. I wanted a campaign that brought together as many people who, like me, believed we could build a better community and better country—young people, new Canadians, people who had never engaged in politics before, people who had never voted Liberal before. And to get them excited and believing that politics mattered.

I started getting a lot of advice from long-time political experts on how I should run my campaign. I was told not to focus on local issues. I needed to stay focused on the Liberal Party message. I was told not to waste so much time on social media. This was 2014 and Twitter was just starting to take off. I was told I needed to go to even more events. But my priority was knocking on doors. I was told I shouldn't open a campaign office until the election was called, usually a month or two before the election (although Harper called the 2015 election seventy-eight days ahead, making my first campaign one of the longest in the country's history). I was told not to bother canvassing students living on campus since young people don't vote and not to prioritize low-income areas because the residents were unlikely to turn out.

In the end, we did the opposite. We ran a campaign that focussed on important local issues like building a footbridge over the Rideau Canal, creating more cycling paths and to restoring respect for public servants. We definitely knocked on student residence doors and doubled-down on those living in the low-income neighbourhoods. I did a ton of social media to raise my profile, engage residents and push out our message. We opened our campaign office almost ten months before the election. And it worked.

← I made this t-shirt. I loved it!

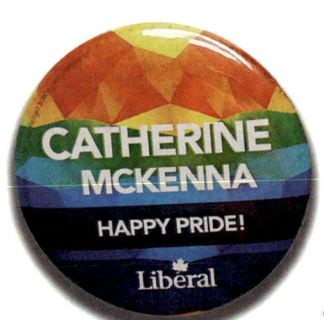

We had a lot of buttons on my campaign.

HOPE BUT MAINLY HARD WORK

The theme of the Liberal campaign was "hope and hard work." As the underdog in what promised to be a gruelling, sixteen-month race, my team and I certainly had to stay hopeful. Mostly, though, we were going to have to work damn hard if we were going to have any chance of winning Ottawa Centre. And we certainly weren't going to win by being negative about the popular incumbent, Paul Dewar. Instead, we'd try to simply outwork him.

The good news is I knew how to work hard. The most useful preparation for a campaign of over five hundred days wasn't my legal education, my work abroad or starting a charity. It was swimming.

Swimming made me tough. It gave me stamina, an ability to power through when things get hard. It taught me about commitment and what it means to be part of a team. It brought me into contact with a lot of different people from different backgrounds. It also gave me an escape from all the noise when I needed to be alone. Swimming also made me disciplined. Local campaigns can be a bit chaotic at times. We were the opposite.

We had an awesome team and we were organized. I had a good foundation from my nomination campaign, but an election campaign is a totally different thing. We needed to knock on doors, fundraise, do community outreach, execute a communications strategy, develop local policy and promote the national platform. It was a lot.

First, I needed a campaign manager. Christine had done a great job on the nomination, but with a toddler and work, she wasn't able to run a full-fledged campaign. Fortunately, at an Ontario Liberal event in spring 2014, I sat in on a session about the importance of engaging volunteers given by a woman named Karin McNair. One of the biggest challenges we'd had with the nomination was properly engaging everyone who signed up to help. Karin was a breath of fresh air. She was a former Air Canada executive, and she spoke about volunteer engagement and how important it was to properly recruit, train and motivate volunteers. She talked in a very practical way that I'd never heard before. I felt a lightbulb switching on.

But as it is with many women in politics, I had to ask her several times if she would run my campaign. She was new to Ottawa Centre and had never run a

I loved these running shoes for door knocking. I wore out three pairs!

campaign before. She wasn't convinced she was up to it. But I had a plan. I got her involved with campaign meetings on my porch and, little by little, she came around. Finally in the fall, she signed up to be my campaign manager.

In the end, what made our campaign successful was not only how disciplined and focused we were under Karin's leadership but also the number and enthusiasm of the volunteers we recruited. That was all Karin. She's very warm, but she's also direct and business-like.

Karin was really good at attracting talent for our core team. We had an amazing group of people with great ideas who I learned so much from. It was humbling that they would spend so much of their time volunteering to help me win. People like Valérie who was from France but lived now in Kanata, a suburb outside of Ottawa. She decided to help on my campaign because she wanted to support a woman and we both cared deeply about climate change. She ended up being a canvass lead out on the streets many nights each week through heat, sleet, snow and rain. Or Andrew, a young person who worked tirelessly through the night inputting and analyzing data about our canvasses, phone banks and volunteers. And Arianna, a University of Ottawa student who became our volunteer coordinator and raced to reach out and train volunteers. She also ran phone banks that reached everyone in the riding. I'll never forget her big smile whenever I came to say "hi" to her volunteers before they started working the phones.

And honestly, the "no jerks" rule on the campaign worked very well. We had a super positive, tight team where everyone supported everyone else. Even though they worked long hours, and occasionally there were some tense moments, everyone got along really well and were committed to the campaign.

We had clear goals, and we ruthlessly measured our progress. Throughout the campaign, we knew exactly how many doors we needed to knock on and how much that worked out to each week. We had a strategy for engaging voters and increasing voter turnout. We had a budget, stuck closely to it, and knew exactly how many dollars we had to spend and how much we had to fundraise. We worked hard to repeatedly win the Liberal Party fundraising award. We leveraged social media in a big way. Yes, we needed some luck and a great national campaign to win. But for the things we could control, it was mostly about hard work.

None of this could have happened without amazing volunteers who are the backbone of every campaign. We knew we needed lots of them. Our goal was to have four hundred volunteers by election day. We started with a base of people from the nomination race, as well as people who signed up on our website or showed up at an event and were interested in getting involved. These were people from all walks of life: moms, kids, seniors, students, new Canadians—even a family from Iran who I had hosted for Thanksgiving one year.

My volunteers were awesome. Volunteers like Bill, a long-time party member, who showed up for almost every single canvass and phone bank. Niny and Sunny who were in their late seventies at the time. Niny would knock on doors even in the foulest weather while Sunny drove their red Prius alongside us. Isabel, who was a neighbour and was always happy to canvass with me. There were Young Liberals from Carleton University alongside new Liberals who had never volunteered on a campaign—just so many people who decided they wanted to get involved in politics and make a difference. We would name a volunteer of the month and award a little trophy to one of our top volunteers to recognize just how much I valued their commitment. But if I could, I would have given an award to everyone.

Even my mother-in-law, Collette, was an indispensable part of the team. She showed up for a month before the election and came to the office every day. She is lovely and very focused. She thought it would be good to create some motivation for the volunteers to hit their phone call targets. (Hilariously, she thought some of them were a bit too chatty). She made a big thermometer and encouraged each volunteer to track the number of calls they made each day. Soon a friendly competition had started. It totally worked!

The days were long and I was still working and of course trying my best to spend as much time as I could with my kids. After leaving the house, I might start with a rally for our volunteers first thing in the morning, then meet with my team, then go out and canvass, then return to the campaign office, have a lunchtime event, talk to everyone who showed up, rally the volunteers again, go home for an early dinner, and then get in one more canvass in the evening. In between all of this, I still had to squeeze in a few hours for paid work. Keeping up that kind of pace isn't just physically demanding, it also requires every last ounce of positive energy because when you're interacting with people, you always have to be on. You can't fake it.

Lots of people showed up at our campaign office to talk about policy, but our policy was to knock on doors. They were told: "You want to talk policy? Go knock on doors with Catherine." I was determined not to overlook any voters, so door-knocking formed the backbone of my days and was unfailingly a highlight. I found canvassing energizing because I loved meeting people and learning about the things they cared about. Every conversation meant we were getting closer to our goal of reaching everyone in the riding. I especially loved talking to people who'd never engaged in politics before. I enjoyed the challenge of trying to get them excited about engaging in politics and believing, as I did, that they mattered. One time, I knocked on a door, and a recent immigrant to Canada answered. When I introduced myself and said I just wanted to have a conversation, he was astonished. "Wow," he said. "In my country, no politician would just come to someone's door and talk to them." We had a great conversation about the problems with our immigration system but how we both loved Canada. Exchanges like this kept me powering through.

But not every day of the campaign was awesome. Some days, it felt like no matter how hard we worked, there was no way we could win. I remember receiving a campaign package from the Liberal Party in December 2014. It had a bunch of numbers but the one that jumped out was eighty thousand. This was the supposed magic number of doors we needed to knock on to have a shot at winning the riding. But by March 2015, after ten months of door-knocking through the often-freezing and wet winter of 2014, we'd only knocked on fifteen thousand doors. After ten months! It was depressing. I had no idea how we would get our numbers up. And then to make matters worse, the Ottawa Citizen kept running articles about how I was a good candidate, but Ottawa Centre was one of the safest ridings in the country and there was no chance the NDP could lose. As one columnist put it, Paul Dewar would have to bite the head off a baby before I had a shot of winning.

This was a tough time but we just kept at it day after day and tried to keep our eyes on winning the long game.

As it turned it out, by the end of the campaign, just over six months later, we'd knocked on one hundred thousand doors in the riding which meant we'd knocked on many doors twice. The secret was having enough volunteers to implement the "snowflake model"–a strategy the Trudeau team adapted from Barack Obama's winning campaign. It relied on training and empowering volunteers to be self-organizing and autonomous so you could have different teams canvassing in different areas of the riding at the same time. This model required many more volunteers, a much greater commitment from them, and a lot of coordination. But we decided to give it a shot, and with some amazing, hard-core field leaders, we built up our snowflake and got the job done.

Hope but a lot of hard work!

A KID-POSITIVE CAMPAIGN

I was told kids had no real place in a campaign, "because kids don't vote." That wasn't going to work for me or my volunteers, many of whom were parents. We made our events family-friendly, with a kids' craft corner in the office. Matt, my eldest, is very crafty, so he took the lead making signs, buttons, and red-and-white rainbow loom bracelets to give to volunteers. Isabelle, then nine years old, loved canvassing. People would be astounded to see her and her friend, Ciara, on their front step, saying, "Hi, I'm campaigning for Catherine McKenna. She's a Liberal candidate. Do you have any issues or concerns?" Once they were shouted at: "The Liberals would do anything for votes! Even send kids out to get them." The door slammed on them and I could hear Isabelle's voice saying, "Thank you. Have a nice day!"

Of course, politics is not for everyone. My son, Cormac, was just six at the time, and he did not enjoy campaigning. He said he would only come to events when there was food. Totally fair.

We even organized a flash dance mob for the day before the election. I'd run into my daughter's dance teacher, who they called: "Kalina Ballerina," while knocking on doors. She wanted to help, as did Jah'kota, a young Indigenous musician who I knew from Canadian Lawyers Abroad. So we invited kids on the campaign to Kalina Ballerina's studio for a short practice before we performed on the street outside my office. So many kids came out with their parents. We turned up Jah'kota's music and everyone did our choreographed dance. It was fantastic! We got great media coverage and signed up even more volunteers to work on election day.

My kids made my volunteers red and white rainbow loom bracelets and in whatever colours the kids who showed up wanted.

WINNING

On Oct. 19, 2015, 522 days after I won the Liberal nomination and seventy-eight days from when the election writ was dropped, it was over. All the door-knocking, phone calls, rallies, events, fundraisers, debates, announcements, videos and tweets. It was done. I vividly remember being out just before polls closed with Yasir Naqvi, then the member of Provincial Parliament for Ottawa Centre, knocking on the last door to make sure the residents voted and doing a hilariously bad high five. I was exhausted but elated. We had left it all on the ice. And we had run an election campaign that was true to who I try to be: hard-working, focused and positive. The polls were very tight so at that point I didn't know if I would win or not. But I still felt happy and very proud of our campaign and the team we had built. Regardless of age, background, or even political persuasion, we were united by a common cause: building a better community and a better Canada.

I went home to watch the results with my family. My kids had made an awesome banner that hung over the TV. I couldn't believe it when I saw the Liberal wave starting in Atlantic Canada. But it wasn't until I received a call from Paul Dewar conceding the race that I realized we'd done it. We'd won. I was the first woman elected MP for Ottawa Centre.

And what a win.

We started as clear underdogs. But in the end, I won with 42 per cent of the vote, the best result in the riding's history. Even sweeter, we had the highest voter turnout in the country, with 82 per cent of Ottawa Centre's residents voting. This meant we had turned out ten thousand additional voters! The one hundred thousand doors we knocked on and the thirty thousand calls we made had paid off. As had the money we'd raised which was more than any other Liberal riding in the country. Our decision to not abandon any part of the riding like others sometimes did—including areas where the voter turnout was traditionally lower—had worked. We even won the Carleton University poll with 488 votes, which far exceeded the total voter turnout of 185 in 2008. Sure, it wasn't a huge number, but we'd engaged a lot of students, and many of them decided to try out politics by working on my campaign. On election day, we had over four hundred volunteers working hard from morning until the close of polls to ensure that every single person we had identified as a Liberal voter showed up.

Around 9 p.m., I arrived with my family at our team's election party at the Clocktower Pub in the west end of my riding. The place was packed with people and cameras. As I walked in to loud cheers, I saw the faces of so many people who had given up dozens or even hundreds of hours to help our campaign. The win wasn't just mine. It belonged to the team, our volunteers, all the people who donated, knocked on doors, and made calls, and everyone who took a chance on me and marked my name on the ballot. People said we couldn't do it, but we did. Hope and hard work paid off.

MY FAMILY IS OFF-LIMITS

The minute I arrived at my election party and saw all the media, I knew everything had changed. Attracting attention during the campaign had been a challenge, but now I was being mobbed. As I made my way through the crowd, with my kids, tightly clutching Cormac's hand (he had his hoodie up over his head, trying to hide), I realized I was in a whole new world.

I remember making a conscious decision that night that while my public life was fair game, family life was not. Under no circumstances would I share it with the public. That meant my kids wouldn't appear on social media or on annual Christmas cards. And after everything that would happen, I was glad that I kept that promise.

My kids and their cousins by one of my signs.

A WINNING CAMPAIGN

BEING ELECTED

AND GETTING STUFF DONE

BEING NAMED TO CABINET

I had never actually thought beyond the election. From the moment I announced I was running, I was focused on winning. I just wanted to be part of the Liberal team that beat Stephen Harper.

Of course, the moment we won the election, that all changed. Immediately, there was speculation about who would be asked by the prime minister to join the Cabinet. I had no expectations. I was a new MP and there were lots of good people to choose from. I was looking forward to settling into my new role as MP for Ottawa Centre.

A week after the election, I got a cryptic email asking me to fill out a disclosure form. It contained basic biographical stuff, but also questions like, "Have you been convicted of an offence?" It seemed that I was likely being considered for Cabinet. But I didn't get my hopes up. I decided at the last minute to go to the Banff Forum to catch up with friends and go hiking in the mountains to get away from it all. I was mentally and physically exhausted, and I knew getting back into nature would be a good tonic.

Soon after I got back to Ottawa, I received another email telling me to come to a meeting in a nondescript building in downtown Ottawa. I was going to be formally interviewed by the transition team. The whole thing was very cloak-and-dagger to keep away journalists who were speculating about who would make the cut for Cabinet. It was awkward when I briefly spotted Jane Philpott, the former chief of family medicine at a major Ontario hospital and also newly elected, as I entered the building and she was coming out. We pretended not to see each other.

I sat in the waiting room wondering what was going to happen. Then I was led into a room and met by two members of the transition team, Peter Harder, a former senior federal public servant, and Marc-André Blanchard, CEO of the law firm McCarthy Tétrault. They asked a number of questions. It wasn't a particularly hard interview. I didn't have anything to hide.

I'm sure a lot of work was going on behind the scenes to build the Cabinet. They had to balance regional perspectives, new and old blood and fulfill the PM's promise to have a gender-balanced Cabinet. It was a challenging exercise.

A few days later, I received a call asking me to come back. This time, when I went into the waiting room, I saw Adam Scotti, the prime minister's photographer.

The cat was out of the bag. I walked into the room, and Justin Trudeau came to the door with a big smile and welcome me in. I saw Gerald Butts, the prime minister's principal secretary, and Katie Telford, his chief of staff, sitting at a table in the corner of the room with big smiles on their faces. It was clear I was being asked to join the Cabinet. I couldn't believe it.

Walking into the room where the PM was and finding out I was in Cabinet. I was ecstatic but nervous!

The prime minister told me how impressed he was by how long and hard I'd worked to get elected, in a riding no one thought was winnable. He emphasized that was a factor in his decisions to put me in Cabinet. And then he told me he had a tough but important job for me. He said something like, "Catherine, I'd like you to be my first-ever minister of environment and climate change, and you're going to Paris for COP negotiations this weekend."

I was thrilled to be asked to be in Cabinet and very excited about the file because the issue was important to me as well as to my kids. I also knew I could draw on my experience as a lawyer and the skills I'd gained in international negotiations at the UN.

But the learning curve, my God. I'm a person who likes to be prepared, and the amount of research I needed to do to get up to speed was daunting. While I had worked a bit on environment issues when I ran Canadian Lawyers Abroad, I was far from being a climate expert. But I was determined that after a decade of climate denial and inaction under Harper's Conservative government, I was going to make sure Canada finally stepped up and did its part to tackle climate change.

THE SWEARING-IN

On the morning of the swearing-in, November 5, 2015, I was told to go to the Marriott Hotel in downtown Ottawa. I was pumped. When you're invited to join Cabinet, you are told you can't tell anyone you've been chosen. You have to wait until the swearing-in. I had no idea who else would be in Cabinet. It was an incredible feeling to walk into the hotel lobby and see my future colleagues. Some I already knew well, like Scott Brison, a seasoned former Cabinet minister and gregarious politician, and François-Philippe Champagne, who had run the Banff Forum with me, and Carla Qualtrough, who I knew from our days as young lawyers in Ottawa and was also a champion swimmer who had competed in the Paralympic Games.

There were also impressive party stalwarts like Carolyn Bennett, a former family physician, the astronaut Marc Garneau, and Stéphane Dion, a long-time environmentalist and the former Liberal leader. Chrystia Freeland, a renowned journalist with deep experience in economics and international affairs, was also there. And there were others who were newly elected like me: Jane Philpott; Patty Hajdu, a single mom who was formerly executive director at Thunder Bay's largest shelter; Bill Morneau, former chairman and CEO of Canada's largest human resources firm; Jody Wilson-Raybould, a lawyer and Indigenous leader; Harjit Sajjan, a police officer and soldier who had been deployed three times to Afghanistan. Some of my new colleagues I recognized from the campaign. Some I didn't really know at all. The idea of a strong team has always been important to me, and I was struck suddenly by the idea that I was going to be part of this incredible group of people. There were lots of hugs, smiles and high fives.

I remember it being the most beautiful day in November, unseasonably warm. It sounds cheesy, but it felt like "sunny ways," the prime minister's slogan, had lit up Ottawa. I had no idea what to wear to a swearing-in and settled on a green dress with flowers for the symbolism of environment and climate change. We were all ushered onto minibuses to go to Rideau Hall for the ceremony, which was hilarious; previous governments had used cars and drivers for each minister, but we were doing things in a new, more accessible way. It almost backfired. The emergency door on our bus accidentally opened as we were on the road, and we nearly lost a new minister out the back before he was even sworn in.

We made it in one piece. We all walked in together along the walkway to Rideau Hall, which was lined with people cheering. And because it was Ottawa and I was local, there were lots of people who knew me and shouted my name. I recognized so many of the volunteers on my campaign—and I hoped it felt like it was their day, too. It was magical. I recently looked at a picture of all our smiling faces. Of course we didn't know it then, but many of them would be gone from Cabinet before the next election.

It's worth pausing on the prime minister's response to a question from a reporter after the swearing-in as to why he had appointed an equal number of men and women to his Cabinet, to which he gave that now-famous answer: "Because it's 2015." His answer was mentioned in all the media reports about the new Cabinet.

Some of my Irish family caught the Cabinet swearing-in and were thrilled that I made it!

At the time, I thought the answer was great. It wasn't defensive or a drawn-out explanation of why it was important to have a gender-balanced Cabinet. It was just a statement of fact. The prime minister was making a point that should have been obvious: half of Canada's population is women, so why shouldn't we be equally represented in Cabinet? It should have been the norm, rather than exceptional. And I'll admit, I laughed when I saw a satirical piece from The Beaverton with the headline, "50 per cent female Cabinet appointments lead to 5,000 per cent increase in guys who suddenly care about merit in Cabinet." It captured the resistance some had to the idea of a Cabinet made up equally of women and men.

Looking back at Trudeau's answer now, the problem is that rather than simply moving on from the fact that the Cabinet was gender-balanced, the prime minister used every opportunity to remind everyone of it. By doing so, not only did he make it seem like it was something novel rather than something that should be the norm, but it also started to sound like it was a marketing ploy or gimmick to make him look good.

Also, by using this framing, he inadvertently undermined the accomplishments of the incredible women who earned their positions based on merit. No one in Cabinet was there simply to "fill a quota." We were there because we were qualified, experienced and ready to serve. But by making it such a big deal, Trudeau put the spotlight on his own virtue rather than the hard work and expertise of the women around him.

It would become a recurring issue. The prime minister liked to remind people that he was a feminist. Inevitably, when issues arose with strong women in Cabinet or caucus, his commitment would then be called into question.

Our Cabinet was diverse in many other ways, too, a point which was often overlooked. It was ethnically diverse; the youngest member was thirty, and the oldest was sixty-nine; there were two persons with disabilities; two were Indigenous; and one minister had come to Canada as a refugee. Study after study has shown that diverse teams make better decisions because they take into account different viewpoints and lived experiences. I noticed this when Cabinet had to talk about really hard issues, like medical assistance-in-dying. It is more than a frame of reference or brand: you need diversity when you're making decisions, especially when those decisions impact the lives of everyone in the country.

TEAM BUILDING

Best team. Ever. Frédérique Caitlin Jocelyn

The good news: I was appointed as a Cabinet minister. The bad news: I had no team and had to get organized fast. The prime minister wasn't kidding when he said I was leaving for Paris that weekend. Suddenly, I had to staff up three offices: my political office to support my role as minister of environment and climate change, my constituency office for Ottawa Centre and my Parliament Hill office as a member of Parliament.

Where to start? First, I needed a chief of staff for my political office. This person plays a critical role. They are there not only to manage your team, provide political and strategic advice, work with the bureaucracy, and get things done, but they basically manage your life—or at least your work life and how it intersects with family life.

I remember talking to the PM's principal secretary, Gerald Butts, soon after the prime minister asked me to be a minister. He was someone who I respected because of his experience in politics and his commitment to fighting climate change. I told him I had someone I thought would be great as my chief of staff. It was Jane McDonald, a long-time friend who also had young kids and had been in my book club before she moved to Winnipeg. She had worked in the private sector on carbon markets, at Environment Canada as a public servant, and was running an environmental organization. He said: "Well, we've already chosen a chief for you." I said, "What do you mean? Don't I get to pick my own?" He kind of joked, "Do you want to fight about it?" I said, "Maybe" (not really joking at all).

In one of the more recent developments in a long line of decisions that have concentrated power in the prime minister's office (PMO), the PM had decided each minister's chief of staff would be picked by the "centre." Marlo Raynolds, a long-time environmentalist who had run in the election for us in a Conservative riding in Alberta and lost, was chosen for me. Marlo was extremely experienced and well respected on climate change and energy issues. I was worried, initially, because he did not know me and my approach to work or life, and I wasn't sure that he wasn't basically there to keep me in line. At the outset, Marlo clearly knew far more than me about climate, and that can make for a strange dynamic. But that's just how the system works. Ministers have to work hard to learn their files and use their best judgment while being surrounded by experts. The bottom line: I was the minister, and I made the decisions. Still, I came to really respect Marlo and we learned to work as a team. In the end, Marlo and I built an incredible relationship and he always had my back. He was methodical, detail-oriented, and cerebral, while I was passionate, focused on outcomes, and often came to issues with a creative, out-of-the-box approach. We developed a very trusting relationship, and together we built an amazing team—I'd say one of the best in politics. I was a pretty tough boss, expecting that we deliver quickly and well, especially after what felt like a wasted decade under the Harper government. The team delivered. And Jane was a part of it, ably serving as my director of policy and a great confidante and friend.

As minister, I had three departments reporting to me, all staffed by highly capable public servants: Environment Canada, Parks Canada and the Canadian Environmental Assessment Agency. As minister, I was not only tasked with developing legislation but also with making and authorizing hundreds of decisions each year. The role of the public service was to provide me with non-partisan advice, and then implement whatever decision I made. On my first day, I personally drafted an email to all of them. I thought it was important—especially after the Harper years, which set back progress on the environment and ignored science and scientists—to make clear that I respected their work and was committed to working with them to deliver on the government's agenda.

The email read:

> Subject: Looking Forward to Working Together
>
> Dear Colleagues,
>
> I entered politics to make the world a better place for my three children, and I cannot think of a better place to work towards this goal. For the Prime Minister, myself, and our government, delivering real results on climate change and the environment is one of our highest priorities. We have an ambitious agenda, and only by working together can we achieve it.
>
> I look forward to receiving your frank and fearless advice and working with you to deliver innovative solutions.
>
> Best regards,
> Catherine McKenna

Next, I had to build my constituency team and find a local office where residents could reach out to me and my team for help accessing services or programs or to advocate for local issues they care about. Scott Brison, my new Cabinet colleague and a long-time parliamentarian and former minister, gave me great advice. He said one of the problems with a newly elected MP immediately becoming a minister is they treat their ministerial files as far more important than the issues facing their local constituents. He told me this can be a minister's downfall because, at the end of the day, everyone is elected by the people in their riding. My constituents needed to be my priority and I found the very best people I could, including several social workers who could help solve problems and empathize with the thousands of residents who contacted our office each year.

CANADA IS BACK

Just a few days after being sworn in, I was on a plane to Paris for pre-COP negotiations. At the time, I had no idea what "COP" stood for. I had to ask my chief of staff. "Conference of the Parties," he said. That wasn't particularly helpful. I immediately banned the use of acronyms by my team.

The Paris climate negotiations took place over two weeks, from the end of November to mid-December. After two decades of failed attempts, the goal was to finally land a global deal to tackle climate change with countries agreeing to limit global temperature rise in line with a clear temperature goal. It was by no means a given that we would succeed. Or that if we did, the agreement was sufficiently ambitious to solve the climate crisis.

COP21 President Laurent Fabius sent me a replica of the gavel he used to conclude the conference.

These climate negotiations were a huge moment not only for me but also for our new government. Canadians and the world were watching. People were skeptical at home and overseas about how committed Canada was to climate action, particularly after the previous Conservative government had been one of the laggards in international climate negotiations, not one of the leaders. I felt huge pressure to deliver.

I spent the night flight to Paris poring over heavy briefing binders concerning the negotiations. The moment I stepped off the plane I was in the glare of camera lights and doing a live TV interview in French. The journalist wanted to know how we could be serious about climate change, given the huge emissions from Alberta's "tar sands." I managed to hold my own and explained that our government was committed to doing the work at home to finally meet our international climate targets.

At my first meeting of ministers later that day, I listened closely to the other speakers. Despite the importance of the topic, it was a stream of technical jargon and more acronyms. No one said anything compelling about why we were here and what we needed to do: fight climate change and save the planet.

I ripped up the speech prepared by officials. It was long but didn't say much of anything. Instead, I decided to be direct. I said three things: first, Canada believed in the science behind climate change; second, we strongly supported developing countries who had done the least to cause climate change, but were paying the highest price; third, I was committed to ensuring that Canada did everything we could to help land an ambitious agreement. I ended by saying, "Canada is back." The room erupted in cheers. Canada's new commitment to climate action created momentum in what were tough negotiations. But it was a moment of clarity for me. It reminded me that it doesn't matter whether you're talking to your swim team, campaign team or a gathering of world leaders: if you want to make an impact and bring people with you, trust your gut, deliver a succinct, clear message, and speak from the heart.

I left the negotiations briefly to return to Canada to be sworn in as a member of Parliament. Before I returned to Paris for the negotiations, a terrible thing happened. On November 13 and 14, ISIS launched a series of horrendous attacks across Paris, including at a soccer match and a rock concert. One hundred and thirty people were killed, and almost five hundred were wounded. Everyone expected the climate negotiations to be postponed or cut short. But the French government of François Hollande didn't back down. They were determined to push ahead. I was assigned two RCMP officers as we boarded a plane back to Paris. When we arrived, there were soldiers with machine guns at the airport and tanks on the street.

I knew it was important to really demonstrate that Canada was back. We did that in part with a Team Canada approach. When I was determining who would be on the Canadian delegation, I was clear that we needed to show that it had a diverse group of Canadians, including a number of premiers from Quebec, Ontario, BC, and Alberta, members of Parliament from all parties, Indigenous leaders, environmentalists, representatives from business and young people. It was a clear show of force from Canada in support of landing a deal.

But "being back" also required that Canada take a serious role in influencing the negotiations. The challenge was that our negotiating team of public servants wasn't used to Canada wanting to play a leading role in climate negotiations—especially a positive one. When I asked who I should meet with, I was asked who I wanted to meet with. This got us nowhere fast.

Here, the US delegation was helpful. These were the Obama years. Their team was led by Secretary of State John Kerry and staffed with heavy hitters who'd been working for years to land a successful climate agreement. They were happy Canada was back on board and that we were ready to work with them to get an ambitious deal. The US team included Brian Deese, President Obama's savvy senior advisor on climate, Todd Stern, their determined and pragmatic lead negotiator, and Sue Biniaz, their incredibly smart and creative lead climate lawyer. They filled me in on the negotiations and helped me figure out where Canada could play a useful role. I learned that a bit of Canadian charm coupled with not being the US could come in handy. That meant approaching like-minded countries, often from Commonwealth countries and the Francophonie, to remind them of our connection and the importance of working together. They could tell I was all in and we worked closely.

As the head of Canada's delegation, I was clear on the elements that reflected Canada's interests and values as well as the priorities we would push to include in the agreement. First, we wanted an ambitious global agreement with a clear temperature target the world would not exceed. While there was general acceptance that global warming should be limited to two degrees Celsius, countries led by the Marshall Islands made the point that many small island developing states would be underwater if global temperatures hit that threshold. I shared their concerns and announced that Canada supported the goal of striving to limit warming to 1.5 degrees. This announcement was well received by the countries most impacted by climate change. We were then asked by Tony deBrum, the foreign minister of the Marshall Islands, to join the High Ambition Coalition of countries, which was leading the charge to strategically push back against countries that were fighting against serious climate action. I considered it an honour for Canada to join.

Team Canada at COP21 in Paris.

We were also working to include language in the agreement that recognized Indigenous rights and Indigenous traditional knowledge. I worked closely with our Indigenous leaders from Canada and Indigenous peoples from around the world to make this happen. Although it would have been much better to have this text in the body of the final agreement, we were all happy to see it in the preamble. This massive team effort also helped build ties between myself and our negotiating team with Indigenous leaders, which carried through the rest of my time as minister.

Canada was also working with other like-minded countries to recognize the disproportionate impacts of climate change on women. UN figures indicate that 80 per cent of people displaced by climate change are women, which is compounded by higher income inequality and financial insecurity for women globally. Also, climate instability leads to greater social unrest and more gender-based violence. On this count, we were also successful.

Canada's greatest success, however, and something I am still very proud of, is the role we played in negotiating Article 6 of the Paris Agreement, which set out the principles for countries to voluntarily cooperate to reach their climate goals including through carbon markets. In a bilateral meeting with Laurent Fabius, the very determined French foreign minister and president of the negotiations, I said I was willing to do just about whatever it took to help move the negotiations forward. He asked me to become one of the fourteen lead minister negotiators tasked with resolving the most challenging outstanding issues. I was charged with negotiating Article 6 or the "markets" text. I wasn't an expert by any means but my trade law background combined with my negotiation experience was extremely useful, as was the support of Canada's negotiating team. I led often tense negotiations about Article 6 over two all-night sessions. It was freezing and, uncharacteristically, there was little food, which was possibly a smart tactic by the French. At one point, one negotiator from a country that didn't believe in markets said if the markets text was included, she would personally ensure I was responsible for the failure of the Paris Agreement when her country refused to ratify it. It was dramatic, but I didn't bite. We got it done.

The final negotiations for the Paris Agreement were unlike any I'd been involved with before: back-and-forth deal-making, speechifying, cajoling and compromising. Nothing was certain until the eleventh hour. The deal hung in the balance, and then almost collapsed because of one word.

When the final draft of the Paris Agreement was released to the exhausted delegates in the conference hall, I heard someone sitting behind me say, "Oh shit." A member of the US team had noticed the use of the word "shall" ("developed countries shall take the lead in cutting emissions") where a "should" should have been. That wasn't a small issue. It was massive. The US argued that the word "shall" made the text legally binding, and it would likely never make it through the US Congress. This had been an issue throughout the negotiations, and nobody knew how this error could have happened. I couldn't believe it. After all this work, the agreement could fail over one word.

Then things got a bit bonkers. Secretary Kerry got up and huddled with Laurent Fabius. Then he went over to Xie Zhenhua, the Chinese negotiator, and spoke with him. Negotiators from a number of other countries, including Nicaragua, came over smelling an opportunity to reopen the negotiations. I asked the Americans what they were going to do. Apparently, someone was trying to reach the Pope so he could make a personal call to the president of Nicaragua to ask him to agree to this one change and get a deal. I'm not sure if it ever happened, as we heard that the Pope was giving a mass at St. Peter's Square at the exact same time. You can't make this up.

Suddenly, Fabius called the room to order and everyone sat down. He said there were some issues in the translation that had to be corrected. An official quickly read out, mostly incomprehensibly, a bunch of translation issues to be corrected—including the culprit, "shall" being changed to "should." Fabius had momentum now and quickly asked for agreement. Then, he forcefully gavelled the conference to a close, ignoring any protests. Everyone on the floor erupted in cheers. We had an agreement.

During closing statements, Marcelo Mena, Chile's vice-minister for the environment (and my new best friend after interminable sessions seated next to Chile), singled out Canada's efforts as critical to getting a deal. I turned and winked at the Americans behind us—they laughed. Yes, our team had killed ourselves to do everything we could to get a deal, but Canada had only been actively involved for about a month. Meanwhile, the Americans had been working around the clock for years—and in the case of Kerry and many of the members of their negotiating team, decades.

The importance of the Paris Agreement should not be understated. Finally, the world had come to agree on an ambitious, legally binding international treaty to tackle climate change. Achieving it was a messy, high-stakes affair, but in the end, multilateralism worked. And France deserved full credit with its efforts over the years to cajole countries to commit to ambitious climate action. Despite a devastating terrorist attack, the French government and the French people did not flinch and still brought the world to Paris because they rightly believed nothing could be more important than getting a deal to tackle climate change.

Later that night, I celebrated with the Canadian negotiating team over a few drinks and bad food in the basement of an Irish pub beside our Best Western. We were exhausted, but very proud. Canada was back.

Now it was time to go home to negotiate a climate deal with the provinces and territories. This was going to be just as difficult, maybe more.

WOMEN KICKING IT ON CLIMATE

There is an untold story from the Paris Agreement negotiations. Or at least one not told often enough. A group of inspiring women helped ensure that we landed not just any agreement but one ambitious enough to save the planet. These women held different roles, but all used their experience, networks and charm to kick ass and push harder for more climate ambition. They were all women fiercely dedicated to finally getting a serious global plan to tackle climate change.

Leading the effort was Christiana Figueres from Costa Rica, the executive secretary of the UN Framework Convention on Climate Change. She is sharp, tough talking behind closed doors, and extremely good at making deals. At the beginning of the negotiations, she said something that snapped us all to attention: "Never before has a responsibility so great been in the hands of so few."

Economist Laurence Tubiana was France's ambassador to COP21. She performed extraordinary diplomatic feats wearing her many different pairs of funky Converse sneakers. It had been her idea to bring all the heads of state to Paris at the beginning of the conference, which put significant pressure on negotiators to reach a deal. She became a role model and mentor.

There were many other women too, including fellow ministers Izabella Teixeira from Brazil, Amina Mohammed from Nigeria, Amber Rudd from the UK and Åsa Romson from Sweden. There was Mary Robinson, the former president of Ireland and United Nations High Commissioner for Human Rights, and already one of my idols for her unwavering support of human rights and justice. At COP21 she kept us focused on the fact that the poorest in the world are also the most vulnerable to climate change. Jennifer Morgan, head of Greenpeace International, brought together environmentalists to demand an ambitious agreement based on climate science. Hindou Oumarou Ibrahim, a member of Chad's Mbororo people and a fierce Indigenous environmental activist fought for the recognition of Indigenous rights and traditional knowledge. Sharan Burrow, from the International Trade Union Confederation was a modern-day Rosie the Riveter, a passionate advocate for workers' rights. She was there to make sure that the energy transition led to good jobs and was fair and just. And Rachel Kyte, the straight-talking, take-no-prisoners head of Sustainable Energy for All, who was pushing hard for credible carbon markets and affordable, reliable and sustainable energy.

There were so many other women leaders from around the world, including ministers, climate activists, business women, Indigenous women and grassroots leaders.

There were also many young women, who were some of the most inspiring and outspoken about the need for climate action. Selina Leem from the Marshall Islands was only eighteen years old when she gave a passionate speech to leaders at COP21. She explained that her her small island home would disappear into the ocean if they failed to act.

All of these women understood that the climate negotiations weren't a zero-sum game. It wasn't about what each particular country wanted from the Paris Agreement, but what we could do together to tackle the biggest challenge the world faced. These women understood that we needed to step up to protect the people and communities we loved. There was no time left for excuses.

Awesome women kicking it on climate!

BE REASONABLE

I first met Jean Chrétien when a friend brought me to a Liberal event at law school. He was working the room, shaking hands, joking with people. You could tell he was comfortable in his own skin. He always said people underestimated him, and he used that to his advantage. He was *le p'tit gars de Shawinigan*.

When I reached out to Monsieur Chrétien, as I called him, during my campaign, he was gracious and agreed to do a rally with me at my campaign office. The media showed up and Chrétien gave a great speech, and then, to my surprise, whole-heartedly endorsed me. It marked a turning point in my campaign. We had momentum.

After I was elected, I'd meet him occasionally for lunch. His law office had a secret staircase we would take to his favourite dining spot, the Rideau Club. We would chat about politics and he would ask me how things were going. Early on, he gave me the best political advice I've probably ever received. Slightly exasperated, he said: *"Catherine, les Canadiens sont raisonnables. Soyez raisonnable!"* I understood exactly what he meant: "Canadians are reasonable. Be reasonable."

He understood that the Achilles' heel of the Liberal Party is arrogance. Liberals, I'm sorry to say, have a tendency to talk down to people, to act like they know what's best for them. He knew people would eventually tire of us if we kept talking about lofty ideals and not living up to them, and if our chief spokesperson, the prime minister, was seen to be preachy and disconnected from the lives of Canadians. He was right.

I first tested Monsieur Chrétien's advice when I had to deal with a "shit" file—literally. Right after being sworn in, I had to decide whether to approve dumping sewage into the St. Lawrence River. Montreal's mayor, Denis Coderre, was desperate for permission to release wastewater to allow critical repairs. Multiple municipal and federal governments hadn't properly invested in wastewater infrastructure, and if they didn't act now, a much worse, uncontrolled release could happen later, with serious consequences.

Sharing a laugh with Monsieur Chrétien.

Coderre called me daily, asking for approval, but I wasn't going to make the decision without asking scientists who could assess the impact of a release and tell us how to minimize any harm. We also reached out to local Indigenous communities. I soon learned that our scientists supported a controlled release. Explaining this to the public would be harder.

But I remembered Chrétien's advice and we held a media event where scientists explained their findings, which also showed that unlike the Harper government, we wouldn't muzzle them. I also explained how our government would invest in better wastewater infrastructure to make sure this wouldn't happen again. It wasn't easy. But by being transparent and reasonable, most of the public understood and I got through it. Monsieur Chrétien was right.

A political cartoon by Yannick Lemay (Ygreck) in Le Journal de Québec, November, 4, 2015.

NEGOTIATING A DEAL AT HOME

As soon as I got home from the Paris Agreement negotiations, the next big file landed in my lap. I needed to deliver Canada's first real climate plan. I knew it wouldn't be easy. At that point I had more passion than expertise, but, somehow, I had to come up with a comprehensive plan that had the support of all of the provinces and territories.

I soon received a sober briefing from my officials who told me where Canada stood in terms of the country's emissions and the various options we had to lower them. Despite decades of promises from various federal governments, Canada had never met its international climate targets. Against our G7 counterparts, we were laggards.

Alberta had the highest emissions of any province, followed by Ontario, Quebec, BC and Saskatchewan. While Canada's emissions made up about 1.6 per cent of global emissions, that still placed us tenth among the world's biggest emitters. Even worse, Canada's per capita emissions were among the highest globally. If every country emitted as much per person as Canada, we'd have crashed the planet already.

The Fort McMurray wildfires that took place in May 2016, in the middle of my negotiations with provinces and territories, were a stark reminder that climate change wasn't just a future threat but a present danger. The devastating fires, which displaced over eighty thousand people and ravaged Canada's oil sands, showed everyone what was at stake. It wasn't just an environmental issue; it was an existential one.

Under the Paris Agreement, Canada had committed to do our part to limit global warming to 1.5 degrees. For the first time, I was determined we were going to have a clear plan to achieve our target. We were going to implement the plan and achieve it. This was another thing I'd learned from swimming. It wasn't enough to have a long-term goal—you need to have a plan and you need to do the work.

Developing a climate plan might sound easy. Essentially, emissions need to go down, and money needs to move from fossil fuels to clean energy—and all of this needs to happen at scale. But decades of rising emissions and delayed action meant we needed to orchestrate a much faster decline in emissions to meet a 2030 target. And it was clear there was no meeting any target without Alberta's oil sands emissions going down.

After weeks of briefings and discussions, I knew it was time to chart a new course for Canada. With the help of my team and the invaluable support of Steve Lucas, a senior public servant seconded to me (who later became my deputy minister), we worked closely with the PMO (especially Gerald Butts, the architect of Ontario's climate strategy) and crafted a set of guiding principles for Canada's climate plan.

Our first principle was to build on the climate progress already underway in many provinces. Canada is a federation and climate action needs to reflect regional realities. This part is often forgotten but in 2016, the four largest provinces—representing 80 per cent of the population—had already implemented a price on carbon pollution either as part of a cap-and-trade system with California (Quebec and Ontario) or as a carbon price (BC and Alberta). There was also other good progress with Rachel Notley's NDP government in Alberta which had capped oil sands emissions and required oil and gas to reduce their heavily polluting methane emissions. Ontario had phased out coal-fired electricity which produced the largest reduction in emissions in Canada's history and Alberta had a plan to do so as well.

The second principle was that we needed to ensure that the transition to a cleaner future was not only effective but fair to all Canadians. This meant we had to invest in retraining and supporting the communities and workers most affected by this transition. We had to create a cleaner, greener economy that benefited everyone. Public transit, energy efficiency and clean technology were areas in which we could make smart investments that would improve lives, save low- and middle-income families money, and create prosperity and good jobs.

The third principle was perhaps the most difficult one: we needed to actually deliver the emissions reductions in line with our target. After looking at the modelling, we decided we should stick with the Harper government's target of reducing emissions by 30 per cent below 2005 levels by 2030. Once we were on a path to reach that target, we could announce a more ambitious one. It was critical to build trust with Canadians and show we were serious about climate action and capable of delivering progress.

We were also determined to engage Indigenous communities throughout our negotiations. I was fortunate to have built relationships with several Indigenous leaders through our work together to secure recognition of Indigenous rights and traditional knowledge in the Paris Agreement. These leaders were critical to developing effective and sustainable climate policies.

I spent that year in extraordinarily intense negotiations with provinces and territories that had no end of drama. A lot of the attention was focused on whether we could land a price on pollution across Canada. This was an important pillar of our plan. When it is essentially free to pollute, there is very little incentive for businesses and people to reduce their emissions.

I did my best to make the case to provinces on carbon pricing and to bring the business community on board. In July 2016, I invited Mark Carney, the former governor of the Bank of Canada, to have a discussion with me in front of a Bay Street audience at the Toronto Board of Trade. I assume most people showed up to hear Carney speak about Brexit, which had happened a few weeks before, but very helpfully, I made sure we also talked about why carbon pricing was a smart strategy for Canada.

I said this to my team all the time. Climate isn't just an environmental thing. It's an economic, justice, national security, jobs, Indigenous, innovation, gender, health, infrastructure thing! They made me a mug.

Meanwhile I was being hammered regularly about carbon pricing in the House of Commons by Conservative politicians. I created the Carbon Pricing Leadership Coalition made up of Canadian companies and financial institutions that supported putting a price on carbon pollution. I was able to round up two of the major banks (which meant that the remaining three had to follow), consumer goods and telecommunications companies, and even one oil-and-gas company, Suncor (which then had much more forward-thinking leadership than now). Besides demonstrating to Canadians that we were working with industry to develop our carbon pricing strategy, it was helpful each time I was slammed about a "job-killing carbon tax" in Question Period to name companies that supported carbon pricing and the number of people they each employed.

By early fall, after many rounds of frustrating negotiations with my provincial counterparts, I knew I couldn't land carbon pricing on my own. I worked with Gerald Butts to line up an announcement by the prime minister about the federal system. We decided the fairest approach was to allow provinces to create their own pricing system (either cap-and-trade or a carbon price) as long as the price went up by $10 every year until it reached $50 per tonne in 2022. The provinces were free to do what they wished with the revenues that were raised, including returning them to taxpayers. This plan meant that Ontario, Quebec, BC and Alberta's plans all complied from the start. The catch was that provinces that didn't comply with this standard would be subject to a federal pricing system. It might surprise some critics to know that our strong hope was that all provinces would decide to develop their own system and would keep the federal government out of it. On October 3, while I was meeting with my provincial counterparts, the prime minister publicly announced that the provinces had until 2018 to introduce their own pricing system, otherwise the federal government would step in.

At the same time, I briefed my provincial counterparts. Several of the ministers were taken aback and stormed out of the room to speak to the media outside. It was a dramatic moment in the negotiations, but sometimes you need to make tough calls. And we couldn't reach our target in a cost-effective way without pricing.

The most apoplectic reaction was from Saskatchewan's premier, Brad Wall. He would not support any price on pollution in Saskatchewan or require action from its oil-and-gas sector. This was a problem given that Saskatchewan's emissions were continuing to rise. He also didn't think Canada should bother reducing its emissions at all. Foolishly, I had some hope that I could bring Scott Moe, Saskatchewan's environment minister, on side. When he unexpectedly decided to come to COP 22 in

Morocco, I organized it so I was sitting beside him at a dinner I was hosting. Shortly after we sat down, I handed him a piece of paper that showed how Saskatchewan could use the revenues from a carbon price to eliminate its provincial sales tax. I thought that was a pretty great idea and it came from my ministerial colleague from Saskatchewan, Ralph Goodale. But Moe ran to the media the second he got back to Canada and said there was no way Saskatchewan would support carbon pricing.

A number of months later on December 9, 2016, during a First Ministers' Meeting that included the prime minister, premiers and Indigenous leaders, Canada's climate plan was officially announced. It included a national carbon pricing framework, a phaseout of coal-fired power plants, improvements to energy efficiency for buildings and transportation, support for clean energy innovation across all sectors and a continued commitment to engage Indigenous leaders in climate action. Every province and territory signed on to the plan except Saskatchewan and Manitoba.

I was proud. The climate plan we announced was the result of months of hard work. It wasn't perfect, but it was a necessary step forward. It showed that, even in the face of enormous challenges, the country could come together to take meaningful action on the most urgent issue of our time.

TURNING OFF MY PHONE

Early in my career as a minister, I knew I needed to get my daily life under control both for the sake of my family and my sanity. I was lucky. Unlike most MPs and Cabinet ministers, I didn't fly back and forth to Ottawa each week. But it also meant I didn't have the extra time at the end of the day to stay late at the office, attend meetings, go to events or just hang out with colleagues over dinner.

While there is no "regular" day in politics, I did try to establish routines. I'd get up early to swim a few times a week. That meant rushing home with wet hair and throwing on work clothes. I'd have breakfast with the kids, help them get ready for school, and like most other parents, rush off to work.

Unlike most parents, though, my job also came with a government driver. I'd pack my government-issued briefcases into the car and jump in where my assistant would be waiting to brief me about the day ahead. I'd try to do my makeup and manage, at most, some mascara and lipstick. My team found this whole routine pretty hilarious.

Depending on the day, I either went to my Environment and Climate Change office in Gatineau or to my office on Parliament Hill. If it was Tuesday—Cabinet day—I'd head to the Hill to meet with my chief of staff and deputy minister, along with members of my team. We'd do last-minute preparations if I was presenting on an issue or discuss what Cabinet items I should speak about. The Cabinet meeting generally lasted two hours, depending on the agenda and if there were any particularly contentious issues. Afterward, I'd meet with my press secretary and get ready to answer any questions from the reporters waiting outside.

Then it was back to my office for a quick lunch at my desk, followed by emails, reading up on files, and reviewing my team's best guess at the questions I'd likely be asked during Question Period—almost always about carbon pricing. After that, I'd go to the dreaded QP prep session with other ministers. I'd try to arrive early to catch up with colleagues in the government lobby of the Commons before the chaos began. And then came the gong show that was Question Period. Afterwards, if I had anything to announce to the media—say, an update on climate negotiations—I'd head to the microphone on my way out of the House of Commons.

That done, I'd race up the three flights of stairs to my House of Commons office for meetings. Cabinet committee meetings on specific policy areas would often follow. Over the years, I sat on many Cabinet committees, including Canada and the World; Canada and the US; Environment and Climate Change and Energy; among others. Treasury Board became my favourite, despite the massive volume of reading material, because it gave me a line of sight on everything the government was doing. I took seriously our responsibility to ensure taxpayer money was spent effectively and inline with government priorities. With Scott Brison as president of the Treasury Board, we were very tough on spending and grilled public servants on why the investment was critical, how it would deliver results, and how it would be managed.

I tried to quickly get out of the office after committee meetings, although it was often hard with my team wanting to speak to me about their files. Eventually I would rush home to have dinner with my kids (often they'd have already had theirs), hang out a bit, help with homework, and get them to bed. I'd try to avoid work calls and emails during this time, but it was hard. After they were in bed or on their way, I would try to catch-up on my inbox and callsheet. I generally fell asleep with my briefing books by my side. The glamorous life, right?

Almost from the start, I felt badly for missing my kids' events and being distracted even when I was home. My youngest, Cormac, would often lift my head from my phone and say, "Look me in the eyes, Mom." That was a wake-up call. I set a rule: home by 5:30 p.m., offline until 8 p.m. Then I would get back to work.

Soon after I was asked in an interview about my work-life balance. I talked about my policy of turning off my phone when I got home to focus on my kids. People stopped me in the street to thank me for setting an important example. Even Melinda Gates praised my decision, although she wished that male ministers would adopt it, too. And guess what? It worked. At least most of the time. Nothing was actually that urgent. The world kept running even when my phone was off.

Examples of things that might happen during a day: preparing for meetings during the drive to work. Leaving Cabinet with my assistant Chantalle. Meeting with Inuit leaders. Walking with my colleagues to a press conference. In my office with Mark Carney (now Canada's Prime Minister). Talking to young people outside of Parliament about Parks Canada (that was my favourite).

BEING ELECTED AND GETTING STUFF DONE

A DYSFUNCTIONAL WORK ENVIRONMENT

While I loved taking my seat in the House of Commons—it reminded me that I had the honour of representing the people of Ottawa Centre—I really hated daily Question Period. It wasn't the pressure of answering questions. That could be stressful, but it was part of the job. What I loathed was the constant shouting, heckling and personal attacks. Partisanship has its place, but this was extreme. It was exhausting and toxic.

I can see why Question Period turns many people off. It feels like a cage match—MPs are yelling at each other and trying to score cheap points rather than engage in any kind of meaningful debate. It's supposed to be about holding the government to account, but more often than not, it's just a chaotic spectacle. The Conservatives, in particular, frequently made absurd and misleading allegations as well as personal attacks. Climate change denial was often at the heart of it.

When I came back from the pre-COP talks in Paris, I was thrown into this bear pit. My director of parliamentary affairs handed me a massive binder filled with answers to possible questions and said, "You have to know all of this for QP—including in French." I was stunned, but went through the entire binder that night, familiarizing myself with likely issues I'd be questioned on—big ones like carbon pricing, and small ones, like protecting *la rainette faux-grillon*, a threatened species of tiny frogs.

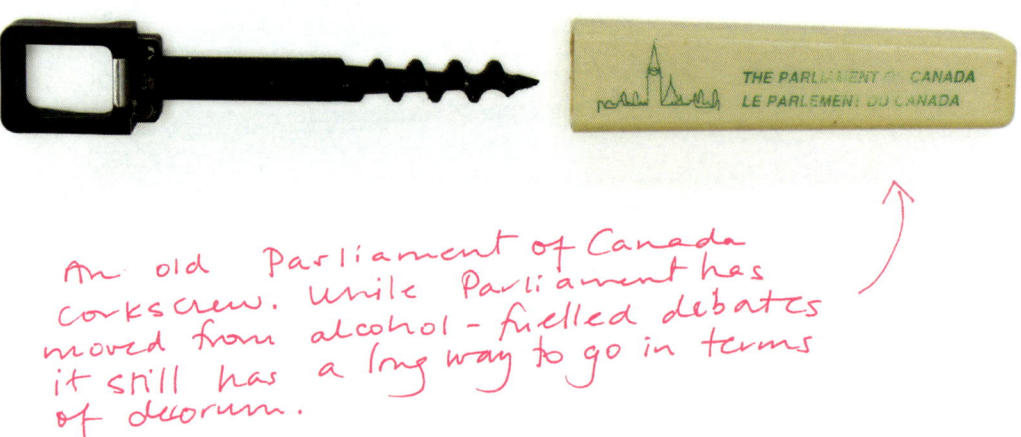

An old Parliament of Canada corkscrew. While Parliament has moved from alcohol-fuelled debates it still has a long way to go in terms of decorum.

Ministers were expected to read from the binder full of talking points, but that wasn't my style. I wanted to give real answers backed by facts. I found it frustrating when other ministers simply read from their binders and tried to dodge the questions rather than engage with them. And too often, ministers used prepared points that didn't answer the question. Holding the government to account for its actions, policies and spending is a critical part of representative democracy, and that requires the government to do its best to respond in good faith.

I also hated the nearly hour-long pre-Question Period prep that ministers would be called to attend if one of your files was in the press. Sure, some ministers weren't great at answering difficult questions. But all the micromanaging made me bonkers.

If you talk to normal Canadians who have watched Question Period, most find the whole thing obnoxious. Some of the old-school MPs love the atmosphere, possibly because it harkens back to a time when Parliament Hill was male-dominated and alcohol-fueled. However, for a lot of us newer members, especially women, it was demoralizing. The worst for me was looking up at the gallery and seeing kids who were on a school trip. They saw members of Parliament screaming and yelling at each other. If we want the next generation to believe in politics, the least we can do is not make it look like a train wreck.

The questions were often just bait—angry, inflammatory statements designed to make me or the government look bad. For example, I was frequently accused of bringing in a "job-killing carbon tax" or "not caring about energy workers." These were not serious questions. They were attacks meant to get social media clicks and fundraising dollars. It made it hard to have a real conversation about the important issues we needed to address. And when I tried to counter with facts, I was often drowned out by jeers.

Pierre Poilievre was the worst for this. For the entire four years I was minister of environment and climate change, he relentlessly attacked me, twisting my words and making misleading claims. He treated Question Period like a young conservative debate club, where his only goal was to score points.

In 2019, I finally snapped at one of his attacks on carbon pricing. I said, "If the party opposite is worried about debt and costs, it should be worried about the costs we're passing on to our kids, the cost of climate change. We've gone from $400 million to over $2 billion because of climate change. Why does the opposition not step up for climate action?" The exchange was heated. The Speaker tried to calm things down, but it was useless. I was shaking by the end of it.

Then to make matters worse, I was delivered a note from a page written by someone in the Office of the Whip or the PMO that read, "Don't sound so angry." Now I was really furious. As my dad would say, "Feck off!" Some people are still uncomfortable with women's anger, especially when it's justified. I'll just say that needs to change.

Later that day, I posted the exchange on social media. I was happy for the world to see how mad I was about Pierre Poilievre's lies and attacks on carbon pricing while the Conservatives had no interest in doing anything serious to tackle the climate crisis.

Fortunately, there were also moments of levity in Question Period. In February 2016, while answering a question in the House, I accidentally implied I had "shared sunny ways" with my Conservative critic, Ed Fast, during COP 21 in Paris. MPs erupted in laughter. I was mortified when I realized what it sounded like and thought about just plowing through my answer. But I realized it was no use. So I just put my head back and laughed, too.

One of my bathing suits. I have a pretty good collection!

PARLIAMENTARY SWIM TEAM

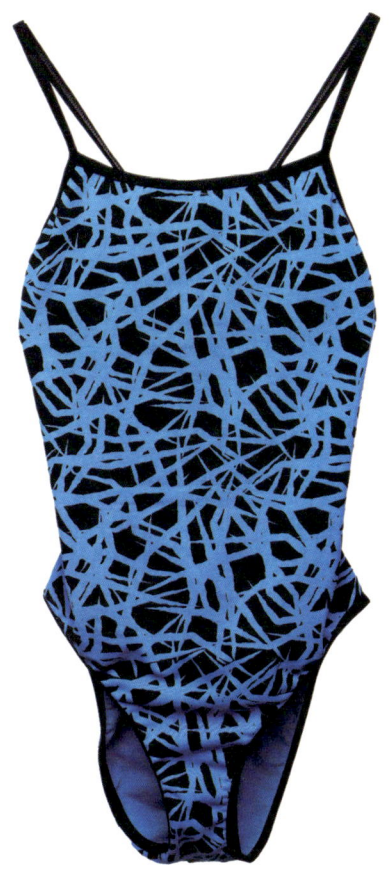

I was thrilled to discover there was a parliamentary swim team. Early every Thursday morning when Parliament sits, MPs and senators swim together at the Château Laurier's art deco pool under great coaches like former national coach, Pierre Lafontaine. It was a rare non partisan space—just colleagues doing laps. You really can't be fancy or a jerk in a bathing suit. I decided to take on the role of swim captain and did my best to round up MPs from almost every party. Green Party Leader Elizabeth May even learned to swim because of these practices. She also tried to lobby me between laps—until I dove underwater to escape!

A STATE VISIT, A CLIMATE DEAL AND A DRESS SOS

When I was first elected, US President Barack Obama was nearing the end of his second term. During that brief year, Canada's relationship with the US was exceptional. We had a true ally in the White House, and the bond between the president and the prime minister was strong. They shared a positive, progressive vision, and the fact that they genuinely seemed to get along meant we could accomplish a lot in a short period. I realized there was a significant opportunity to work with the US on climate, both bilaterally and globally.

This work got underway when President Obama invited the prime minister for an official visit to the United States. The date was set for March. It was a special honour and would be the first state visit by a Canadian leader to the US in almost twenty years. Climate was going to be a major focus. I was pretty chuffed when the US climate negotiator, Todd Stern, who was part of a White House briefing about the visit, praised my leadership in Paris. I was determined to use the state visit to announce joint commitments with the US that would help advance Canada's national climate plan. When you agree with your largest trade partner to take specific climate actions at home, it's harder for people to say the measures will hurt Canada's competitiveness.

While the media buzzed about the state dinner, I was almost entirely focused on securing a climate deal for the visit. I hadn't given the dinner much thought. I figured I'd just wear a dress from my closet. Then, just days before the visit, several people—including my sister, Maureen—asked me which Canadian designer I was wearing. What? I was negotiating a major climate deal, and now I had to scramble to find a Canadian-designed dress? The weirdness of being a woman in politics.

I couldn't find anything that suited the occasion nearby. But I put the word out, and through friends of friends, I was put in touch with some of the people at the sensational Canadian label Greta Constantine. They had one beautiful red ballgown close to my size. I bought it without trying it on, and it arrived the night before I was leaving. While I finalized the climate agreement text, I rushed to a local seamstress who made last-minute adjustments.

BEING ELECTED AND GETTING STUFF DONE

Getting my state dinner dress fitted while working on the text for the Canada–US statement on climate.

*The President and Mrs. Obama
request the pleasure of the company of
The Honorable Catherine McKenna
at a dinner in honor of
The Right Honorable
Justin Trudeau, P.C., M.P.
Prime Minister of Canada
and Mrs. Sophie Grégoire Trudeau
to be held at
The White House
on Thursday, March 10, 2016
at seven o'clock*

Black Tie   *Southeast Entrance*

Chatting with President Obama before the State Dinner. To think a year ago I was still knocking doors.

The visit to Washington was full of ceremony. On March 10, we were formally welcomed at the White House with a nineteen-gun salute. While I didn't get to attend the actual Oval Office meeting between the prime minister and the president, I did get a glimpse inside—it really is oval, smaller than it looks on TV, and pretty awe-inspiring—especially when you think of all the different presidents who governed there. Later that afternoon I had the chance to meet President Obama. He seemed really genuine and at ease. I'd seen him at the Paris negotiations, but this was the first time I'd met him. He has a magnetic, slightly mischievous smile. I was a bit starstruck. I'm not sure what we talked about other than climate—although we did share a laugh.

At the end of an absolutely perfect day, we had a press conference in the Rose Garden. It was clear that the president and prime minister liked and respected each other. Several media outlets used the term "bromance." Whatever you called it, the bond between the leaders was crucial to getting big things done.

I was thrilled when they jointly announced the new Canada-US statement on climate, energy and the Arctic. The agreement meant we would cut methane emissions and work on a global deal to phase out hydrofluorocarbons (HFCs)—gases commonly used in refrigeration, air conditioning and aerosol sprays. I worked closely with the US and the head of the Environmental Protection Agency, Gina McCarthy, to make this happen. We also committed to signing the Paris Agreement on Earth Day, April 22, and to work on a new climate and science partnership to protect the Arctic and its peoples.

Later that day, we attended a state luncheon in honour of Prime Minister Trudeau hosted by Secretary of State John Kerry, with performances by the US Army Band, US Air Force Band, and Canadian singer-songwriter Rufus Wainwright. Everyone from Lorne Michaels to Secretary Henry Kissinger was there.

I bought these from the White House gift shop!

Afterward, it was back to Blair House, a historic guesthouse where the prime minister and his team were staying. It had probably never seen the kind of chaotic joy that the three Trudeau children running around the house brought to it. The night before, the Weeknd had dropped by to see the prime minister, adding to the excitement. I walked into the room to find the Weeknd chatting with the prime minister, who was holding his son Xavier. Not exactly a typical day for a girl from Hamilton.

That evening was the state dinner. The flowers in the majestic East Room where the dinner was held were dazzling and the food was exceptional with thoughtful nods to Canada like mini poutine with duck and a pecan cake with maple syrup and cotton candy on top. There were Canadian celebrities everywhere: Ryan Reynolds, Michael J. Fox, Mike Myers and Sandra Oh.

What impressed me most was how warm and authentic the president and Michelle Obama were. You could tell they were a true team—not just politically, but also in prioritizing their family. When President Obama made his toast to the prime minister and Sophie, he choked up as he talked about his daughters, Malia and Sasha. He reflected on how they were just ten and seven when he was elected, and now Malia was off to college. He said something that really resonated: "We're not here for power. We're not here for fame or fortune. We're here for our kids. We're here for everybody's kids—to give our sons and our daughters a better world."

After dinner, Michelle Obama hosted us in the State Dining Room, where we watched singer-songwriter Sara Bareilles perform her song "Brave" with the Washington Performing Arts Children of the Gospel Choir. It was incredibly moving, and it was clear how seriously Michelle took her role as First Lady and used her platform to promote diverse voices. Those girls sang with so much heart: "But I wonder what would happen if you / Say what you wanna say / And let the words fall out / Honestly I wanna see you be brave."

That message struck a chord with me. And while it was absurd to worry about what I was wearing, I did quietly love my Canadian-made ballgown—even if no one asked who designed it.

GIVE YOUNG WOMEN THE MIC

COP statements are often long and uninspiring, but with Donald Trump's election days before COP22, I wanted ours to have an impact. I asked Maatalii Okalik, then president of the National Youth Council, to join me and share how climate change threatened Inuit culture and existence. Though UN rules allowed only the country representative to give the statement, we ignored them. Dressed in traditional sealskin, Maatalii spoke powerfully about justice and Indigenous rights—proving that sometimes, the best move is ceding the mic.

A beautiful Inuit made sealskin necklace that I bought in Iqaluit. The Inuit earrings were a gift.

THE TRUMP YEARS

On March 25, 1969, during a speech to the National Press Club in Washington, DC, former prime minister Pierre Elliott Trudeau famously remarked that living next door to the United States was in some ways "like sleeping with an elephant." He told his audience, "No matter how friendly and even-tempered is the beast, if I can call it that, one is affected by every twitch and grunt." His observation vividly captured the delicate stance Canada has to maintain in its dealings with its much larger, more powerful, and often unpredictable neighbour. And as history shows, decisions made by the US that seemingly have nothing to do with Canada often have massive repercussions for our country.

After living the Canada-US relationship up close during the six years I was in government, I preferred to put it in dating terms. It was new and great during the Obama administration. When Trump came along, it turned abusive and erratic and, quite frankly, exhausting. Then Joe Biden won and the relationship was back on good footing, but we couldn't forget the bad times or stop worrying about what the future would hold.

During the 2016 US presidential election, all ministers were warned about the need to be careful about what we said about Donald Trump. It was clear he was going to be a problem for Canada. He had said in the campaign that he thought the North American Free Trade Agreement (NAFTA) between the US, Canada and Mexico was a "disaster" for US workers and their economy, and he wanted to rip it up. That was a big problem given that the US was Canada's largest trading partner, and trade with the US contributed significantly to our economy and to Canadian jobs. Trump also denied the science on climate change and labelled it a hoax by the Chinese designed to make US manufacturing uncompetitive.

I'd had my first heads-up about the possibility of Donald Trump being elected president when Scott and I were invited as the Canadians to a conference outside of San Francisco in December 2015. It was an interesting group, mostly composed of senior tech executives, some politicians, and other policy leaders. They were worried about Trump. They said he was getting a lot of attention and had a way of connecting with folks. I didn't believe it. I thought there was no way Americans would choose Trump, a businessman and former reality-TV host, over Hillary Clinton, a former first lady, senator and secretary of state.

On November 8, 2016, I was at an election party in the ballroom of Ottawa's Château Laurier hosted by the US ambassador to Canada, Bruce Heyman. My ten-year-old daughter, Isabelle, was with me. We were both waiting for the announcement that Hillary Clinton had won. I was chatting with Finance Minister Bill Morneau and a few others when I felt Isabelle pulling on my sleeve. She asked: "Isn't this bad?" I looked at the results, and they didn't look great. I said, "Don't worry. It's early and Hillary will pull it off." About fifteen minutes later, I realized it wasn't looking good. At that moment, my cell phone rang. It was my chief of staff, Marlo. He said, "I'm watching TV, and the cameras are on you, and you look very nervous. You better leave now!" I slipped out, as did Bill Morneau. The last thing I wanted was for some journalist to ask me what I thought about Donald Trump becoming president.

The world changed that night. Now we had a president who opposed most of what we stood for and was obsessed with renegotiating NAFTA. It felt crushing to watch Hillary Clinton give her concession speech:

> "To all the women, and especially the young women, who put their faith in this campaign and in me, I want you to know that nothing has made me prouder than to be your champion. I know we have still not shattered that highest and hardest glass ceiling but I know someday someone will and hopefully sooner than we might think right now."

At that moment, it didn't feel like the glass ceiling would be broken anytime soon. Under Trump, there was no talk about the new, ambitious things we could do with the US on climate or anything else. Our focus was on how to avoid a full-on trade war. And my personal focus was trying to keep the US in the Paris Agreement.

During the Obama years, my counterpart in Washington was the EPA secretary, my terrific friend Gina McCarthy, a no-nonsense Bostonian with the accent to match. We did a lot of good things on climate in the short time we had together and we had fun. In Austria, where we were in frustratingly slow negotiations to amend the Montreal Protocol which phased out super polluting chemicals used in coolants like refrigerants and air conditioners), we teamed up late in the night to hand out chocolate to any negotiator who would budge on their position. It put people in a better mood, and a few countries took it as a sign to actually negotiate. Our job done, we scrounged a bottle of wine, found an empty room and caught up.

Trump's pick for the EPA couldn't have been more different. Scott Pruitt was a climate denier supported by the coal industry. As attorney general of Oklahoma, he'd brought in a slew of anti-environment policies and sued the EPA multiple times. And now he was running it.

I went with Marlo to the EPA headquarters in Washington, DC, and the atmosphere was terrible. It felt largely deserted. There were boxes in the hallway for all the people leaving the agency. We sat down at a table in Pruitt's office, and I tried to break the ice by talking to him about the Blue Jays. I'd done my homework and knew he liked baseball. Then I gave him my pitch about the benefits of the Paris Agreement and emphasized the economic benefits and jobs for the US. Pruitt wasn't paying attention, and I was getting more and more annoyed. When the meeting was finally over, I said to Marlo, "What the heck was that?" And he said, "Didn't you see? He had a March Madness game on the TV just behind you." Give me a break.

Things went from bad to worse when Trump announced on June 1, 2017, that the US was pulling out of Paris because the agreement would "undermine" the US economy and put the US "at a permanent disadvantage." The only saving grace was that under the agreement, the US couldn't officially withdraw until the day after the next US election. I'm not sure exactly how that happened or whether it was a coincidence, but I think I have to give credit to my friends on the US climate negotiating team.

Of course, our government was laser focused on the NAFTA renegotiations, which started in August 2017. After over a year of tense and at times dramatic negotiations, there weren't many major changes to the original agreement except for some concessions related to supply management, which was always a hot-button issue in Quebec, and a welcome increase in the North American content requirements for vehicles to be eligible for preferential trade treatment. However, the process was extraordinarily painful to Canada's economy and specific sectors because of tariffs Trump imposed on imports of Canadian steel and aluminum to apply pressure for a deal. We were prepared and retaliated against the US with similar tariffs. It also took a toll on our government. Everyone was exhausted. Almost every Cabinet meeting involved a NAFTA discussion and many emergency meetings were held.

The only upside of this period is that Canadian leaders really came together. Politicians of all stripes, from ministers to premiers to mayors, were sent to Washington, DC, or border states or cities, to remind Americans that Canada was the largest market for US goods and a huge percentage of the US economy and American jobs relied on this trade. Once again, Team Canada was back in action. We established a multi-partisan advisory council that included former politicians, business leaders and former prime minister Brian Mulroney, who knew Trump well and provided sage advice. We finally signed CUSMA (the Canada-United States-Mexico Agreement) in November 2018. Ultimately, our strategy of preserving the core structure of NAFTA and standing firm on Canadian interests worked.

While I weighed in on the negotiations as a Cabinet minister, my main focus in terms of NAFTA was negotiating a new environment chapter. Given my background in trade law, I hoped the agreement could be improved in a number of important ways, especially given Canada's long history working with the United States to protect the Great Lakes and improve air quality. I assembled a top team of Canadian advisors, but in the end, it largely came to naught. The new environment chapter included no mention of climate change, and while it says that each country should have measures to protect the environment, it doesn't prevent a country from lowering its environmental standards unless it is done to create a trade or investment advantage.

One positive thing that came out of it from an environmental perspective, for which Chrystia Freeland deserves a lot of credit, was the elimination of NAFTA Chapter 11. It gave foreign companies the ability to sue governments over changes to regulation or policies that hurt their profits, even if the changes were for legitimate reasons like protecting the environment. Canada had been a frequent target of these actions.

One of my most vivid memories of how impossible it was to manage the relationship with Donald Trump was when we hosted the G7 Leaders' Summit in Charlevoix, Quebec, in 2018. I was there for the session on climate change that took place once Trump had left. At the press conference after the summit, a reporter asked Trudeau if he'd stood up for Canada against Trump in the meeting. Trudeau responded, "We're polite, we're reasonable," and in reference to US tariffs on steel and aluminum, added, "but we also will not be pushed around." Not a big deal and a pretty obvious answer.

Immediately after the press conference ended, I went with a few friends from the PMO to debrief. Only a few minutes had passed when I looked at my phone and saw a new series of tweets from Trump slamming the prime minister: "PM Justin Trudeau of Canada acted so meek and mild during our @G7 meetings only to give a news conference after I left saying that 'US Tariffs were kind of insulting' and he 'will not be pushed around.' Very dishonest & weak. Our Tariffs are in response to his of 270% on dairy!"

My colleagues left to clean up the mess while I called my kids to see how their days had gone.

NO ONE COUNTRY CAN STOP PROGRESS

With Trump likely pulling out of the Paris Agreement, I shifted my focus to doing whatever I could to help ensure the rest of the world continued to move forward on climate action. I developed a two-pronged strategy: first, bring major countries together to fill the void left by the US; second, work with US states like California to show progress was still possible.

For over a decade, the US had convened the Major Economies Forum (MEF), which brings together the world's biggest emitters for frank discussions to advance climate action. With Trump in office, I assumed it was over. I saw an opportunity for Canada to step up and create a new group, but it would require getting the EU and China on board.

At the Bonn Climate Change Conference in Germany in May 2017, I invited Miguel Cañete, the European commissioner for climate action and energy, and Xie Zhenhua, China's special envoy on climate change, to dinner. While Canada had significant differences with China, especially on human rights, it was the largest emitter in the world and the second-largest economy after the US. It was committed to the Paris Agreement and we needed China to step up.

At dinner, I pitched my big idea: replace the MEF with a new forum, the Ministerial on Climate Action (MoCA), at least until a new US administration could be elected in four years. It would be led by Canada, the EU and China. I think they were surprised by my audacity, but I tried to be charming and make my case. They were concerned about how the US would react. I was blunt: "Look, I've tried to sell them on the merits of the Paris Agreement and the benefits to the American economy and jobs, but they aren't buying it." After a long discussion, they agreed to co-host MOCA.

When Trump finally announced the US was withdrawing from the Paris Agreement, I had my response ready for the media: "In the United States, businesses support the Paris accord, cities support it, and everyone's moving forward—both in the US and around the world. It's unfortunate that the US administration is pulling out of the Paris Agreement, but you can't stop progress." That September, Canada hosted the first MOCA, with senior representatives from about thirty countries and discussed how they could work faster on climate. It was a remarkable achievement and helped to prove that Canada could still punch above its weight and lead.

Canada was phasing out coal. The U.S. was promoting it.

With the US government MIA on climate, I reached out to the governor of California. California isn't like any other state. Its economy is the fifth largest in the world. I met with Governor Jerry Brown, a Democrat. I'd heard he could be a tough character and often didn't engage much in meetings. I did some reading up on him and learned he had once studied to be a Jesuit priest, just like my uncle Dermot. I somehow worked my uncle into the conversation and soon we were talking about Catholicism and climate. Then he said, "Well, I guess we better talk business. What about those tar sands?" I replied, "Well, in Canada, we call them oil sands." He smiled and said, "Oh, don't worry. I don't consider 'tar' a bad word. When I was a kid, I'd pick the tar off the road when it was freshly laid and chew it like gum." I had no idea how to respond. We both burst out laughing and it marked the start of a great relationship. I also met with Mary Nichols, head of the California Air Resources Board and we worked together on electric vehicles and expanding carbon markets. It was helpful to be able to say, in the face of US government inaction on climate change, that we were working with the state of California.

In San Francisco, Canada's consul general, Rana Sarkar, took me to a great climate event hosted by Laurene Powell Jobs, the wife of the late Steve Jobs and a major powerhouse in global philanthropy. She was very kind and told me how much she admired Canada's action on climate change. She unexpectedly invited me to join her onstage to talk about our government's agenda. I'd prepared nothing, but went up anyway and told the audience that Canada was absolutely committed to climate action and ready to work with California to reduce emissions and create economic opportunities. The crowd cheered. They were hungry for positive climate news after Trump's election. Later that night, I ended up sitting beside MC Hammer at a private dinner she hosted. I had grown up listening to his music and now we were talking about how to raise kids. Only in America.

During this time, Canada also played a leading role in several other global initiatives. With Claire Perry, the UK's environment minister, we discussed the need for a global push to phase out coal—the most polluting fossil fuel. Canada had already announced it would phase out coal by 2030, and the UK was on a similar path. On the back of a cocktail napkin, we developed a strategy. We created the Powering Past Coal Alliance to accelerate the phaseout of coal power. Michael Bloomberg, a long-time climate leader, generously stepped up to help fund the initiative. Nineteen countries signed on at the launch at the UN Climate Summit in Bonn in 2017. It was a great contrast to the competing US event which was focused on promoting coal.

Finally, as part of Canada's climate leadership, we focused on nature protection in the lead-up to a global summit in 2020 (which would be delayed by the COVID-19 pandemic until 2023), where the goal was to protect 30 per cent of the world's nature by 2030. I decided Canada should take the lead, given our strong progress on nature conservation in partnership with Indigenous peoples. We hosted a Nature Champions Summit in April 2019, and Harrison Ford, a long-time nature conservation advocate, agreed to participate. He was a complete pro. He even did a public interview with the prime minister and joined me for a press conference. It was unforgettable standing next to the man I knew as Han Solo as he he lauded Canada's leadership on nature and the environment, lamented the situation in the US, and called for young people to step up.

CLIMATE BARBIE

I'm sorry guys.
It's over.
I'm not letting this one go.

I said this to my team in September 2017 as we sat in the overcrowded lobby of our nondescript midtown New York hotel after a long day at the United Nations. I had looked at my phone and saw that my Twitter feed had exploded. I scrolled through and quickly figured out why. A former Conservative minister and current MP, Gerry Ritz, had taken a shot at me online by referring to me as Climate Barbie. It wasn't the first time I'd heard that insult or much worse. There was an active campaign against me led by right-wing rage-farming outlets and amplified by their followers that started basically the moment I was sworn in.

Being called Climate Barbie might not seem so bad especially after the blockbuster Barbie movie, where director Greta Gerwig helped recast Barbie in a feminist light. But this was way before that, and I certainly didn't appreciate being called a Barbie. I never liked or played with Barbies, and I didn't look or act like a Barbie. Ritz was trying to make me out as a bimbo: a woman who didn't have the brains for the job and who'd been picked solely because of her gender and blonde hair. And it was layered with climate denial. He didn't believe the science behind climate change. I had to hand it to him: misogyny and climate denial all wrapped up in one stupid viral tweet.

I'd done a good job until then ignoring the hateful, sexist, and too-often violent tweets against me. My team, made up of a lot of smart, strong women, were protective of me and didn't want me to see all of it, much less respond. Their logic, which wasn't wrong, was that a response would bring even more attention to the attacks and likely increase them.

Left: This is one of the Barbies sent to my office with a mocking note almost certainly by a grown man.

I expected a backlash from the haters on social media, but I knew I could handle it. I was Irish and from Steeltown. I'd learned to stand up to bullies. Ritz was trying to discredit me and knock me off my game—but that wasn't going to happen.

I took a few minutes to carefully write and rewrite my response. I was thinking like a lawyer and wanted to be careful, but direct with my choice of words. I pressed send and said to my team, "Tweet's out."

My tweet went viral. There were some haters, but regular people, many who had followed my journey into politics, responded positively. It also attracted international media coverage. Clearly this incident hit a nerve.

But I wasn't in politics to fight Conservative politicians who were sexist and denied climate change. It was annoying and a distraction. I was just trying to do my job. It was hard enough tackling climate change. I resented also having to take on the mantle of being a woman in politics, too.

The Climate Barbie insult started soon after I became a minister. It was coined by Rebel Media, a rage-farming far-right platform whose business model is largely based on attacking progressive politicians and real journalists and then suing anyone who dares call them out. I was one of their favourite targets.

Not long after the Gerry Ritz incident, I was going into a press conference after a meeting with all the provincial and territorial ministers of the environment. One of my staff whispered to me as I walked up to the mic: "Rebel Media is here." I was furious. I knew they were only there to get a clip they could use repeatedly to mock me to their followers, who would join in, all amplified by bots and trolls and social media algorithms. On the spot, I made a call. I turned to my ministerial colleagues, "Sorry, I'm going to have to call this out."

The first question was from Rebel Media. I used every ounce of energy I had to stay calm, keep my voice even and low, and speak slowly. I knew that to pull this off, I couldn't sound angry or upset. When you're a woman in politics, you learn that if you don't do that, you'll be seen as emotional—or worse, "shrill." It was like I was back on the starting blocks in swimming with everything going in slow motion. Looking back, I can tell my voice is almost shaking and I am uncomfortable. Before answering his question, I asked if he would commit to Rebel Media never calling me Climate Barbie again. I said "there are lots of girls who want to get into politics, and it's completely unacceptable that you do this."

The exchange was caught live on TV, and the exchange again went viral on social media, largely in a good way. Many commentators and regular people spoke up against Rebel Media and its demeaning attacks on me. One man later stopped me in the street and said: "Thanks for doing that. I showed the clip to my kids and said, 'That's how you stand up to a bully.'"

My response wasn't so much for me, but for every woman in politics and my kids. Anyone who wants to go into politics, especially women, shouldn't have to put up with constant abuse.

PINKY PROMISES

As minister, I made hundreds of pinky promises with children who cared about climate action where we mutually committed to do our part to tackle climate change. I thought it was important to remind them they weren't alone. Even after leaving politics when I was no longer accountable to my former constituents, I knew I was still accountable to them.

I did hundreds of pinky promises with kids across the country.

MAKE TIME TO DO WHAT YOU LOVE

I would never have survived politics if it hadn't been for swimming. It was my refuge where I could glide through the quiet water, free from pressure. As environment minister, I was lucky to oversee national parks which gave me opportunities to swim, no matter the temperature. Once, at a Parks Canada announcement in Cape Breton Highlands, I was told there was no time for a dip. I secretly changed into my suit anyway and ran for the water, as an RCMP officer assigned to my security detail chased after me. Swimming kept me sane and reminded me of Canada's incredible natural wealth.

Left: Swimming in Forillon National Park, July 31, 2018.

OUR COMMON HOME

"Once we start to think about the kind of world we are leaving to future generations, we look at things differently; we realize that the world is a gift which we have freely received and must share with others. Since the world has been given to us, we can no longer view reality in a purely utilitarian way, in which efficiency and productivity are entirely geared to our individual benefit. Intergenerational solidarity is not optional, but rather a basic question of justice, since the world we have received also belongs to those who will follow us."

— Pope Francis, *Laudato si'*, 159

Although I have my share of issues with the Catholic church, I respect the Jesuit order of Catholic priests. I admire their focus on social justice and their more open-minded and intellectual approach to moral issues. This was very different from many of our local priests who were often vocal in their attacks on abortion, divorce, and homosexuality.

I first learned about Jesuits from Uncle Dermot. He was the eldest of the McKenna boys and announced at the end of high school that he had a calling to become a Jesuit priest. My grandmother could not have been prouder. In Ireland at that time, having your eldest son decide not only to enter the priesthood but to become a member of the Society of Jesus, the Jesuits, the most learned of Catholic priests, was a huge blessing.

Dermot was quiet and reflective, a contrast to his louder and more boisterous brothers, led by my father. He was an idealist who was driven by a desire to do his part to help the poor and marginalized. He helped to found an Irish cooperative in Dublin that gave new graduates entrepreneurial skills to start businesses so they could stay at home rather than go abroad to find work. When I was older and visited Ireland—including during my time as a minister—Dermot and I would go on long walks and talk about the connection between climate and justice, and how unfair it was that those who had done the least to cause climate change were the ones most affected by it. He was so proud when Pope Francis, the first Jesuit Pope, wrote the encyclical, *Laudato si'* (*Our Common Home*) in 2015, in advance of the Paris Agreement negotiations. In it, Pope Francis calls for urgent global action to address the environmental crisis. He explained that climate change is not just an environmental issue but a profound social, economic and political challenge. Pope Francis called for climate justice and highlighted how environmental degradation disproportionately affects the poor and vulnerable. His message was clear: we must act now to protect our planet and ensure a just and equitable world for future generations.

In June 2017, after attending the G7 Environment Ministers Meeting in Bologna, I visited the Vatican. I wanted to understand how Catholics could work together within the Church to engage more Catholics to fight climate change. Fortunately, there was an incredible Canadian Jesuit priest from the Ottawa area, Father Michael Czerny, who was at the Vatican. He was later made a cardinal by Pope Francis in 2019. Father Czerny had spent decades working on human rights and social justice issues and was then working for the Vatican's Migrants and Refugees section. He kindly brought me into a workshop that he was running on migration and I saw how he inspired all the participants. He spoke about how climate change is having an impact on the rise of migrants globally who often live in poverty and are forced to move because of the destruction caused by climate change. When we chatted at the end of the class, he presented me with the most wonderful gift: a signed copy of *Laudato si'* from Pope Francis, inscribed in meticulous handwriting: "To Hon. Catherine McKenna, please keep on caring for our common home. God bless you and pray for me. Francis."

The next day, I attended a mass in St. Peter's Square where I was given an audience with Pope Francis. He blessed a Jesuit cross that I had bought for my uncle Dermot and I thanked him for his gift. I looked him in the eye and told him, "Don't worry, I will work with you to care for our common home." He smiled and said "That is very good."

One of my most cherished possessions: a copy of *Laudato si'* inscribed by Pope Francis.

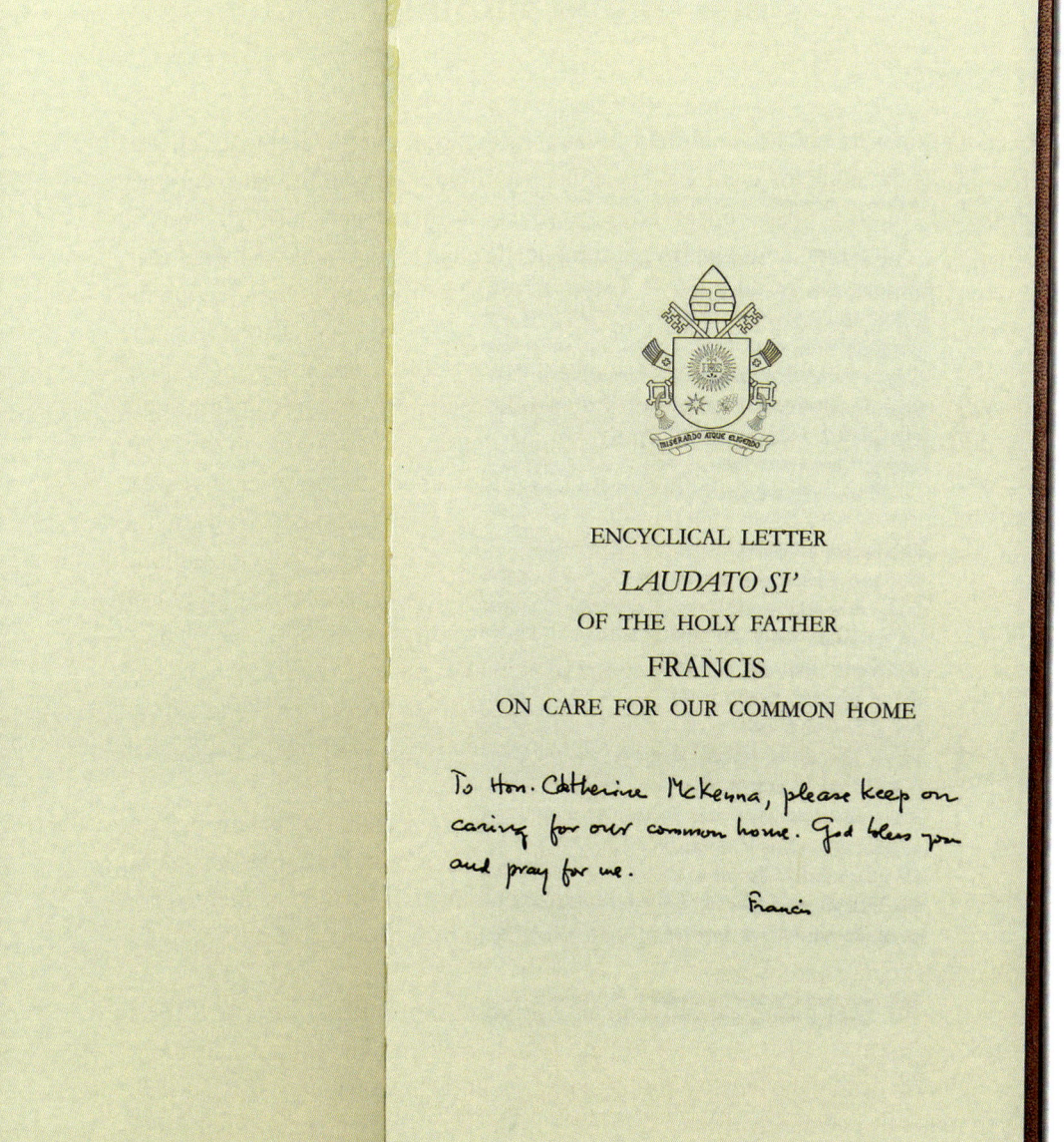

ENCYCLICAL LETTER

LAUDATO SI'

OF THE HOLY FATHER

FRANCIS

ON CARE FOR OUR COMMON HOME

To Hon. Catherine McKenna, please keep on caring for our common home. God bless you and pray for me.

Francis

HARD THINGS ARE HARD

An escalating price on carbon pollution was at the heart of our government's climate plan. It was the most efficient way to reduce significant emissions. And, contrary to popular belief, it was a conservative approach. Rather than requiring people or business to reduce their emissions by a set amount through more expensive regulations, it relied on market forces to drive change. In other words, rather than paying the carbon price, you could choose to take steps to reduce your emissions (e.g., by making your home more energy efficient, taking public transit, buying a more energy efficient car or using cleaner industrial processes). As a result, I thought it would appeal to Conservatives. It wasn't just theory. It worked in many other places. By 2018, close to 50 countries and 25 regions had carbon pricing or were implementing it. And it wasn't a new idea. Under President George H.W. Bush, the US implemented cap-and-trade to combat acid rain by putting a price on sulphur dioxide emissions and allowing companies to decide how to reduce their pollution. Those who did more than required could sell their allowances to other companies. This created an incentive for many companies to upgrade their facilities to reduce pollution. The result was that sulfur emissions went down faster than predicted and at a much lower cost than projected. It was very effective at tackling the problem in an innovative and flexible way.

But there was a catch. While we had announced Canada's carbon pricing system, we had to resolve what would happen to the money collected by the federal government in provinces that refused to implement their own consumer carbon pricing system. Would we keep it to use for green initiatives, give it back to the province or rebate taxpayers?

One of the best pieces of advice came from a Republican, George Shultz, former US secretary of state under Ronald Reagan. When I met him in California, he convinced me that the key to gaining public support for consumer carbon pricing was to make it revenue-neutral. This would mean that all money collected would be returned to the public in a transparent way. This approach, he argued, would create an incentive for people to reduce their emissions in order to save money. It would also help make the whole thing more palatable. I agreed. Our modelling also

Another of my favourite sayings. My team put it on a pillow!

showed that this would be a progressive approach—80 per cent of Canadians would get more back than they paid, especially low- and middle-income Canadians. So, to me, this was a win, economically, politically and environmentally.

But pushing this idea internally wasn't easy. Some people, particularly in the PMO, wanted to invest any new revenue in green projects. I argued that if we went down that path, people would see it as a tax grab and challenge how we spent the money. Finance Minister Bill Morneau was on my side, but I needed the prime minister's approval. The challenge was that after months of repeated requests, the finance minister and I simply couldn't get a meeting with him. This was a flagship government policy, yet getting half an hour to discuss it seemed impossible.

In the end, the revenue neutral option prevailed largely because Liberal MPs spoke out in a caucus meeting and urged the prime minister to give the money back to people. Thanks to their support, I was able to convince the prime minister of the merits of our plan. It was a big win for our team.

However, there were still significant hurdles, many of our own making.

I had expected carbon pricing revenues would be returned to people through clear, quarterly rebate cheques (or automatic deposits) from the Canada Revenue Agency (CRA). But when I pushed for this, I was told by public servants it wasn't possible. Instead, the money would have to be returned when people filed their taxes. This meant it would be a once-a-year payment lumped together with other benefits and deductions. In other words, it would be hard for people to see. (Incredibly, it was only after COVID, when it was clear that the Canada Revenue Agency could do a lot of things that didn't seem possible before, that they finally agreed to move to quarterly automatic deposits.)

Speaking of unclear, there was also the debate of what to call the payments. A number of different names were discussed, which of course had to make sense in both official languages. To me, calling it a rebate seemed like a no-brainer. Unfortunately, the Department of Justice flagged a legal risk and insisted we go with the less-than-ideal "Climate Action Incentive." Years later, shortly before the policy was cancelled, the payments were ultimately renamed the "Canada Carbon Rebate."

Then we hit another stumbling block. A number of the major banks refused to clearly label the quaterly deposits when they went into people's accounts. For many, it was labeled as CanGov or CanRevenue or something equally cryptic. People couldn't make the connection with our climate policy. Unbelievably, the government refused to compel the banks to properly label it properly. This was after my time but I was furious.

I also knew we needed a massive public education campaign about carbon pricing. But we hit another roadblock with officials arguing that such advertising would be too "political." I pushed back hard, without success. It was partly our government's fault. We had introduced strict restrictions on government advertising when we were elected. We didn't want to see a repeat of the massive use of tax dollars by the Harper government to advertise the Economic Action Plan.

In retrospect, our restrictions backfired. I wasn't sure how providing factual information about a carbon rebate that Canadians needed to apply for when they did their taxes qualified as political. The consequence was that most Canadians never heard the facts about how carbon pricing worked and didn't appreciate that the majority of people who paid the price received more money back than they paid. Instead, they were fed misleading statements or outright lies by Conservative politicians like Pierre Poilievre, who repeatedly called the carbon price a "job-killing tax" that needed to be "axed."

Out of options, I reached out to H&R Block. I noticed they had signs in their windows advertising the "Climate Action Incentive" which they would help their customers claim when preparing their taxes. This could be a great opportunity. I asked our MPs to visit an H&R Block office in their riding with a family from their constituency to film a video with an H&R block employee explaining the Climate Action Incentive to the family including how much money they could expect to get back. This campaign was cheap, simple, truthful, and focused on people, not politicians. But at best, it only reached thousands, not millions.

It didn't help that journalists constantly framed carbon pricing as costly and the enemy of affordability. Remember: for most people, carbon pricing made life a little more affordable because they got more money back than they paid. But Conservative politicians were gleeful in their lies. Let's be real. Carbon pricing did not drive inflation or the affordability crisis in Canada. The exorbitant prices charged by fossil fuel companies did.

Another serious problem was the flawed analysis by the Parliamentary Budget Officer (PBO) on carbon pricing. This was seized on by Conservative politicians. The PBO concluded that the consumer carbon pricing would raise costs in the short term, mainly through higher prices for energy and transportation. But they screwed up. The PBO's original analysis also included the pricing system that applied to heavy emitters in its calculations. The PBO also failed to account for any benefits from reduced emissions, and it did not estimate the cost of alternative policies. Instead, it simply compared doing nothing to tackle climate change versus carbon pricing, as if doing nothing was an option. Had the analysis compared carbon pricing to other policies, like regulations or subsidies, it would have shown clearly that carbon pricing is the most cost-effective way to cut emissions. Period. The PBO also ignored the high cost of inaction and overlooked the long-term benefits of reducing emissions, such as fewer extreme weather events and lower health care costs. Nor did it consider how carbon pricing revenue would help offset costs, especially for low- and middle-income households. It was flagrant malpractice, but the damage was done.

By the time I left the Environment portfolio after the 2019 election, you could see that momentum on carbon pricing was being lost. This was a fight that you had to keep fighting. Because the price rises every year, you had to keep defending it, over and over. But the government's efforts were half-hearted. And while environmental organizations should be applauded for supporting carbon pricing at the outset, once it was in place, many of them moved on from defending the policy to demanding that the government do more.

Incredibly, the most damaging attack on carbon pricing was self-inflicted and happened two years after I'd left politics. In October 2023, the prime minister announced a pause on carbon pricing for heating oil. I was stunned. This wasn't just a policy shift—it was a blatant, politically motivated move designed to shore up support in Atlantic Canada, where heating oil is common. With the Liberal Party's Atlantic caucus standing behind him, the prime minister argued that the decision was necessary to address affordability, especially in the face of rising energy costs. When I saw him standing behind a podium with a sign that read, "Making Life More Affordable," I spit out my coffee. As I told journalists when I spoke out against the decision, the reason heating oil—and gas—cost so much wasn't because of carbon pricing, again where all the money is returned to people, but because energy companies were jacking up prices. If the prime minister really cared about affordability, why not introduce a real solution to high energy costs, like giving every Canadian a free heat pump to get off fossil fuels? It could have even supported Canadian manufacturers in the process.

The announcement was beyond cynical. It was stupid. It created confusion and resentment outside of Atlantic Canada. People in other provinces where the federal pricing system applied asked, "Why are we still paying the carbon tax on natural gas while Atlantic Canada gets a pass?" The "pause" played into the hands of critics.

It also undermined the government's climate goals and sent the message that action on climate change could be delayed whenever it became politically convenient.

The government's cynicism discouraged Canadians who were genuinely committed to ambitious action on climate change. Defenders of carbon pricing, who saw it as a necessary tool for reducing emissions, felt crushed.

Mark Carney, Justin Trudeau's successor as prime minister, would eventually kill the consumer carbon price, arguing that it had become too divisive an issue especially when Canadians needed to be united against Trump's tariffs and sovereignty threats. It was a tough pill to swallow. However, by that point, especially after the cynical "pause" on heating oil, carbon pricing had suffered a serious blow. It had become a distraction and was impeding action an almost every other front. And if Liberals lost the election because of it, we stood to lose all of our hard fought progress on climate of which the carbon price was only one part.

In the end, Canada lost a climate policy that worked to reduce emissions in the most cost effective way, ensured that most families were better off (especially middle- and low-income ones), while creating an incentive for people to save even more money by choosing more energy efficient options, and which provided an opportunity for businesses to innovate and develop clean solutions. Losing a policy which leads to one of the most significant reductions in Canada's emissions makes hitting the country's climate target even harder.

But let's consider this one battle lost and not the war. Progressive politicians need to be much tougher and more strategic if we're going to do big things that matter, especially on climate. Hard things are hard.

THE RESISTANCE

In 2018, Maclean's, a national newsmagazine, ran a cover story in its November 7 issue titled, "The Resistance." Five of the country's conservative leaders—all male—defiantly posed on the cover as a combative, fight-ready group in blue suits and ties. The cover headline read: "A powerful new alliance of conservative leaders is taking a stand against the Liberals' carbon tax plan. Welcome to Justin Trudeau's worst nightmare." The piece described how they had united to oppose Liberal climate policies, particularly carbon pricing.

Once again, the so-called "resistance fighters" conveniently forgot that it was premiers of the largest provinces that had introduced carbon pricing and that most Canadians were already covered by a provincial program when our government was elected. But working with their big-spending friends in the oil and gas industry, they were determined to sink the federal policy.

As the fight escalated, I spent a lot of time thinking about how to build a "resistance to the resistance." I knew we needed different tactics and so we built a diverse coalition including environmental and conservation groups, religious organizations, youth groups, economists, farmers, doctors, health care professionals, labour leaders, Indigenous groups, cities and citizen action networks.

These groups activated their networks on social media, organized supportive campaigns and events, wrote op-eds and launched letter-writing campaigns to MPs. Several of them also joined as interveners in the carbon pricing litigation, and backed the federal government's position.

In the end, the resistance lost—in court, at least. In 2021, the Supreme Court of Canada delivered a majority decision which declared the federal carbon pricing law constitutional. The court ruled that climate change poses "a threat to the future of humanity" and affirmed the federal government's authority to impose a minimum price on greenhouse gas emissions across the country.

It was a relief. But, of course, the resistance didn't go away.

Cover of Maclean's Magazine, December 2018.

TERMINATING CLIMATE CHANGE

Politics can be surreal. One afternoon in early 2019, I was deep in a meeting on carbon pricing with my officials when a FaceTime video call popped up on my phone. The caller? Arnold Schwarzenegger, casually smoking a cigar. I had met him once at a climate event in Paris, and he offered to help me if he could. He made a video explaining how California's cap-and-trade system cut emissions while still growing the state's economy. My tweet with his video read: "Being tough means being tough on climate change! #TerminatingClimateChange."

I managed to take a screenshot of Arnie when he called me on Facetime out of the blue!

LEADERSHIP

In September 2018, I was leading the G7 environment ministers meeting in Halifax. At the press conference, the first question was whether I'd do what David Suzuki demanded—and resign. He wanted me to follow the French environment minister, Nicolas Hulot, who had quit live on air, claiming his government wasn't serious about climate action. I was stunned. I knew Suzuki was angry, but couldn't he see I was in the fight of my life—defending carbon pricing and climate policies against a wall of Conservative opposition? And resigning? How would that help? I replied, "I'm no quitter. Resigning is easy. What we're doing is hard. This is a long-term transition to a cleaner future." But the criticism stung.

Shortly after, I was in my constituency office when an assistant handed me the phone saying the prime minister was on the line. I picked up the phone expecting to hear from Justin Trudeau. To my surprise, it was former prime minister Brian Mulroney. He launched right in: "Catherine, How are you doing? Ignore the criticism. Just keep on going."

I loved that he took the time to call to lift my spirits and encourage me to keep fighting the good fight. Mulroney had been through many tough fights in his day. He knew what it took to take a bold leadership stance, and that it doesn't always make you popular.

Mulroney became one of my biggest mentors on protecting the environment and fighting the climate crisis. The carbon pricing plan I was trying to implement was similar to the same market-based approach he advocated to tackle acid rain.

In 2017, he joined me in Montreal where we stood shoulder to shoulder with government officials, scientists, environmentalists and industry leaders from around the world to celebrate the thirtieth anniversary of the Montreal Protocol. In 1987, Mulroney hosted the international conference in Montreal that led to the ground-breaking agreement to phase out the production of substances that depleted the ozone layer. That experience reminded me that good ideas are good ideas, no matter what side of the political spectrum they come from.

In November 2019, former prime minister Brian Mulroney was presented with an environmental leadership award at the fiftieth anniversary Gala Celebration of Pollution Probe in Toronto. I wasn't able to make it, but I later read his speech and

On my way with Brian Mulroney to the 30th anniversary of the Montreal Protocol on November 20, 2017.

it touched me. We were two very different people from different eras and different political parties, yet he understood leadership on climate the same way I did.

My favourite excerpt:

As our politicians gather in Ottawa for the opening of a new Parliament, I would encourage them to dream big and exciting dreams for Canada. They should keep their eyes on the challenges confronting Canada's golden future and avert them from constant and misleading public opinion polls and focus groups that dictate the nature of many of their public policies, often choosing the easy way out.

Otherwise, when they leave office and history says: "What visionary or courageous policies did you introduce that improved Canada's environment and perhaps inspired the world?" If the answer is "none, but I was very popular," then, they will have an eternity to reflect on the tough, unpopular but indispensable decisions for Canada's progress they avoided, in order to bask in the fleeting sunlight of high approval ratings that served only their own personal vanity and interests.

They must realize that there still is a place for daring in the Canadian soul.

As St. Thomas Aquinas admonished leaders everywhere, and for every age: "If the highest aim of a captain were to preserve his ship, he would keep it in port forever." That was not my way when I was prime minister and it cannot be our way now. In fact, Minister Catherine McKenna has worked in a highly challenging area for the last four years in a competent manner in which she sought to advance our national interest as she saw it.

There is a quotation from the book of proverbs carved into the Nepean sandstone over the west arch window of the Peace Tower of the Parliament in Ottawa that serves as both an inspiration and a warning for all who seek to lead. "Where there is no vision, the people perish."

Where so many Conservative politicians were bashing me and our climate policies, Mulroney's kindness made me well up. Here was a decent man who had often taken hard and deeply unpopular decisions, saying, in effect, just keep going.

NATURE

In 2017, I went kayaking with Moosa, an Inuk elder, by a glacier in the Qikiqtani Region of Nunavut in Canada's High Arctic. It is a place where Inuit have lived for millennia and one of the most magical and ecologically significant areas in the world teeming with narwhal, beluga, polar bears and large colonies of seabirds. We were on board a ship with the Students on Ice expedition that brought Inuit youth with youth from around the world to experience the Arctic, learn about the Inuit, and foster a commitment to sustainability. Moosa was spending much of his time teaching Inuit youth how to build kayaks. That skill had diminished in many communities and Moosa was committed to revive it with youth to help increase their connection to traditional ways. While we paddled on the water, Moosa spoke about the deep connection between ocean health and Inuit well-being.

The trip was made even more special when we announced a partnership with Inuit to move forward on creating Tallurutiup Imanga (Lancaster Sound), Canada's largest marine protected area, realizing the vision of Inuit leaders to protect their waters.

Left: Kayaking with Moosa in the Qikiqtani Region of Nunavut in Canada's High Arctic, August 2017.

OUR PARKS AND PROTECTED PLACES

When I first became minister of the environment and climate change, I didn't immediately realize I was also responsible for Parks Canada. At the time, my primary focus was on landing the Paris Agreement. Once I understood that I was responsible for Canada's nature file (along with other ministers, of course), I was thrilled. As I told everyone, "Parks Canada is my happy place."

I often reflect on how fortunate we are as Canadians. We have the longest coastline in the world, nearly 20 per cent of the world's freshwater, and more than seventy thousand wildlife species. Our boreal forest is the largest continuous forest on earth, and our Arctic is home to unique species like narwhals, walruses and Arctic foxes.

One of the most satisfying tasks during my mandate was making Parks Canada's sites free to visit to celebrate Canada's 150th anniversary. It was not only extremely popular, I was convinced that by discovering our amazing natural spaces, Canadians would connect with them and understand how important it is to protect them.

Of course, it's not just about protecting nature. It's about recognizing and respecting the stewardship of the land and waters by Indigenous Peoples. In this regard, I was very fortunate to have two incredible Indigenous lawyers on my team, Jesse and Katherine. They showed the rest of us that building trust and relationships with Indigenous Peoples and communities was more important than simply achieving conservation targets. It's also about ensuring that nature, climate, the economy and jobs, and Indigenous knowledge and experience go hand-in-hand. They helped me build partnerships with Indigenous communities across the country where we worked together to create a new network of incredible Indigenous protected areas and support Indigenous guardians as stewards of their traditional lands, waters and ice.

During a trip to the spectacular Torngat Mountains in Northern Labrador, the national Inuit leader and friend Natan Obed helped me start to see things differently. When we were on a ship looking out at icebergs and spotting polar bears, I talked about the need to protect nature. Natan corrected me gently. "For us, it's not about protecting nature. It's about our people and our relationship to the land, ice and all living things," he said. "Inuit live here in the place we call 'Inuit Nunangat'—

meaning our homeland." Governments and even nature conservation organizations have been slow to understand this.

The trip changed how I thought about Canada's Arctic. What makes the Torngats so special is not just their breathtaking beauty, but the fact that they are sacred to the Inuit. Standing at the edge of a fjord, looking out over the water and ice, it was impossible not to feel a sense of awe.

A ceremonial drum given to me in March 2018 by the Indigenous Circle of Experts to accompany their report setting out how Indigenous-led conservation can help Canada fulfil its stewardship goals.

In Gwaii Haanas National Park in northern British Columbia, I travelled with my family to Haida traditional territory, where we paddled in a Haida war canoe as a Haida youth drummed and sang. Later, we visited a Haida village site with towering totem poles. Speaking with Haida guardians—elders and youth responsible for protecting the land—continued to profoundly change how I thought about conservation. For Haida people, and Indigenous peoples more generally, protecting their land is inseparable from their culture and identity. Their knowledge, combined with Western science, creates a holistic and ultimately more sustainable approach to conservation.

In August 2019, our government created Thaidene Nëne National Park Reserve in the Northwest Territories in partnership with the Łutsël K'é First Nation. Thaidene Nëne means "land of the ancestors" in the Dene language. Before the announcement, I camped overnight and I got a small glimpse of this incredible place that covers 26,525 square kilometres and includes lakes, rivers, wetlands and forests and is filled with caribou, muskox, bears, Arctic fox and lynx. The next morning, I went for a swim in the very chilly waters and looked up to see an eagle circling overhead. A Dene ranger told me eagles symbolize good luck. I certainly felt lucky to be there.

I came to understand that as we face the twin challenges of climate change and biodiversity loss, working alongside Indigenous communities is essential. Protecting nature isn't just about ecosystems—it's about respecting the cultures, traditions and wisdom of the Indigenous peoples.

ONLINE HATE HEATS UP

"Climate change denial and misogyny seem to go hand-in-hand."

On April 1, 2019, the day the federal carbon tax became law in New Brunswick, Ontario, Saskatchewan and Manitoba, I received a torrent of angry and hateful messages and tweets. They came from the usual suspects: climate deniers; haters calling me a liar for whatever I happened to say or do about climate change; trolls making derogatory and sexist comments about my looks, even the fact that I sometimes ride a bike wearing a dress, and, of course, calling me Climate Barbie.

Things took a darker turn that day. Besides the higher volume of tweets, I also noticed they were becoming more hateful and savage. Conor Anderson, a climate scientist and PhD candidate at the University of Toronto's Climate Lab, conducted a data analysis of replies to my tweets on Twitter which you can read at conr.ca. He found that April 1, the day when carbon pricing took effect in those four provinces, had by far the highest volume of tweets directed at me.

My team and I could tell that the frequency and offensiveness of the replies to my tweets had intensified significantly. I wasn't just Climate Barbie, I was a "traitor," an "enemy," a "communist piece of garbage." I wasn't just a blonde bimbo, I was a "stain on this country" who should "rot in hell."

Many of the tweets were violent. One popular meme featured a Barbie doll being crushed by a sledgehammer. Another one had the message, "Tick Tock, Barbie Bitch." And it didn't stop with me. The messages threatened my family as well and described different ways we would be attacked and how my kids should contract fatal diseases. I didn't know it at the time, but my son, Matt, not only saw these tweets, he would sometimes respond and try to defend me, while disarming the attackers with humour. When I found out, I told him to stop. There was no winning. But this hit me hard. I was worried about the impact on my kids, especially Matt who was exposed to all this hate. However, unless you are prepared to log off of social media completely, there's no real way to protect your kids, especially teens, from much of the bad stuff.

Why did I get all this hate? I knew that carbon pricing was a deeply symbolic issue for people. Change is hard and takes time. Some people wanted it to happen overnight because of their legitimate concerns for the planet's future. Others didn't want it to happen because they worried about their or a loved one's job.

I was also keenly aware of deeper psychological currents driving this. As climate minister, and a woman using her political power to advocate for climate change policies, I was a target for hate on two fronts: a deeply entrenched, misogynistic hatred of women and a fear-of-change-driven antipathy to climate policies. Conor Anderson's analysis found that the content of the replies on my Twitter account included many anti-female slurs including "Barbie," "bitch" and "cunt." He concluded that the evidence showed that "Climate change denial and misogyny seem to go hand-in-hand."

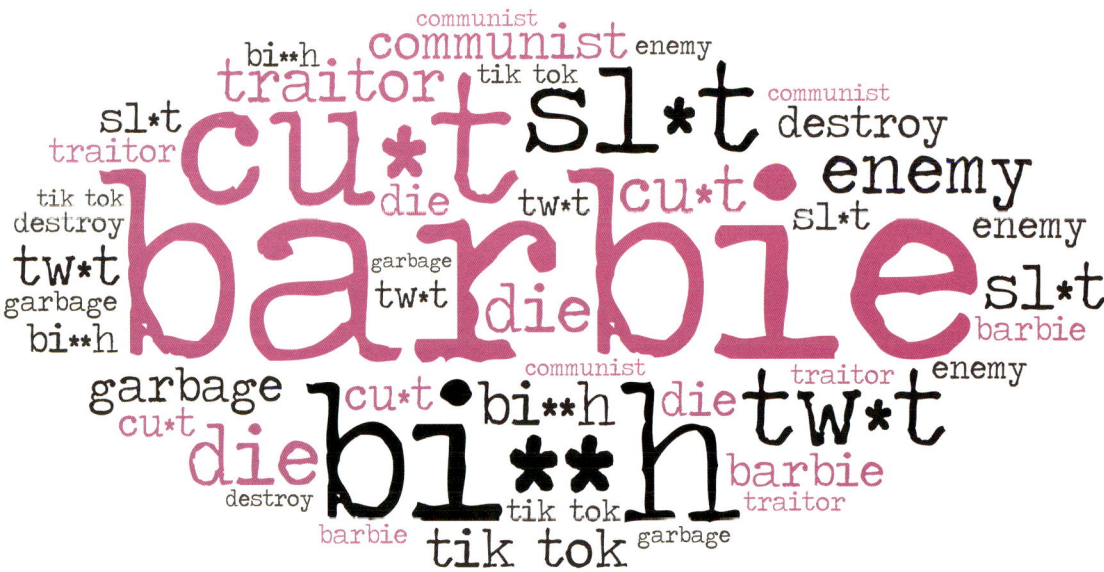

Study upon study has found that women who use their political power to push for environmental action are targeted much more frequently than their male counterparts, and the attacks they endure are far worse. Much of the nastiness and vitriol emerges from insecurity and fear, especially in male-dominated industries directly affected by environment and climate policies. As I assume many of them understood it, here I was, an outsider, and a woman, no less, suggesting that they might lose a job at a place where their fathers and grandfathers had worked for generations.

Maybe but let's be real. A great part of the sentiment driving the attacks and misinformation against me originated with high-profile Conservative politicians like Pierre Poilievre and Andrew Scheer, along with their provincial counterparts. They would slam me and our government's policies, saying that I didn't care about workers, Canadians, or families because we were bringing in a "job killing carbon tax." Rage farming, disinformation outlets such as Rebel Media and Ontario Proud would push the video clips or retweet or repost the posts from these politicians. Then trolls (real people), and bots (not real), and bot-fuelled campaigns would amplify the anger and fury against me, as would the algorithms used by social media outlets like Twitter and Facebook which made it possible for vastly more people to see the angry responses and weigh in. It was endless.

State-sponsored disinformation was likely a culprit, too. A 2019 CBC/Radio-Canada analysis of 9.6 million tweets from accounts since deleted found that "Twitter trolls linked to suspected foreign influence campaigns stoked controversy over pipelines and immigration in Canada." These trolls were suspected of having originated in Russia, Iran and Venezuela.

One of the things I really disliked was when a TV journalist asked to do an interview about online hate and then would surprise me by reading out hateful or violent tweets that people had written about me. It was a bizarre and unsettling experience to hear horrendous things about myself live on camera and then be forced to explain how they made me feel and why I thought people said these horrible things.

As tough as I am, the volume of hate towards me was jarring and upsetting. It hurt that some people who had never met me, who had no idea what I was like, not only hated me, but let's not mince words, wanted to hurt or even kill me or my kids. They couldn't see that I was just a regular person doing the best I could at a very hard job. I tried to rationalize that all women working on climate were subject to hate and that it wasn't really about me, but I think it took a toll on me, one I didn't realize until I left politics. While there were still haters, I felt a massive weight lift off my shoulders when I left because I no longer felt I had to care. It wasn't my job anymore.

It was also terrible for my staff. They saw all of it and wanted to protect me but they couldn't. Regular people who followed me and replied to my posts were attacked as well.

Let's put this in the language of "freedom" used by a number of those who think I should just have put up with these attacks because I was in politics: it wasn't just my freedom to express myself without being subject to hate, attacks, and threats of violence that was being compromised, it affected the freedoms of regular Canadians to express themselves, as well. Many people told me they had stopped replying to any of my posts and even following my account because the viciousness was so intense.

I started to worry about the threat of violence in real life. I met with the RCMP, Canada's national police service, and other agencies to see what they could do. Their reaction was demoralizing. A very senior member of the RCMP said to me that the solution was to get off social media. While that might seem like a reasonable idea now, in 2018, Twitter was a great way to reach journalists who used the platform religiously, and it was one of the best platforms to communicate directly with constituents and Canadians.

My team reached out to the platform's Canadian representatives and they told us to report anything worrying. We explained that given the volume, that would take my staff every minute of every day. I asked how their algorithms worked and why instead of amplifying hate and violent posts they weren't using their algorithms to identify and remove them. I received no answer. My team did its best to report the most offensive and worrying posts. Little was ever done.

I decided to take a different approach. I started blocking the worst accounts, partly because they were impeding reasonable discussions and were using my account to amplify their hate, but I also wanted a list of possible culprits to give authorities in case anything happened to me or my family. Yes, that's what it came to.

In early 2021, I received notice that Rebel Media was taking me to federal court alleging that I had violated the Charter right to free expression of one of its employees by blocking them. Of course, it wasn't just any employee. This is a woman who claims credit for coining the phrase "Climate Barbie" and had spent years harassing me.

Where many government cases like this often settle, I said, "Absolutely, no way." Rebel Media's argument was as absurd as it was offensive. To give into the argument that their employee's freedom of expression was violated if that person couldn't attack me day in and out was preposterous; it was also dangerous for democracy. Who in their right mind would go into politics, especially women, and sign up to be a punching bag for right-wing rage-farming outlets?

We commissioned an expert in online violence against women in politics, Dr. Gabrielle Bardall, a fellow with the Centre for International Policy Studies at the University of Ottawa, to conduct an analysis of the tweets against me. What she found was extremely telling. Her report outlined that I was targeted by a "sustained and hostile violence against women in politics (VAWP) campaign" instigated by Rebel Media. It noted that "violence against women in politics exists at the crossroads of 'dirty' politics and gender-based violence, targeting women who participate in public or political life, either specifically because they are women, or [by using] ... sexist threats or sexual harassment or violence." The report also highlighted that violence against women has "distinctly gendered impacts" on the exercise of civil and political rights. These include fewer women running for office, more elected women resigning or retiring early, and greater difficulty recruiting female candidates.

The report also made a critical point: "It is well documented that abuse, incivility and harassment on social media often spill over into offline and physical harm. This creates another reason for credible fear and intimidation. Minister McKenna clearly faced such a credible concern." The expert report concluded I had the "right to mitigate abusive attacks by using blocking functions."

I was fully prepared to go to court but Rebel Media dropped its action against me when I left politics. I assume they realized I not only had a solid case against their allegations but also against them. This is partly why I was so disappointed when a similar case against Stephen Guilbeault, my successor as minister of environment and climate change, was settled with an agreement to unblock the head of Rebel Media and pay a settlement. Sometimes you need to fight your harassers.

Of course, I wasn't the only woman working on climate who was attacked on social media. Basically, any woman who is working in the field gets targeted. The former environment minister of Alberta, Shannon Phillips, also spoke out against violent tweets attacking women in politics. On May 25, 2016, she retweeted a post from a man who said: "My boot would look nice on @SPhillipsAB's face," and wrote, "I have no idea why women might think twice about entering politics." Earlier the same year, police charged a man who made death threats to staff in her office, allegedly because he was angry about the carbon tax her NDP government brought in. Shannon's experience was particularly egregious. She was even targeted by members of the local police who conducted unauthorized surveillance of her because they didn't like her politics.

My friend, Katharine Hayhoe, a Canadian-born climate scientist and director of the Climate Center at Texas Tech University, is also the target for endless sexist abuse online which range in her words from "disparaging to downright vile." On August 18, 2023, she wrote: "As a female climate scientist, blocking is the only thing that makes my engagement here on Twitter/X possible." Blocking, she explained, ensures that she doesn't have to see comments from people who repeatedly call her "a whore" and tell her to kill herself; limits the traffic in disinformation and hate on the platform; frustrates trolls and starves them of the energy they derive from engagement with her; and makes her account seem more credible by ridding it of negativity and hate. I couldn't agree more.

The situation has only became worse under Elon Musk's ownership of Twitter which soon became X. The real threat to freedom of speech is when women and other victims simply stop standing up and speaking out about online abuse. When we look back, I think we will see how irrational this twenty-year experience in unregulated social media has been.

MAKING A BIG MISTAKE

Throughout 2017 and 2018, I was pushing hard to sell our climate plan and carbon pricing. By spring, 2018, the issue had really heated up. That April, Evan Solomon invited me onto CTV Question Period, his Sunday morning political talk show. Evan and I are long-time friends. He always added this disclaimer when I appeared on his show.

He began with a few softball questions before getting to the meat of the interview. He asked how I planned to handle provincial opposition. I took that to mean Conservative politicians in provinces who were vocally opposed to carbon pricing and campaigning against it–especially in Saskatchewan, Alberta and Ontario. I should have seen it coming but I let my feisty Irish side get the better of me. "Let's be clear," I said. "Climate change has huge costs, and I have no time for folks who are saying we shouldn't take action." Uh-oh.

The moment the words were out of my mouth, Evan pounced: "Your job is to have time for people who disagree with you." I clarified that I always have time for Canadians who disagree with me. I had conversations with them every day. What I didn't have time for were politicians who were merely opportunists and had no real plan to tackle climate change. It was an important distinction that got lost in the moment, and the damage was done. CTV clipped my remark, omitted my clarification, and the Conservatives used it in a new set of attack ads.

I had tripped up and the timing couldn't have been worse. I was laser-focused on communicating to Canadians that carbon pricing wasn't just important to tackling climate change–it would put more money back into the pockets of 80 per cent of Canadians. Now, there was a clip out there making me look like an elitist snob who had no time for ordinary Canadians.

It was a sharp reminder that I always had to be hyper disciplined when speaking in public. I had to choose my words very carefully. But at the same time, I always wanted to sound real in an interview, not like a robot spewing talking points. But in politics, it's a fine line between sounding like a real person and saying something that can be misinterpreted or twisted. Still, I hate this aspect of modern politics because controlling every single word that comes out of your mouth makes it harder to be authentic. But here I got it wrong. Big time.

Watching the bedroom fan. Turn, turn, turn.

Worst, and what upset me most, is that I came across as someone antithetical to who I am, and how I was raised to be—a regular person from Hamilton who was trying my best to tackle climate change.

That night, I couldn't sleep. I lay in bed, with my dog Skoki at my side, just staring at my ceiling fan, worried about the damage I'd done. One screwup, and it felt like I was jeopardizing everything. It made me sick to my stomach.

Evan and I remain friends. He was a great journalist, and he's now on the other side of the mic as an elected MP. All I can say is, good luck!

YOU'RE NOT TOO MUCH

> "We have to always be extraordinary, but somehow we're always doing it wrong."
>
> —America Ferrera as Gloria in *Barbie: The Movie*

I struggled with imposter syndrome in my twenties and thirties. I often felt like I didn't belong in the room or, if I did, I wasn't smart enough to speak up. I'd sit quietly, convinced that others had better things to say.

It's hard for my friends to believe now, but I almost never spoke up in law school. I'd sit at the back, taking notes while many others eagerly raised their hands. The one time I did speak, it was in my favourite class—constitutional law. I decided to push myself by taking the class in French. I was nervous and accidentally used the informal *"tu"* instead of the respectful *"vous"* with my favourite professor, Armand de Mestral. It was mortifying. After that, I never spoke in class again.

In my thirties, I made a decision: I would force myself to speak up. I started going to international relations conferences—an area I knew well. I'd wait until the end of the Q&A, then gather the courage to approach the mic. My hands would shake, and my voice would crack, but I'd get my question out. And after, I'd beat myself up, thinking I'd sounded foolish. It was painful, but it was the only way to overcome the self-doubt. Eventually, I realized something. When the mostly male speakers asked questions, they often went on with long, self-important introductions and wasted everyone's time. My questions were shorter and sharper. Of course, even in my thirties I was still often mistaken for an intern. I remember going to a business conference when I was running Canadian Lawyers Abroad and at lunch I was seated by the organizers at the head table beside the CEO of a large Canadian company. He turned to me, said hello, and then "joked" that he hoped he was allergic to the soup so I could give him mouth-to-mouth resuscitation. Barf. I remember being furious. I could feel the blood rushing to my face (I'm sure I was bright red), and smiling but not smiling as I tried to take in what he said.

You'll find this on my fridge. I love it!

When I hit my forties and entered politics, things didn't get better. In a way, they felt even worse. By now, I was used to being in the room and often one of the only women at the table. But something strange would happen: when I spoke up, there was often a reaction that while subtle, was there. A glance, a sigh, someone cutting me off. And I'd find myself thinking, "Wait, what's going on?" You could almost hear the guys thinking, *we don't want to hear what you have to say. You're too much—especially about climate*. Often, it came in the form of male business leaders saying to me, "You don't understand," like I was twelve years old, rather than a former corporate lawyer, international negotiator, minister and climate leader.

And it hasn't stopped, even now, having been in Parliament for six years with three degrees, running my own company, working on climate change globally, and having raised three kids. I recently had a call with a retired CEO from a large international oil-and-gas company who went on and on about how committed the oil-and-gas sector was to climate action. He concluded by telling me I didn't really understand them. I paused for a bit and said: "Funny that. If you've spent four years as Canada's environment minister, you understand the oil and gas sector's position on climate pretty well."

But understand this. It is not you. It is them. And it is real.

I've seen this happen with so many other strong women, too. It's as though we are expected to sit at the table, but not ask for much. There is this constant, invisible pressure to tone it down. And for racialized and Indigenous women speaking from personal experience, it gets even worse. You can almost see many men checking out.

This dynamic had an insidious effect. It made me second-guess myself: "Am I speaking up too much? Am I being too forceful?" But I knew that when I did speak up, it was because I had something to say. Not because I enjoyed hearing my own voice.

Here's what I believe is going on: it's fine for women to be at the table as long as we don't push too hard. As long as we smile, agree, and keep things easy. But if we try to make things happen–that makes some men uncomfortable. And let me tell you, most men don't like to be made to feel uncomfortable.

I'm not sure how we fight this. Many men probably don't even realize they're doing it. If you point it out, they might be offended or dismiss it. But there's still an old boys' club at play. A lot of men are fine with women being at the table as long as we don't challenge the status quo. The reality is women often bring a different perspective, and from my experience, it is often more creative, more ambitious, and more practical. We must speak up. It's not "too much." In fact, it is usually exactly the right thing to do.

WHEN THE TEAM COMES APART

By January 2019, four years after we'd been elected, we were all exhausted—Cabinet, caucus, the PMO, and, presumably, the prime minister himself. We'd worked hard and accomplished a lot. I was proud of the climate plan and carbon pricing system we had developed. We created the Canada Child Benefit, which cut child poverty in half and Canada took in forty thousand Syrian refugees. We cut taxes for the middle class, legalized marijuana and adopted the UN Declaration on Indigenous Rights. We had even managed to revamp the trade deal with the US and Mexico to replace NAFTA. By any measure these were real achievements.

But there were setbacks. We abandoned our promise on electoral reform. Scandals hit, notably when the ethics commissioner found the prime minister violated conflict-of-interest rules when he visited a private island owned by the Aga Khan. Then there was the disastrous 2018 trip to India, full of embarrassing diplomatic missteps. Still, headed into the election year, we were in decent shape. It was all manageable, until the SNC-Lavalin affair exploded.

There are many different perspectives on what happened, but the basic facts are as follows. SNC-Lavalin, now Atkins-Réalis, a major Canadian engineering firm, was facing criminal charges for bribery and corruption related to its business in Libya. It was seeking a settlement agreement where it would admit wrongdoing and pay a fine rather than proceed to a criminal trial. In February 2019, Jody Wilson-Raybould, who had been minister of justice and attorney general, until she was shuffled to veterans affairs in January of that year, accused the prime minister and his officials of pressuring her throughout the fall of 2018 to intervene in the case. She argued this was improper interference in the justice system and refused to intervene.

It was a train wreck. Wilson-Raybould resigned from Cabinet along with the treasury board minister, Jane Philpott. The prime minister's principal secretary and the member of the team with the most executive political management experience, Gerald Butts, also resigned, even though he didn't have much to do with the file. He took a hit for the prime minister and the government, but his sacrifice went largely unacknowledged. Now we had a gaping hole in our government. Gerald had been the person with the overarching vision for our government's agenda, and he had a deeper

Cabinet members hanging out waiting for the prime minister to arrive for an official photo at our Cabinet retreat in Winnipeg, January 21, 2020.

sense for what policies would fly with regular people than most. Butts grew up the son of a coal miner in Cape Breton and his roots provided a good reality check. The former head of World Wildlife Fund Canada, he was also a climate champion working at the centre of government. We didn't always agree but I knew without him it would make it much harder to get things done. Most importantly, he seemed to be the only person in Ottawa who could speak frankly to the prime minister.

After Butts left and with everything in complete meltdown, I asked Katie Telford, the prime minister's chief of staff, if she had thought of either our United Nations ambassador Marc-André Blanchard or our ambassador the US, David McNaughton as potential successors. She responded, "that's really interesting that you would suggest two men over sixty." My jaw dropped. My first thought was, "Marc-André isn't over sixty." My second thought was incredulity that she was suggesting I wasn't a good feminist because the two most competent and loyal people I could think of happened to be men. My third thought was, "Oh shit. Our team is in real trouble." In the end, the prime minister never did appoint a new principal secretary.

In August 2019, six months after the story broke, the ethics commissioner concluded the prime minister and his officials had violated the Conflict of Interest Act by improperly pressuring Wilson-Raybould.

In my view, the SNC-Lavalin affair showed that we had failed as a team. If politics is ultimately about relationships, and if you're the prime minister, you have to tend to those relationships. It's a disaster if you don't, and we could all see it up close.

Building and maintaining a strong team isn't easy. It takes skill to get the best out of everyone and keep the focus on the bigger goals. While people often think Cabinet works as a unit, it's really a collection of individuals, each with their own personalities, egos and motivations. After a few years, cracks are bound to appear. Cabinet meetings, including our retreats, were overrun with Memoranda to Cabinet through which the public service outlined issues and recommended actions, effectively filling up our agenda. Instead of discussing strategy and prioritizing files, identifying risks to our ability to deliver services to Canadians, or assessing global developments that could derail our agenda, Cabinet discussion bogged down in bureaucratic minutiae. And increasingly almost every decision was left "ad referendum," meaning the final decision was left to the finance minister and prime minister.

With lengthy mandates and high expectations, ministers were stretched thin. Most had families, and striking any work-life balance was tough. I did things that I thought might help build the team, like hosting an annual Christmas party or inviting ministers to my house to hang out. But it was far too little. We needed leadership.

Our biggest problem? The prime minister was aloof and just didn't seem interested in his ministers or caucus members beyond his childhood friends, Dominic LeBlanc and Marc Miller. I think he believed Cabinet ministers were basically interchangeable and that it mattered little who was in a particular role. This was entirely different from his predecessors like Jean Chrétien and Brian Mulroney, who were constantly on the phone lines with their Cabinet ministers and caucus members. They burned up the phones because they wanted to cajole but also to know what was going on and hear different opinions. They understood that it mattered that they acknowledged personal or professional milestones. Basically, they liked their team and drew energy from its members.

Justin Trudeau was different. It was almost impossible for ministers to reach the prime minister even though he said he was always available. He existed in a fortress. He had said at the start that he, Gerald Butts, and Katie Telford were a team, so when they spoke, they spoke for him. While that sounds great, there can be only one team leader, especially on a sensitive issue that needs a clear decision from the boss.

I like to think that the prime minister could have learned a lot about leadership from my UofT swim coach, Byron MacDonald, who built and nurtured many winning teams over decades. It's not just about recruiting talented people. As a leader, you are responsible for fostering team spirit and making sure that members feel part of something bigger than themselves. Building pride and unity as a team, inspiring people to do the hardest things and to be in position to win—none of that can be delegated.

In the aftermath of SNC-Lavalin, it was clear: the prime minister hadn't built a true team and now that team was coming undone.

COLLISION

On June 17, 2019, I rose in the House of Commons and tabled a motion declaring that Canada was in the midst of a national climate emergency. It passed with support from all major parties, except the Conservatives. I was proud of that moment. For me, it was a long overdue recognition of what the science and people across the country had been saying for years: that we could no longer afford to delay serious action on climate change.

But less than 24 hours later, Cabinet announced the expansion of the Trans Mountain pipeline, tripling its capacity. I was floored by the timing.

To the outside world, this must have looked like pure hypocrisy. One day, a government declares a climate emergency. The next, it approves a major fossil fuel project.

What people often don't see is that governments aren't monoliths. They're made up of individuals—elected officials from different places, with different constituencies, different pressures, different responsibilities and different beliefs about how to move the country forward. And sometimes those forces push hard in competing directions.

The decision to declare a climate emergency and expand the capacity of a pipeline reflected real concerns—about science, about equity, about the economy and jobs, about national unity. But putting them side by side made our contradictions impossible to ignore.

Inside the government, I fought hard to align our climate ambition with our decisions. We had an aggressive climate plan that included carbon pricing, methane regulations, phasing out coal and a new impact assessment process that better protected the environment and Indigenous rights while ensuring good projects got built faster. But it never felt like enough, and it was never easy.

I was very reluctant to support the pipeline expansion. But at the time, I convinced myself that approving it was a necessary compromise to maintain a national climate consensus that included Alberta. I believed it could buy space to implement the rest of our plan – that if we made progress on climate, invested all the revenue from the pipeline expansion into Canada's clean energy transition and showed that we cared about jobs and workers in resource communities, then

On the streets of Ottawa with tens of thousands of people as part of the global climate march on September 27, 2019.

Canadians would come along with us. Even environmentalists, I hoped, might see the bigger picture.

Looking back, I have serious doubts about both the pipeline and our conciliatory approach to the oilsands. After all, the oil sector didn't meet us halfway—or anywhere close. Emissions kept rising. Promises to act were broken. Companies returned record profits to shareholders—many outside Canada—while demanding more subsidies at home.

The truth is, there's no winning when you're caught between regions, industries, and ideologies—especially on an issue as complex and existential as climate change. But it's also true that while politicians fight and make compromises, the climate crisis continues to get worse.

Meanwhile, massive climate marches were underway. That September, I decided to join tens of thousands of people in Ottawa—many of them young people—for the global climate strike. Despite everything, I felt welcome. No one shouted at me. Instead, many thanked me. That day was a turning point.

It reminded me that pressure from the public matters. That government often needs people in the streets as well as different voices at the Cabinet table. Because while professional lobbyists are constantly working to shape policy behind closed doors—often with deep resources and endless access—climate activists and young people who will bear the consequences, just don't get that same airtime. If governments keep hearing mainly from industry, they'll act like it. That's why we need more than a registry of lobbyists—we need parity. Every time a minister meets with a business leader, they should also meet with a young person who wants more climate action or someone who represents the public interest and the planet.

That climate march helped me remember why I entered politics in the first place. Not to win every argument. Not to be perfect. But to fight with others who care—to keep pushing, to keep showing up even when it's hard.

The truth is, all governments are messy. Progress is rarely linear. But public pressure works. So keep fighting.

A BRUTAL ELECTION

When the 2019 election was called, I was exhausted, as was everyone else in the government. It had been a long four years. Yet with the media framing the election as a "carbon tax election," I felt a huge weight on my shoulders and I knew I couldn't coast. I had been doing everything I could to convince Canadians to support a price on pollution. If the Conservatives won, carbon pricing and many other climate policies were toast. We had to fight hard.

When I knocked on doors, I told constituents I was running because I believed we still had a lot of work to do for Canadians, especially on climate change. It was a tough sell. People were not excited. Already the enthusiasm for our government and also in the prime minister was fading fast and this was still before the pandemic. At the door, many people were mad that we broke our promise on electoral reform; others had issues with the prime minister's judgement. But mostly it was just general disappointment. Sunny ways had clouded over. My constituents seemed happy enough with me and what we'd done on the environment and climate change, but it just didn't feel like it had in 2015.

In mid-September, we were doing a student canvass at Carleton University when a member of my campaign team, Murielle, pulled me aside and said, "Look at this." She showed me a picture on her phone. I couldn't really tell what I was looking at. It seemed to be the prime minister. But his face was painted. He was wearing some kind of weird outfit. Then I saw the headline containing the word "Blackface." I looked at Murielle, a young Black woman. "I think we should get out of here," she said. We left immediately.

This was bad. Murielle was shaken and angry but she later told me that those feelings dissipated quickly. She later told me that she and her friends vented but then made light of the incident because, sadly, these are experiences that Black people have grown accustomed to and expect to happen time and time again. But what really frustrated Murielle was that it was now on Black Canadians to either channel the outrage or offer forgiveness on behalf of the entire community.

On my red bike to the press conference.

With my friend Greg at the super tough press conference. Greg is amazing.

The next morning I was supposed to do an event with my friend and Liberal colleague Greg Fergus announcing our campaign commitment to transform an old rail bridge into a pedestrian and bike crossing. Greg was chair of the Parliamentary Black Caucus. I called him up, thinking the media would only want to grill Greg on Blackface, and said, "I guess we're not doing this announcement." Greg said, "Of course we're still doing it." Apparently, he'd already talked to the prime minister. He told Trudeau he was disappointed and that Trudeau had screwed up. He'd have to work to rebuild relationships with Black Canadians, and that he should really ask himself why he ever thought, even in his twenties, that Blackface was a fun idea.

We rode our bikes down to the bridge and made the announcement. A lot of media showed up, but no one cared about the bridge. Greg was asked about the photos. He said he had spoken to the prime minister the day before and explained why his actions were hurtful. And he emphasized that had he done Blackface while PM, Greg would have been furious. But he concluded that the prime minister as prime minister had always fought racial discrimination and supported Black communities. And because of his track record, many in the Black community were willing to forgive him.

It was a huge deal that a well-respected Black Liberal member of Parliament was vouching for the prime minister so soon. Greg didn't have to be the first person out in front of cameras standing up for the prime minister. He did it not to save the prime minister, but because he thought that what we were doing as Liberals was too important to throw away. And he was right.

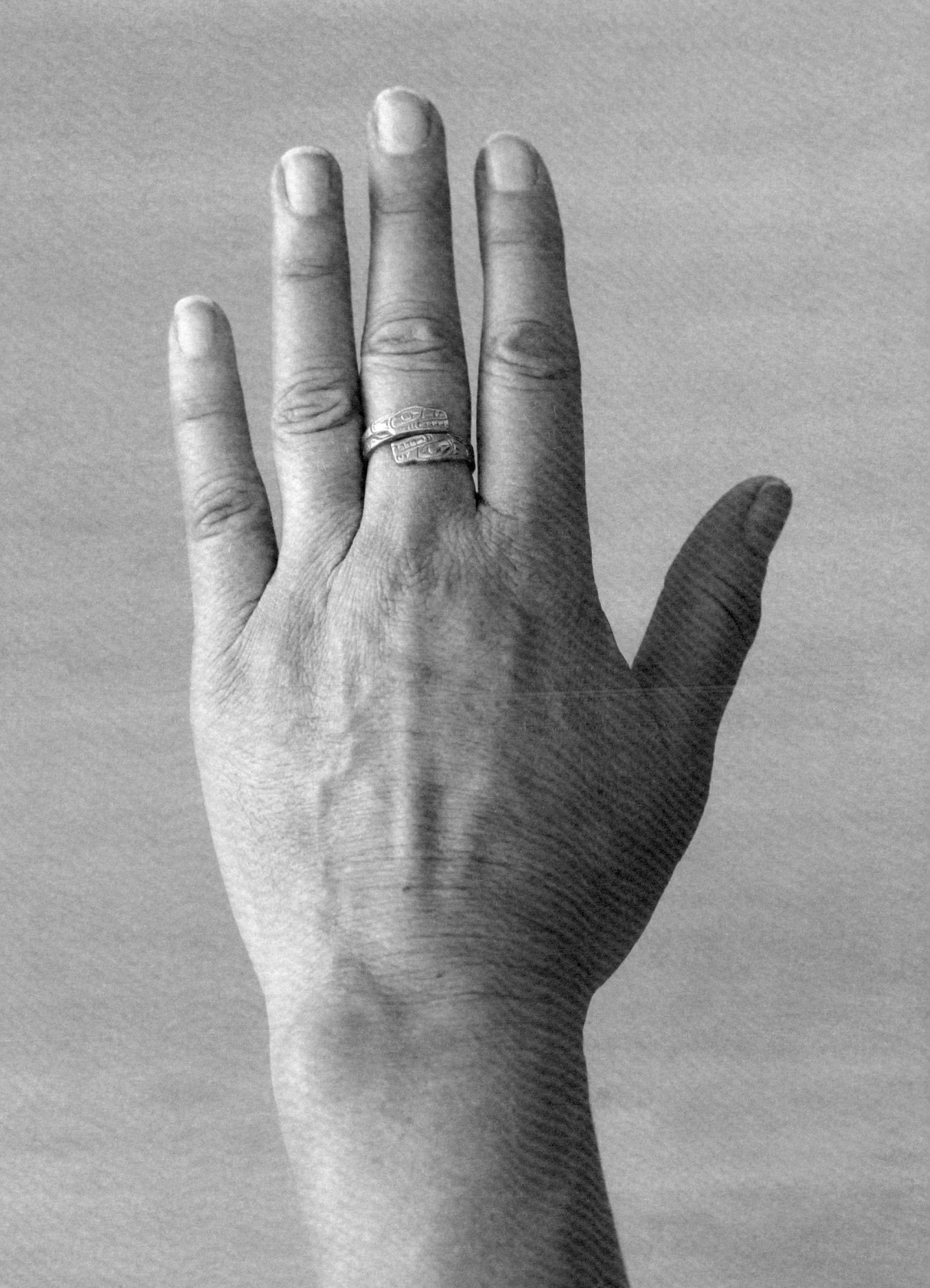

TAKING OFF MY RING

One of my indispensable volunteers, and an Ottawa Centre Liberal legend, Isabel Metcalfe, said to me she always tries to be very positive and understanding when she canvasses with politicians because you never know what is really going on in a politician's life. Truth.

Scott and I had been growing apart for a while. In Ottawa, people sometimes compared us to James Carville and Mary Matalin—a well-known American couple with very different political views. While it was true that, as a Liberal and a Conservative, we often backed opposing ideas, we also shared a deep interest in public policy and improving the country. Over time, however, our differences went beyond political preferences, and it became increasingly clear they weren't going away.

Eventually, Scott and I made the difficult decision to separate. We told the kids together and reassured them that we loved them and that we would continue to live close to one another.

Going through a marriage breakup is an incredibly lonely experience. Doing it in the political spotlight is even more so. I pride myself on being an open person, yet through this period of time there were things I wasn't telling people, and possibly even things I couldn't admit to myself.

Even after it was done, I didn't want to tell anyone else except for my family and closest friends, not simply because it hurt but also because I had to keep our personal family lives from becoming a news story.

In July 2019, I took a much-needed break from the election campaign from hell, gathered up the kids, and headed with them to Vancouver Island with my close friends, Caroline and Matt, and their kids. I needed distance from the campaign. I was desperate to get away from it all and spend some time in a tent with my kids.

One day, when we were wandering around the shops in Victoria, I spotted a beautiful gold Haida ring engraved with an image of a wolf. The shopkeeper explained to me that wolves are family-oriented animals. To the Indigenous People on the West Coast, they are seen as loyal guardians and protectors. Something about the symbolic, fierce protectiveness of the wolf and the exquisite craftsmanship of the ring spoke to me in the moment. It seemed like the right time to take off my wedding band and put on this new one. I felt better. Maybe not a transformation. But at least a new chapter had begun.

YOUR FRIENDS WILL SAVE YOU

My advice to any woman going into politics: cherish your girlfriends and keep them tight.

At one point, I stopped going out. It was just easier. I loved the people of Ottawa Centre, but it was hard to escape politics in Ottawa. Whether I was grocery shopping, having a meal with friends or going for a walk with my kids or my dog, people would come up to me. I was becoming more and more guarded. Although most of the time they were polite and friendly, I just didn't want to talk about politics. And I knew my kids resented that their time with me was always getting interrupted by small talk. It also didn't help that Scott and I had separated.

I really don't think I could have survived without my girlfriends. They knew me before I got into politics, and I knew they would be there once I got out of politics. Politics was just my job. They helped me hold everything together when I wasn't sure I could. Having a good laugh with them over a glass of wine reminded me that no matter what happened, no matter how bad things seemed, things would somehow be ok.

My book club became a lifeline to me. We had our meetings once a month. I'd try to make it if I wasn't travelling, too often not even knowing what the book was. But my girlfriends didn't care. At our gatherings, I wasn't a politician or a minister—I was one of our gang. When I had a particularly terrible day, I'd send an email with the subject line: "Emergency drinks at my house at 8 p.m." Whoever could make it would drop by for a glass of wine and Miss Vickie's potato chips (jalapeno or salt and vinegar). I might rant for a bit but I never really got into the details; the fact they were always there for me was the most amazing thing.

When things were really unbearable and I needed to escape, I'd call my mom and sister and we'd plan a weekend away. Like me, my sister had a lot going on at home with three kids, and my mom and dad were busy, but my mom and sister always made time. We'd meet up somewhere halfway between Ottawa and Toronto. I'd try to turn off my phone and just hang out. I knew they knew how things were

A weekend canoeing with my good friends Rebecca and Deirdre once a summer was exactly what I needed.

hard at work and at home. That's why they did everything they could to be there. I loved them for it.

Once each summer, I'd really try to get away from it all, into nature, with my university friends, Rebecca and Deirdre. Since leaving university, we'd gone on several summer camping trips to Algonquin Park. We'd bring a canoe, a food barrel and packs and go on a weekend adventure. Being out in the wilderness with them, especially with no cell service or internet, was the best thing ever. They were far outside the Ottawa bubble, so we didn't spend time on politics. We'd cover a lot of ground in the canoe, paddling and reminiscing about life, catching up about our families and kids. We'd swim, make campfires, look for moose and deer, and just hang out.

WHAT KEPT ME GOING

In politics, I received countless letters—some positive, some negative, some downright nasty. The best ones, by far, were from kids. They cared so much about the environment and they would share their fears, their hopes, and their ideas to make things better—from using metal straws to organizing park cleanups. On tough days, I'd pull out a few of these notes and be reminded why what I was doing mattered. Like this one from Alexandra, which never failed to cheer me up.

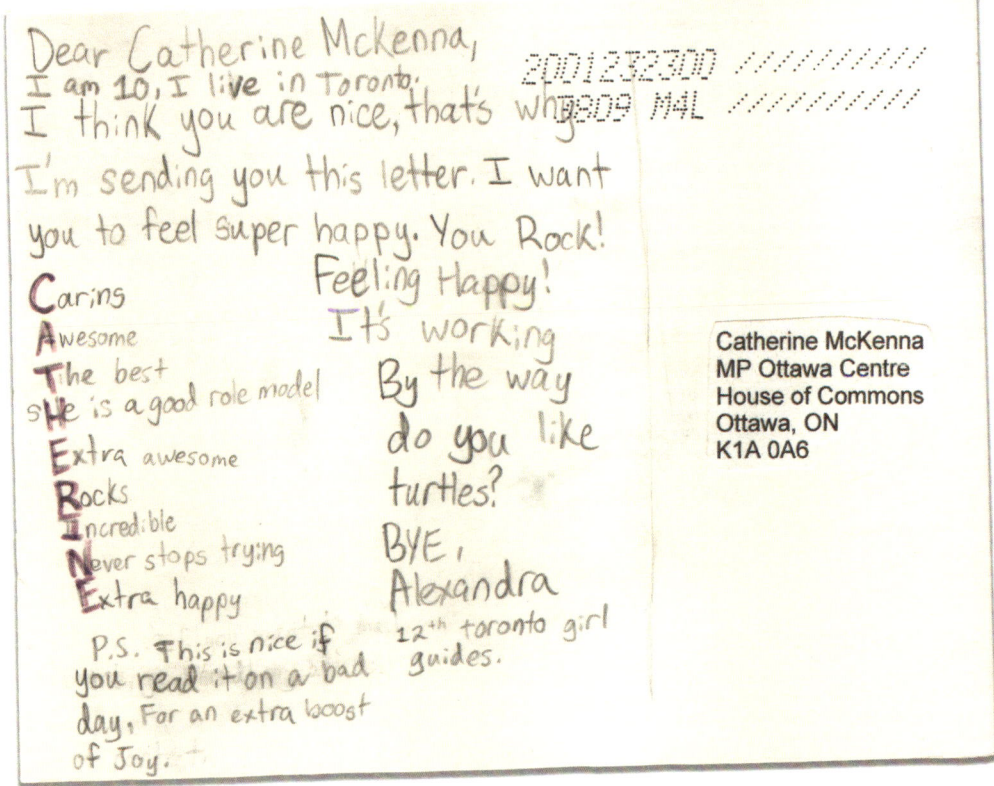

I loved all the encouraging mail I received from kids like Alexandra!

MY KIDS ARE THE BEST

I hated the 2019 election. My party was unpopular, the scandals were relentless, the online hate was worse than ever and my marriage was over. My kids knew how hard it was, so they made me the best possible present: a ten-day countdown calendar on one side, with drawings and motivational quotes on the other to keep me going. Quotes like: "Winners make a habit of doing stuff that losers don't want to." And on the last day: "It's finally over. We are so proud of you." I cried. My kids kept me going.

Ten day countdown calendar from my kids.

WHEN WINNING DOESN'T FEEL LIKE WINNING

In the end, we won the 2019 election. Barely. The Liberal Party won 33.12 per cent of the vote which at the time was the lowest vote share ever for any party forming a government or at least until the 2021 election. We still managed to remain in government albeit a minority one.

I should have felt happier. I'd won handily in my riding, and the majority of voters had chosen a political party that supported carbon pricing. That was a huge win in policy terms. I celebrated at a local pub with my incredibly devoted campaign team and hundreds of volunteers who once again killed themselves knocking on doors, making calls, inputting data, fundraising and buoying my spirits. And there was a lot of family there. McKennas show up. But it was also true that Canadians hadn't given the Liberal Party much of a mandate. They had sent us a message: shape up or you'll be gone.

I spoke honestly that night about how important it was to do better: "I think one of the lessons that is emerging from today's result is the need for a more positive political culture in our country. We all have work to do to bring people together and remember the value of being open to different ideas from coast to coast to coast." What I left out was that we needed to start listening better and with a lot more humility.

Afterward, someone sent me a column from the Abbotsford News. It noted that at a post election party for Conservative MP Ed Fast, who'd been re-elected as MP for Abbotsford, the TV coverage turned to my speech and a few of his supporters actually clapped when I said we all had work to do to bring people together.

Ed had been my critic on the Conservative benches. I took it as a sign that if his supporters were applauding me, it meant that maybe there was hope that despite political differences, people could still be decent and get along.

Left: Speaking at my election victory party with my family behind me on October 22, 2019 at Craft Beer Market at Lansdowne Park, Ottawa.

THE C WORD

It turns out I spoke too soon.

A few days after the campaign I was happily walking Cormac to school, which was something I hadn't been able to do for a long time. I knew that because he was in Grade 6 and was soon moving on to middle school, this was likely the last year he'd let me walk with him. Halfway to the school, the phone rang. It was my campaign manager, Kyle. Someone had spray-painted "cunt" on my campaign-office window. Already, the media was on-site. He told me to try to get ahead of the story by coming by as soon as possible and speaking to them. I said nothing to Cormac, dropped him off, and drove to my office.

And sure enough, there it was, written in angry red letters over my face on a giant poster in the window. Cameras rolled while I walked into my campaign office. I was overwhelmed to see everyone there looking ashen-faced, especially all the women on my team who had come in that morning to help box things up from the campaign. They did not deserve this.

The women lined up behind me as I looked straight into the camera and said: "We've just been through a really divisive campaign with a lot of negative rhetoric, and this is really beneath us as Canadians. It isn't about me; it's about what kind of politics we want in our country. That someone would do this—I don't even have words to describe what kind of person would do this. It's the same as the trolls on Twitter. It needs to stop. We need to come together as a country and have real discussions about real issues, but doing it in a way without vitriol, without hate, without anger."

I acknowledged I was a bit shaken. "Look, I'm tough, but I'm really sick of this. I'm angry and quite frankly really disappointed."

When the press conference ended, I hugged my team. I felt sorry that they had to go through this, especially after such a brutal campaign. Many constituents dropped by, especially women, to say how horrified they were. Some dropped off cookies and little gifts to cheer me up. It was the nicest thing after the worst thing.

I went home and stewed. I called my mom and tried to act tough and downplay it. I knew she would see it on TV and worry. I told her it was probably some teenagers who did it as a joke or on a dare. She wasn't having it. "Absolutely not. This was done by a man who doesn't like you."

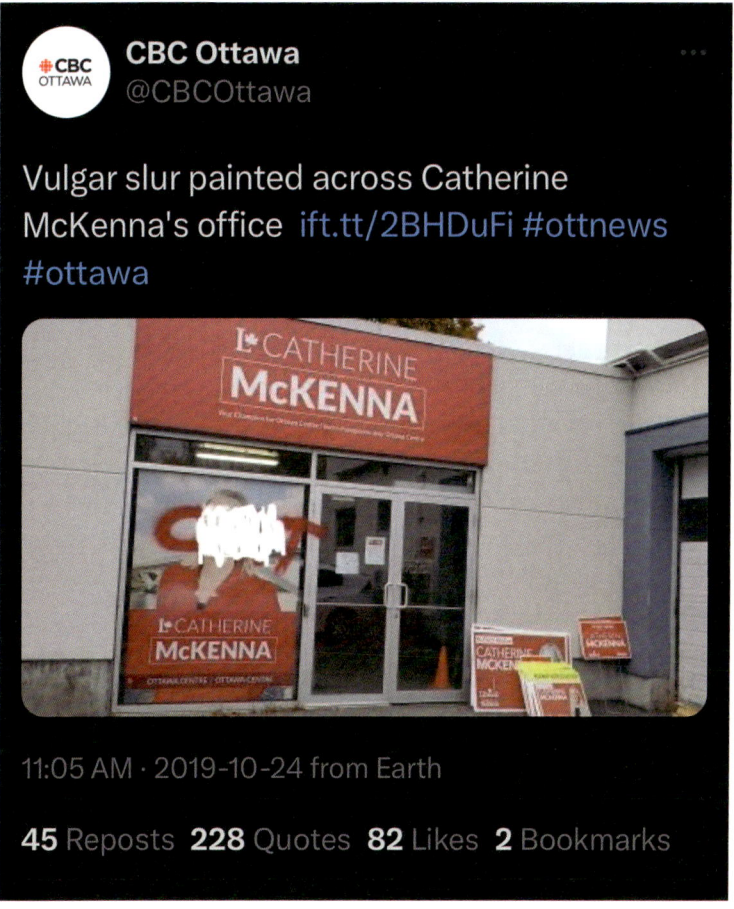

CBC Ottawa tweet about the incident at my campaign office on October 24, 2019.

I figured my older kids would have heard what happened through social media by the time school was done. We'd have to sit down and talk about it so I could hear how they felt and put their fears to rest. I hoped Cormac wouldn't find out at all–I didn't want him to worry. Of course, by the time they got home, they'd all heard. They said, "Mom, don't worry about us. How are you doing?" And then, finally, I started to cry. I tried to hide it because I didn't want them to see me breakdown. I love them so much. Now I felt a surge of grief. I was worried about everything they had to go through because I entered politics. And my darkest, ugliest, and now constant fear was that someone would try to harm them.

DANCE IF YOU WANT TO

With growing security concerns, I was starting to feel like I'd become almost a prisoner in my own home. But I love dancing and fortunately for me, Ottawa's legendary pinball and perogies place, House of TARG, has 80s and 90s nights, once a month on Fridays. At one point I decided I had to go with my girlfriends. It was time to live it up like I used to before politics, starting with the local dances in high school.

I'm a big New Order fan, but I'll dance to almost anything fun that was played when I was in high school and university: U2, Green Day, Madonna, Eurythmics, The English Beat. People recognized me, but no one hassled me. Blowing off steam doesn't make you a worse politician—it made me a better one. If we want normal humans in politics, we can't set impossible standards. Just ask the former Finnish prime minister, Sanna Marin.

House of Targ posters promoting their infamous 1980s dance parties.

BE IN POLITICS TO DO SOMETHING, NOT BE SOMEONE

With the election behind us I wondered if I'd be asked to join Cabinet again, and if so, in what role. I liked environment and climate change, but I was the second-longest-serving environment minister, and I wondered if it was a good thing for anyone to be so closely associated with a file, especially such a polarizing one. I thought the drama needed to be dialled down a bit, and if that meant moving me out of environment, fine. Whatever came next, I wanted it to make a real contribution to tackling climate change and building a cleaner future for Canada. After all, meaningful climate action depends on many parts of government—not just environment, but also foreign affairs, national security, justice and innovation. Once again, I was called in to speak to the transition team, this time with Anne McLellan, the former deputy prime minister under Paul Martin, and Isabelle Hudon, our ambassador to France. Interestingly, they asked if I had any advice for the government. I was diplomatic, but frank. I said a lot of our challenges were because we weren't acting as a team. There was a gulf between the prime minister and his ministers and Liberal caucus members. People felt that their perspectives, and those of their constituents, weren't being heard and that it wasn't clear that we were working toward a common goal. They asked what I would want if I could choose my file. I said I was happy to continue at Environment and Climate Change or move to another serious portfolio where we needed to drive climate action and the energy transition.

A few weeks later, I was again called into that nondescript building in Ottawa to talk about Cabinet posts. I walked into the room and sat down with the prime minister. I could see Katie Telford on the other side of the room. The atmosphere had changed. Neither was upbeat or excited like 2015. The meeting lasted about thirty seconds. There were no pleasantries to start, not even a "How is your family doing?" "I'm sorry someone wrote 'cunt' on your office," or "Good job on landing carbon pricing." Instead, the prime minister said, "Catherine, I'd like you to be the minister of heritage."

I was stunned. It made no sense. Heritage was an important portfolio but entirely disconnected from anything related to our climate priorities. I told the prime minister that I serve at pleasure and got up to leave.

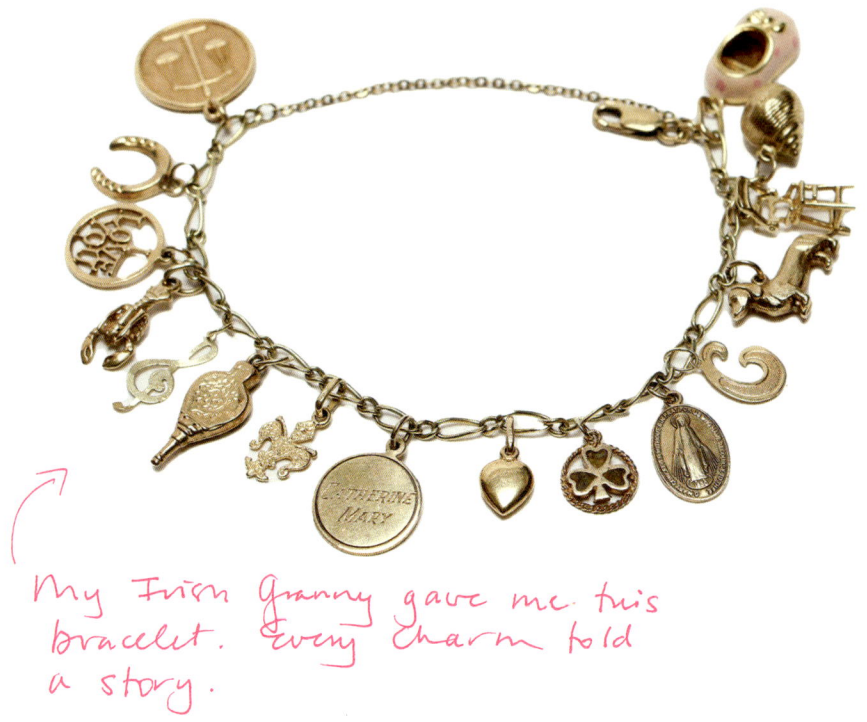

My Irish Granny gave me this bracelet. Every charm told a story.

My head was spinning. My comment and body language must have given it away because Katie ran after me and said, "You know, you get to spend a lot of money at Heritage." I stared at her. I could not have cared less about spending money. I wanted to work on climate change which the prime minister had said was one of his biggest priorities.

I went home confused. I thought, "Maybe I'm missing something." So I read the mandate letter for the previous minister of heritage. And there was nothing there on climate, directly or indirectly. I thought maybe there'd be something about reforming competition laws, something I had a background in. Maybe that's why the prime minister wanted me there. But no. I couldn't understand why he thought I would be good at this file. It's always an honour to be considered for Cabinet, but I had absolutely no relevant experience or connection to the portfolio.

Then, from somewhere inside of me, I thought, "Do I even want to do this anymore?" I didn't care about the trappings of being a minister. After four years of working domestically and internationally on climate change and learning so much,

I knew how much more we needed to do. I wasn't in politics to be someone. I was in politics to do something. And heritage just wasn't it. If that meant no longer being a minister and focusing on being the best member of Parliament for the people of Ottawa Centre, so be it.

I called my sister to make sure I wasn't bonkers. I worried people would be disappointed in me if I decided against joining Cabinet. She said, "Catherine, this is your life. You've got do what is right for you." That settled it.

I asked for a call with the prime minister, which I learned annoyed people at PMO. My chief of staff, Marlo, took an angry call from Katie. She basically told him to get me in line. "Have you met Catherine?" he asked. I loved him for that answer.

The prime minister called. I was nervous. I looked down at the gold charm bracelet that my Irish granny had given me. It gave me strength and when I looked at it, I was reminded of so many stages in my life. I was prepared. I'd thought hard about the three things I wanted to say. First, I told the PM it had been an honour to serve in Cabinet and that I was proud of what we had accomplished on climate. Next, I said that despite my request to keep working on a file relating to climate change, he hadn't seen a role for me in that capacity, and I respected his decision. Lastly, I asked him to accept my decision not to serve in Cabinet, but to support me as I worked on climate as a member of Parliament.

It sounded like he was reading from a script or at least something someone had hastily written down for him. He said that heritage was a really important climate file, without elaborating, and to take some time to think carefully about my decision. I paused. It was one of those moments. I wasn't sure if I should say what I wanted to say, but screw it, I thought. "Respectfully, prime minister, I think you should take some time to think about what I said." And that was it. The call ended. I was shaking, but I knew I had done the right thing. It was my life.

A few days later, just after being sworn in again as an MP in front of my family, friends and members of my team and many volunteers, I received a call from the prime minister. He got right to it. He said, "Catherine, I'd like you to be minister of infrastructure." I was tired and I was about to go to lunch with my kids, so I said, "Can I think about it?" He said I had an hour. I called back half an hour later and said "Yes."

Game on. This was my chance to keep going on climate and to help build a cleaner future for Canadians.

INFRASTRUCTURE IS CLIMATE

When I took over the infrastructure portfolio, many people—mostly journalists—asked me how it felt to move from working on climate change to focusing on infrastructure. I was surprised by this question because infrastructure and climate change are intrinsically linked. What we build today will determine whether we meet our climate goals—will it reduce emissions or increase them— and how resilient our communities are to the impacts of climate change.

My son Cormac made this wind turbine for me when I became infrastructure Minister. I kept it in my office.

Consider what happened to the town of Lytton, BC. In June 2021, it was devastated by a fire, the day after recording Canada's highest-ever temperature—49.6 degrees Celsius (121°F). This tragedy made it obvious that Canada needs to do much more to protect people and infrastructure in the face of climate change.

I also wanted to ensure that every dollar spent achieved multiple outcomes. My mother's thrifty ways taught me to stretch every dollar, which meant ensuring that each tax dollar contributed to growing the economy and creating good jobs, building a cleaner future and improving lives. Infrastructure is an unparalleled tool for making a real difference in Canadians' lives—whether it's better broadband or clean energy for remote communities, new community centres, expanded affordable housing, improved public transit or clean drinking water for Indigenous communities.

My office also moved to tackle the massive backlog of infrastructure project approvals. Despite a sixty-day target for reviews, the system was clogged, delaying investment and frustrating communities. We increased staffing, and I received weekly updates and detailed timelines on every project. Within a few months, we cleared the backlog.

I realized early on that Canada's approach to infrastructure investment too often focused on short-term goals, rather than long-term vision. This wasn't the way to build a resilient future, especially one that addresses climate change and supports a competitive, low-carbon economy. We needed a road map—a comprehensive plan outlining major projects and how to fund them with limited taxpayer dollars. This would be key to leveraging the private sector investment needed to address Canada's infrastructure deficit and build our future.

Inspired by the UK's approach to infrastructure, I launched a national consultation called "Building the Canada We Want." It was designed to collect feedback from Canadians about how to make every dollar count and deliver both immediate and long-term outcomes. This consultation covered everything from affordable housing to clean energy, high-speed broadband and high-speed rail. From the beginning, I was focused on making sure that climate considerations were integrated into every infrastructure investment.

At the same time, the amount of control the prime minister's office was trying to exert over its ministers was becoming unbearable. But after four years in government, I'd learned a few lessons. When one of my staff members said I had to make a policy decision I didn't agree with because the PMO said so, I'd tell my staff that if I didn't recognize the person's name, I was going ahead with my plan because I was the minister. In the unlikely event that the message was coming directly from the PM's top advisors, I'd tell my chief of staff that if it was really important to them, they could call me to discuss it. We'd been told by the prime minister that it was government by Cabinet. Well, I was the Cabinet minister, so the buck stopped with me. I knew that jousting with PMO was hard for my staff, but I think they understood why it mattered.

Things were going well until March 2020. The COVID-19 pandemic hit, turning the world upside down. It was a challenging time, but not without some successes. We developed a bold green infrastructure investment plan that included major investments in electric buses, bicycle and walking paths, urban green space and public transit systems. Our focus was to kickstart the economy and create jobs, help communities recover, and build a low-carbon future.

I also worked throughout 2020 and 2021 to reform the Canada Infrastructure Bank (CIB), created by our government in 2017 as a new model for financing public infrastructure by partnering with the private sector. When I arrived, the CIB had delivered one project—the REM light rail system in Montreal. We knew it could do more. We brought in the legendary Michael Sabia, a leader with deep experience in finance and infrastructure, as chair and appointed Ehren Cory as CEO. The CIB began working with pension funds and private investors to finance projects like a major battery storage project with an Indigenous community in Ontario and an innovative irrigation project in Alberta. By the time I left, the CIB had financed or funded $14 billion in projects, with almost 70 per cent of the financing from private sector partners which included funding for Indigenous projects across the country.

I'm proud of the work we did to help rebuild Canada. After the pandemic, we had a choice—and we decided to invest in things that would matter for years to come. I like to think that one day, a father and daughter riding a new subway line might talk about how it got built. Maybe the father will say, "There was a tough time when everything felt uncertain. But instead of pulling back, we chose to build—so people had jobs, and life got a little easier."

The word "infrastructure" is a bureaucratic term that doesn't capture how transformative the things we build truly are. Investments in new affordable housing or better public transit can change lives. I saw this firsthand when we built a footbridge in Ottawa Centre across the Rideau Canal. It quickly became an essential part of daily life for students, workers and local businesses. It wasn't just about concrete and steel; it suddenly changed how people connected and lived.

BEING ELECTED AND GETTING STUFF DONE

DON'T MESS WITH MY FAMILY

Catherine McKenna
Aug 10, 2020

Please see my statement regarding the incident that took place at my office in #OttawaCentre:

Thursday's incident was not a one-off or an isolated occurrence.

My family, my staff and I deal with abusive behavior on a regular basis.

That is unacceptable and I am commited to working across party lines to make it stop.

Social media platforms need to accept a share of the responsibility as well.

These people just want attention. The only attention they should get is from law enforcement.

The proper authorities have been notified.

👍😮😢 771   638 comments 74 shares

When I left the Environment and Climate change portfolio for Infrastructure, I thought the attacks, harassment and hate would end. They didn't. In fact, what was happening online was often happening in person.

People would call my office and yell at my staff. We would get disturbing threats in letters or packages with bizarre contents. My neighbours, who were always watching out for me, noticed strange incidents like when a car with some men inside pulled up in front of my house and took selfies with my house as a backdrop. I reported the incident to Ottawa Police Chief Peter Sloly, who immediately took my concerns seriously, and explained that the video was likely meant to be a "trophy" that was later posted online.

Of course, some of this had started before. There was the infamous incident involving the c-word written on my campaign office. Another time, my kids and I were headed to a movie near our house one night. I was walking and my kids were skateboarding. A guy driving his car by the theatre stopped in front of us. I thought he was going to ask for directions. Instead, he started swearing, "Fuck you, Climate Barbie," and began videotaping and continuing to hurl abuse at me. I knew that as soon as he left us, he'd post that video of my kids and me online. It was terrifying, because now it involved my kids.

And it wasn't just folks who were on the right of the political spectrum. At an event in Victoria, BC, where I'd come to announce that we planned to make a major investment in conservation projects across the country over the next three years, activists screamed at me, called me a "climate criminal," and tried to arrest me. It was jarring. Thankfully, the RCMP intervened.

But most of the time, I'd report the incidents to the RCMP and it didn't seem like there were any real solutions. I'd hear that the issue was outside their jurisdiction and a matter for parliamentary security or even the Ottawa police. At one point, the RCMP installed a panic button in my house, but I was told it wasn't actually monitored twenty-four hours a day. I asked them if it was better to just call 911. They said if the incident was outside of office hours, that was probably a good idea. I know they were under-resourced, but seriously? I eventually decided to hire an agency to review my house for vulnerabilities and suggest what I could do to make it safer.

I just wanted to do my job but in the back of my mind, I was thinking about what happened to United States Representative Gabby Giffords in 2011 when she was shot during a local meeting. She was critically injured and left with a severe brain injury. Six other people were killed. The perpetrator was a twenty-two-year-old man who was obsessed with Giffords. Then there was Jo Cox, a British member of Parliament who was fatally shot and stabbed right by a fifty-two-year-old male constituent.

He was a white supremacist who shouted "Britain first" when he attacked her. This happened right before she was set to do meetings with her constituents. And this was before the appalling 2020 plot by members of a far-right militia to kidnap and kill Gretchen Whitmer, the governor of Michigan. The male plotters used threats such as "Just cap her" and "Grab the fucking governor, just grab the bitch." In her book, *The True Gretch*, Governor Whitmer spoke about the serious toll the incident took on her family. I got to know Whitmer when I was infrastructure minister and we worked on files together. I can confirm that she is no shrinking violet and wasn't going to let all the threats, attacks and even the kidnapping incident get her down.

My final straw came in August 2020, during the pandemic, when a man came to my constituency office. We'd chosen an office that was on a main street and accessible and open to the public—that was important to me. He came to the door and when one of my staff opened it, he started hurling abuses while filming the whole thing. It was during COVID, so when my staff member opened the door, she explained that the office wasn't open to the public. He then started yelling profanities, before my staff member was able to close the door.

Initially, my staff didn't tell me, because I was with my kids at my parents' house in Hamilton. They didn't want to upset me. They did tell the RCMP, but heard nothing back. Then I saw the video posted on Twitter. I was beside myself. My poor staff member. Not only did I need to protect myself and my family, I needed to protect my staff.

I have to give huge credit to the Ottawa Police. They immediately took the incident seriously, with the Ottawa hate crimes unit launching an investigation. Chief Sloly told me that they were looking out for the guy, as they knew from his social media that he was still in Ottawa.

I issued yet another statement, noting that this incident wasn't a one-off for my staff, myself or my family. I said it needed to stop because it would only discourage more women from entering politics.

I headed back to Ottawa the next day with my kids. I was worried about our safety. I called my chief of staff and said that I needed him to tell the prime minister's office that I wanted a meeting with everyone who was responsible for my security. I said, "We're not doing this anymore. I'm on my own with my kids, and I've got some guy screaming at my staff and he's looking for me. It's time the people responsible for my safety took it seriously."

A meeting was hastily organized with the various security agencies and departments for the next day. It was like I wasn't even there. First, they spent time passing the buck about who was actually responsible for my safety at different times of the day and in different places. The RCMP reminded everyone that they only provided security when they deemed there was a significant risk. I asked for my risk assessment which they refused to disclose and cited security clearances. I reminded them I was a minister and had top-security clearance. Then more excuses. (Incredibly, I would later learn that my colleague, the defence minister, Harjit Sajjan, was also denied access to his risk assessment). Next, I listened to each agency explain how it was only responsible for my security in specific circumstances. I lost my cool. I said, "I don't give a damn about jurisdiction. I'm one person and whether I'm on the Hill, off the Hill, traveling for work, at home, or at a park with my kids, I'm only being targeted because of my job. It's not a random thing that my campaign office was targeted or that my constituency office was targeted or that people harass me and my family on the street or take weird pictures in front of my house."

I was furious. "If anything happens to me or my family, I'm holding all of you responsible."

"So let's just get real. Do you know where this guy is currently? The one hurling abuse at my staff? Do any of you know?"

Someone answered, "Ma'am, for all we know he could be in Calgary."

"He's here in Ottawa," I exploded. "The Ottawa Police know where he is."

At some point the RCMP increased security and took the protection of ministers, including myself, more seriously. I still think about Gifford, Cox and Whitmer. Canadian politicians of all parties and backgrounds are much more vulnerable than we admit. I sincerely hope someone doesn't pay an unconscionable price.

LEAVING ON YOUR OWN TERMS

I have three children, so I'm always worrying, "Where are things going off the rails? Which of my kids is having a hard time with school, friends or life?" I often wake up at night and lie there, staring at the ceiling. I know it's not particularly productive, but I know a lot of moms who do the same. As my mom says, "You are only as happy as your least happy child."

Like so many kids during the pandemic, mine were struggling. Infuriatingly, students in Ontario had to spend more time at home and online than in any other jurisdiction in North America. They were bored, irritated and pretty down because they couldn't see their friends or do any of the normal things teenagers want to do. The teenage years are enough of a challenge for kids and their parents without throwing a pandemic into the mix.

Kudos to parents who figured out how to keep their kids motivated during that time, because I sure couldn't. I could barely motivate myself. Ten months in, I had completely run out of ideas. I ordered a bunch of board games that were lying around unopened because no one felt like playing, including me. I rented a friend's cottage at one point, thinking that maybe spending part of the winter in the wilderness would break up the monotony and offer us a change of scenery. That distraction lasted a few weekends, then we were on lockdown again.

I tried to rally the kids to go for a walk now and then to get some fresh air, bribing them with slushies at the convenience store, but they didn't want to walk, and who could blame them? When I was a teen, the last thing I wanted to do was spend time with my parents.

I worried about my youngest son, Cormac, in particular. I was on his back constantly about how much time he was spending online. One day, he just looked at me, laughed, and said, "Love me less, Mom. I'll be okay." That made me laugh, too, which I needed.

Harping on my kids about their lack of motivation probably wasn't the best strategy, and I lightened up a bit. I still felt like a terrible mother.

Slowly, I realize now I was being too hard on myself. Everyone was struggling then. It was a global pandemic, for God's sake! But it was hard not to worry because I could see how frustrated and down my kids were. They'd been through so much.

It wasn't just the pandemic. They had gone through their parents' breakup. They had to watch their mom get attacked daily at her job. I started to think I owed them more than what I could accomplish fighting for their futures in the political arena. I started to think I owed them my time.

Plus, I was lonely. I felt cut off from so many of the people I loved. I was longing to hang out with my friends, parents and siblings. My dad was over eighty, and I worried about how much time we'd have left to spend together. So I'd stare at that dumb ceiling fan trying not to count the hours I wasn't sleeping. As it did for so many people, the pandemic magnified all my worries.

A crisis is also an impossible time to try and set any kind of healthy boundaries around work. I'd tried to put boundaries around my time, but that strategy quickly fell apart. Problems didn't just seem urgent. They were urgent. Businesses were closing in my riding. Many of my constituents were struggling. Our most vulnerable residents were scared and not sure how to access the services they desperately needed. It was never-ending.

Within Cabinet, we were taking nonstop decisions based on information that seemed to change daily. It felt like wartime, especially for ministers on the frontlines, including Patty Hajdu, who, as minister of health, was tasked with overseeing the country's public health response. Anita Anand, minister of public services and procurement, was working day and night to acquire vaccines and other critical supplies. Bill Morneau was designing programs to support individuals, employers and businesses stay afloat in the pandemic. Incredibly, we saw things that in most normal circumstances would take years to deliver happen within days or weeks. We were doing everything we could to support Canadians and save our economy. And in retrospect, some of the most consequential decisions made were the right ones. We got vaccines in people's arms and money in their pockets. It wasn't perfect, but Canada's economy bounced back faster than just about any other country.

The bottom line was that the stakes were stratospheric during the pandemic, and the demands on my time were even more crushing than normal, which left me scant time or energy to devote to my kids when they needed me more than ever.

When women take on demanding jobs, they often say, "I'm a mom first." But if you have a job that requires you to be on call 24/7, those words are empty.

January 2020, ten months into the pandemic, something had to give. My kids needed me, and I needed to be there for them. I was tired of always only being half there, because I was too distracted to give them my attention. I was also deeply aware of how little time was left with them. My eldest was going away to university in a year. My other two would soon follow. Plus, I was turning fifty that August. Was this really how I wanted to spend the next decade of my life?

Landmark birthdays can be tough if you're not in a place in your life that you want to be when one rolls around. But they also serve as markers of sorts. It seemed to me that at fifty, you really had to be significant to yourself, not other people. This was the time to make decisions on your own terms and not be what other people thought I should be. And so, as I stared at my ceiling one night in January, I asked myself whether it was time to leave politics. I spent the next six months thinking that through.

In politics, you're surrounded by people who talk about issues and politics around the clock. They think the work they're doing is vitally important, and often it is. The bubble absorbs so much of your time and energy that it can be difficult to imagine returning to life outside it. That's especially true of people who rise to senior positions and grow accustomed to having an office, a staff, the trappings of power, and a long line of people clamouring to talk to them. That was never my thing. In truth, I found it claustrophobic. I didn't like being bossed around by the prime minister's office. I didn't like being managed by my staff (awesome as they were). I didn't like every second of my day being programmed. I got into politics because I wanted a new government and to help make a difference. I had made a promise to myself, at the very start, that I would leave when I felt I had done what I'd come into politics to do.

Politics is important and honourable, but I'm not sure it should be the whole of a person's life. We all have friends and families; we have causes that are separate from and sometimes even bigger than politics; we should have other kinds of work we like to do, other things we want to learn, and other experiences waiting for us. Politics is important, but there are lots of ways to make change.

By the spring, I knew it was time to move on. It wasn't easy to admit. I felt an obligation to the people in my office, my campaign team, the voters in my constituency, and the many volunteers who helped get me elected. If I'd asked, I knew most would have advised me to keep going. They would have said there was more to do, and I'd be bananas to leave a senior Cabinet position after working so hard to get there.

And let's be real. I was comfortable, but I wasn't rich. If I didn't run again in 2021, I'd be one month short of qualifying for my parliamentary pension. It was a lot of money and future security to leave on the table. Of course, I knew I couldn't just stay a month and then check out, so I'd have to commit to another term. And I

Riding my bike on the Flora Footbridge on June 28, 2021 to announce that I was leaving politics.

A copy of an editorial cartoon by Graeme MacKay in the Hamilton Spectator on June 29, 2021. He wrote on it, "From a proud Hamiltonian to another..."

just couldn't do that. I remembered my grandfather. He refused to take his pension for his time with the Irish Volunteers and said he didn't fight for Ireland's independence for a pension. And while I don't begrudge anyone theirs, I didn't run or get into politics for the money. Ok, I thought. That's settled.

But I also worried that people would get the wrong idea about why I would leave. They might think I wasn't tough enough and couldn't handle the heat. The attacks were awful, especially the personal ones, but I wasn't being driven out. In fact, the haters made me want to stay.

There was one thing I wanted to do before I left: land a massive deal with Doug Ford's Conservative government in Ontario to build more public transit, which included new subway lines in Toronto and a new light rail transit line in Hamilton. In a way, it was ironic that the last thing I would do was a deal with a politician who had been such a nemesis on climate. But we got it done, a historic $12-billion investment in transit projects throughout the Greater Toronto and Hamilton areas, where almost one-fifth of the country lives. It would reduce congestion, cut pollution and create thousands of jobs. That was a high note on which to end.

I set June 28, 2021, as the day. I kept my plan totally under wraps because I wanted to control my own story. I asked a friend who managed events to organize the press conference by the footbridge our government had funded in the heart of my community. I felt very zen about the decision, and you can see that in the picture of me riding my bike to the announcement, with a big smile on my face. Just me and my bike, riding over a bridge the community and I had built together.

In my statement, I talked about why I got into politics, what I'd accomplished. Canada's first meaningful climate plan. Historic investments in infrastructure to improve lives. But I also talked about why it was the right time for me to go. I thanked my parents, my family, my team and the people of Ottawa Centre. I then addressed any girls and young women who might be thinking about politics and whether it's for them:

> "Do it. And when you do it, don't be afraid to run like a girl. I'll be there cheering you on. Every positive lesson you've learned in life will serve you well in politics. Get into politics to do something, never to be something. There's a lot to dislike about this business, but you can make a bigger difference in the lives of more people than you can anywhere else."

I promised that in the future, I'd be 100 per cent focused on climate change, and that was it. I got back on my bike, and went to a coffee shop with my kids to start my new life.

EPILOGUE

EPILOGUE

STILL SWIMMING

To mark my fiftieth birthday and the start of a new chapter after politics, I decided to swim a few kilometres in all the Great Lakes and raise money for an incredible water charity, Swim Drink Fish. With some cajoling, a few of my old U of T swim teammates joined me. We started with Lake Huron and ended in Lake Ontario, celebrating with friends and our swim coach, Byron. Later, when I was able to go to the United States after the pandemic, I visited our former Ambassador Bruce Heyman and swam in Lake Michigan at sunrise, completing the journey.

Great Lakes swimming with Mike, Rebecca and Steve to celebrate my 50th birthday.

MY LIFE NOW

At the Ottawa airport on September 21, 2021 on my way to New York City Climate Week wearing the "Citizen" T-shirt Pete gave me to celebrate my new life.

It's been four years since I left politics. I'm happy to report that life is good. My kids are thriving. Matt and Isabelle are off at university, with Cormac next in line. Scott rented a house a block away after we split and we're good co-parents. Having more time with my kids has been a blessing. Hands down, it's the best part of this new phase of my life. We've been able to travel more together. Recently, we went to Costa Rica and fulfilled a life-long dream to see the rainforest. My kids come and go and when they're all home we hang out and don't do much of anything. Just having the chance to be present in their lives, for as long as I have that chance, feels like the most incredible luxury.

EPILOGUE

A few of my good friends decided to start setting me up on dates with nice guys, but it was my friend Hillary from university and who has known me for over thirty years who nailed it. She introduced me to Peter MacLeod in the summer of 2021. We started talking and that was it. I fell in love. Pete's an amazing dad. He built an organization focussed on the future of democracy, and, yes, he likes open-water swimming, too. Honestly, it couldn't be a better match. We got married in the summer of 2024 on the shore of Lake Ontario and when everyone left, we jumped in.

Sadly, my dad didn't make it to our wedding. We lost him in April 2023. His death was unexpected and devastating for our family. In February, he began to feel unwell, saw his doctor, and was diagnosed with aplastic anemia. It's a rare and serious blood condition we were told could develop quickly or gradually, be manageable or grave.

We thought he'd rally and fight it off, like he always did. He was a robust eighty-four-year-old, still playing golf, still engaged in his community, still making people laugh. He was our strong, invincible, athletic dad, and nothing could sap his fighting Irish spirit.

Two months later, he was gone. It was hard to comprehend how such an incredible life force vanished from our lives. The only saving grace was that I was able to see him more after I left politics, and we spent a lot of time together during the last months of his life. I'm also very proud of my mom. In spite of the grief, she just keeps going. She's a great Granny to all her grandkids, a great mother, as well as a great friend.

A few months after my dad died, my mom, my sister Maureen, and I travelled to Ireland to visit the Irish McKennas. We shared many drinks, laughs and tears reminiscing about our crazy, hilarious, beloved dad. And yes, I swam at the Forty Foot with my cousins to celebrate his memory.

Today, I'm devoting all my work time to climate action. My life can be hectic, but in a way I like, and it's enormously rewarding. For the first time in a long time, I wake up every day excited to go to work. The day after I left politics, I flew to New York to speak at Climate Week, not as a minister or a representative of Canada, but as me. To mark the occasion, I wore a navy T-shirt Pete had made for me with the word "Citizen" printed across the front.

When I left politics, I knew I wanted to take what I'd learned about fighting climate change and apply it on a global scale. I was approached to run climate foundations or to go in-house with large companies to support their climate action, but I wanted to do my own thing and be an entrepreneur again. So, I founded my

I first crossed paths with António Guterres, the UN Secretary General, 20 years before. He is one of my heroes!

company, Climate and Nature Solutions. I have a great team and awesome clients ranging from large companies to cleantech start-ups to organizations working with Indigenous people on large-scale nature conservation. They are all working hard to do their part to build a better world.

Then, unexpectedly, one of my climate heroes, UN Secretary-General António Guterres, asked me to chair a group of experts from around the world to set clear standards for net-zero pledges and call out corporate greenwashing. As he put it, "The world is in a race against time. We cannot afford slow movers, fake movers, or any form of greenwashing." We worked our butts off over six months and with our amazing group of global experts, we launched our report, *Integrity Matters*, with the UN secretary-general at COP 27 in Egypt.

I was affiliated with the Columbia Climate School for a few years where I worked with super smart young people working on climate, and now I'm associated with my alma mater, the London School of Economics, working with its Just Transition Finance Lab. I'm constantly inspired by the passion of young people to tackle climate change.

After I left politics, the French government awarded me the Légion d'honneur for my work on the Paris Agreement. It was the most wonderful thing. The ceremony was hosted by the Canadian ambassador to France, Stéphane Dion, whose "Green Shift" plan had inspired me years before, alongside Kareen Rispaal who was our former ambassador to Canada and a friend. The award was presented by Laurent Fabius and Laurence Tubiana, who I had met eight years before when they led the Paris climate negotiations, and I was such a newbie that I didn't even know what COP stood for. Life.

When I travel in Canada, people sometimes recognize me. Recently, when I was sitting at the Toronto airport waiting for a flight, a man came up to me. He said he didn't want to disturb me. He wanted to give me a note. Uh oh, I thought. He looked friendly but my guard went up—a legacy of what I'd had to deal with.

I opened up the note cautiously and read it. It spoke about how he was a Conservative but he found the abuse that I faced and that other female politicians faced unacceptable and spoke up against it. He concluded, "I hope you take consolation that you and others like you are making it easier for the next generation of women (including my three daughters)."

I teared up. Here was a man from a different political party who didn't support most or maybe any of the policies but who could still respect me as a person, and think of me as a role model to his daughters. Monsieur Chrétien was right. Canadians are reasonable. We're fortunate to live in a country where most people are kind too. We can never lose that.

Ms. McKenna,

I did not want to disturb you so I thought I would write this note instead. Because I identify as a Conservative, in all likelihood, we probably would disagree on many issues. I find it quite disturbing the level of abuse that you and many other female politicians must endure. →

Fairmont

EPILOGUE

It is unfortunate and unacceptable and I make a point of speaking out when I see it.

I hope that you take consolation in the fact that you and others like you are making it easier for the next generation of women (including my 3 daughters!)

Luigi

↖ The nicest note!

WOMEN LEADING ON CLIMATE

> "What if I told you that the most powerful force against climate change is a woman."
>
> —Vanessa Nakate, Ugandan climate activist

After a decade of working on climate, I'm more convinced than ever that empowering women is one of the most effective ways to make real change. From boardrooms to classrooms, negotiating rooms to communities, and on the streets, women are stepping up to demand urgent action and push for change. They speak hard truths, challenge the status quo, and refuse to back down. And while the journey is often lonely and the work is incredibly hard, women are pushing us forward, one step at a time.

The facts are undeniable: women are two and a half times more likely to demand government action on climate. They're 60 per cent more likely to use their voices to advocate for change and twice as likely to engage civically on the issue. Companies with more women in leadership roles are more likely to take decisive climate action, including disclosing their emissions. Women leaders in government, business and civil society are driving progress.

Look at Greta Thunberg. What started as one young woman's solitary protest in front of the Swedish Parliament grew into a global movement that mobilized millions of people and pushed governments—including the one I was part of—to take stronger climate action.

Reflecting on COP21, it's clear that women played a pivotal role in the success of the Paris Agreement. The women I met in Paris weren't just there to participate—they were leading, negotiating and shaping the course of those critical discussions at every level. Their leadership was integral to the deal we struck.

I also saw the power of women firsthand again in 2018 when I hosted the "Women Kicking it on Climate Summit" as Canada's minister of environment and climate change. Women from around the world came together to ensure that the Paris Agreement's goals were met and to push for ambitious solutions. The energy in that room was electric. The connections we made helped move the global climate agenda forward, reinforcing that women's leadership is not just important, it's essential.

EPILOGUE

After leaving politics, I founded "Women Leading on Climate", a global network of women leaders committed to driving climate action. In 2024, with the We Mean Business Coalition, we launched a global network at Climate Week in New York. Our event was a resounding success. We set a clear agenda: to demand global leaders triple renewable energy, phase out fossil fuels and develop new, bold climate plans. Leading climate champions, including Laurence Tubiana from France, Patricia Espinosa from Mexico and Jennifer Morgan from Germany, delivered powerful messages about the urgency of collective action. Ana Toni from Brazil spoke about the leadership of Brazilian women on climate and announced the formation of a local network ahead of COP30 in Brazil.

One of our victories came when women leaders, led by Maria Mendiluce, CEO of the We Mean Business Coalition, successfully called out the Azerbaijani government for excluding women from the COP29 organizing committee. It was absurd, given that women make up half the population and are at the forefront of advocating for more ambitious climate action. Following our push, women were appointed. It was a small but important victory.

At COP29, we presented an advocacy letter to UN Secretary-General António Guterres, signed by women leaders from business, politics, and civil society, urging bolder climate action and committing to support his efforts. We also launched the #WomenLeadingonClimate social media campaign, reaching 14.6 million people led by voices from leaders such as Vanessa Nakate, Sophia Kianni, Arizona Muse and Tori Tsui. This campaign empowered women around the world to share their stories, call for more ambitious climate leadership, and demand policies that prioritize climate justice.

Women Leading on Climate will continue to grow and push for bold and transformative change. At a time when many countries are backtracking on climate commitments, women's leadership is more crucial than ever.

Join us at womenleadingonclimate.org

CONCLUSION

CONCLUSION

Life is messy, and as I reflect on its twists and turns, the wins and the losses, I've come to appreciate the unpredictable beauty of it all.

We're all navigating a world that demands we be perfect, yet often rewards us most when we embrace our imperfections. That's the truth I've learned: it's not the neatness of the plan or its execution that makes life meaningful. It's the moments of courage, the willingness to step into the unknown, and the conviction to be true to yourself—even when the world is telling you to be something else. Sure, I've had to make some tough calls, and like everyone, I've made mistakes, but I've learned to trust the messy, unpredictable journey that got me here.

One thing that stands out to me is how much strength can be drawn from others, especially women who step up, speak out, and refuse to be silenced. We need more of those voices—loud, clear, and unapologetically themselves—because the challenges ahead are immense. Whether it's fighting for gender equality, confronting climate change, or simply demanding respect, our voices are our greatest source of power. I've seen the power of collective action, the magic that happens when women come together, amplify each other, and lead with conviction. It's a force that can't be ignored, and it's the key to tackling the world's most pressing issues.

So, as we each find our own way, remember those lines from the Nike ad: "It's never too late to have a life. And never too late to change one." There will be setbacks, moments of doubt, and times when you feel like you're failing. But I promise you—when you choose to live on your terms, stop trying to meet everyone else's expectations and dare to get messy, the world opens up in ways you can't predict. Keep pushing forward. Because in the end, the journey is where you'll find your real significance. And that's something worth fighting for.

ACKNOWLEDGEMENTS

I've done some hard things in life, but writing a book is definitely up there. There wouldn't be a book without the support of so many wonderful people: friends, colleagues past and present, team members, volunteers, supporters, fellow climate warriors, and of course, my family. I'm deeply grateful to all of you.

And to all the others who've been part of this journey–Byron; my swim crew; my book club; the amazing women leading on climate; and everyone in Ottawa Centre–thank you.

Of course, this book reflects my memories to the best of my recollection, and I take full responsibility for any errors.

The idea for this book began as a way to stay sane during COVID. It was dreamed up with my swim friend–and one of the most creative artists and writers I know–Leanne Shapton, the extraordinary art editor at The New York Review of Books. Leanne encouraged me to think differently about what a book could be: a collection of objects and images, each with a story. That approach helped me dive into the unruly archive of things I'd collected over the years and just start writing.

Leanne introduced me to Ken Whyte, my publisher, who she knew from her early days at the National Post. From the beginning, Ken got it. When others questioned why I couldn't write a more conventional political memoir–with a few glossy pages of photos in the middle–he backed the vision. Thank you, Ken and Sutherland House for believing in the power of Canadian voices and stories. And thanks as well to my agent, Sam Haywood whose support provided the space to shape this book in a way that felt true to me.

I'm also incredibly grateful to Kate Hall for designing the book. She found a way to bring clarity and style to what began as a messy collection of images and ideas.

My heartfelt appreciation to all the talented photographers I've worked with in politics and beyond: Adam Scotti, Alex Tétrault, Blair Gable, Martin Lipman, Fatima Said, and David Pike who shot the cover photo. And thank you to the amazing members of my social media team who captured the highs and lows of political life–especially Jocelyn Lubczuk, Riley Lange, Chantalle Aubertin, and Murielle Pierre. I want to thank Liz Renzetti and Wendy Dennis for their early editorial assistance and Kathleen O'Grady for her meticulous eye.

I'm especially grateful to the friends who offered edits, comments, and encouragement. A special nod to those who read every page, especially Joanne Chianello and Caroline Pitfield. Your generosity and insight made this book better.

And then there's my family. The Irish McKennas are the best because they always show up—whether it's braving the Forty Foot or raising a glass at the pub. To Michael McKenna, for painstakingly documenting our family history (building on Aunt Shirley's wonderful work), and to Siobhàn and Dara McKenna for ensuring there was nothing in here to cause serious offence—or family feuds. To Sean, Maureen, and David: thanks for putting up with me bossing you around as a kid and for still always being there for me, now that being the oldest isn't quite the flex it used to be.

Mom, writing this book made me appreciate just how much you did for our family—and for me. You always put us first. And Dad, I imagine you looking down, hopefully proud, and maybe even smiling at how those lessons you taught—especially that hard things are hard—continue to serve me well. I think of you, and miss you, every single day.

To Rosalyn, part of our family from when Matt was a baby until today, there is no way we could have survived and thrived without you.

To Matt, Isabelle and Cormac—my amazing kids. I know every parent says this, but you truly are incredible. You've always been there for me, in good times and bad. You're hilarious (and yes, "THC"—The Honourable Cathy—still makes me laugh), you're kind, and you care. Watching you grow up is hard—but watching who you're becoming is the most beautiful thing in the world.

And Pete—thank you. For that first date. For swimming with me. For believing in me and in this book. For believing that politics can be so much better. And for making our life together. You are the best dad to Quinn and the best partner to me. I love you.

Lastly, my deepest thanks go to my beloved country, Canada, which has given me and my family everything.

PHOTO CREDITS

To the best of my knowledge, all of the photos are mine, family photos or photos taken by my campaign or political team except where stated below. All photos of objects were taken by Blair Gable.

5-6: Nike ad from the early 1990s, "Significant to yourself"
39: Pictorial Press Ltd/Alamy Stock Photo
65: Provided by French G7 Leaders Summit Press Office
79: Scott Gilmore
89: Scott Gilmore
118: Alex Tétrault
129: Nike ad from the early 1990s, "You will tell them yes"
152: Alex Tétrault
154: Adam Scotti
165: Adam Scotti
180: Alex Tétrault (top middle), Jennifer Adler (bottom right)
190: White House photographer
205: Adam Scotti (top right)
225: Martin Lipman
242: Alex Tétrault
257: Alex Tétrault
275-276: Alex Tétrault

INDEX

A
Abbotsford, British Columbia, 258
Afghanistan, 85, 156
Alberta, Canada, 80, 160, 163, 164, 174, 175, 177, 234, 236, 245, 267
Alkatiri, Mari, 92
Anand, Anita, 273
Anderson, Conor, 230, 231
Arctic, 191, 226, 227, 229
Atlantic Canada, 147, 217, 218
Australia, 90, 91, 92

B
Baie-Comeau, Quebec, 34
Bali, Indonesia, 71
Banff Forum, 124, 126, 153, 156
Bardall, Gabrielle, 234
Bareilles, Sara, 192
Baumann, Alex, 46
Bennett, Carolyn, 156
Biden, Joe, 194
Biniaz, Sue, 164
Blair, Cherie, 74
Blair, Tony, 74
Blanchard, Marc-André, 153, 242
Bloomberg, Michael, 200
Bonn Climate Change Conference, 198, 200
Bono, 50
Borges, Niny, 92
Bourlamaque, Quebec, 14
Brison, Scott, 124, 156, 161, 181
British Columbia, 164, 174, 175, 177, 213, 229, 251, 258, 266, 269
Brown, Jerry, 199
Burrow, Sharan, 169
Bush, George H.W., 213
Bush, George W., 121
Butts, Gerald, 124, 154, 160, 175, 177, 241, 242, 244

C
California, United States, 175, 194, 198, 199, 200, 213, 221
Cañete, Miguel, 198
Carleton University, 141, 147, 248
Carney, Mark, 176, 180, 218
Carville, James, 252
Champagne, François-Philippe, 124, 156
Chirac, Jacques, 67
Chong, Michael, 124
Chrétien, Aline, 67
Chrétien, Jean, 52, 67, 122, 171, 172, 243, 284
Climate Barbie, 2, 20, 202, 204, 230, 233, 269
Clinton, Bill, 67, 92
Clinton, Hillary, 67, 194, 195
Coderre, Denis, 171, 172
Cohen, Andrew, 124
Collenette, Penny, 132
Collins, Michael, 11
COP21, 155, 162, 165, 169, 184, 185, 287
COP22, 178, 193
COP27, 284
COP29, 288
COP30, 288
Copps, Sheila, 52, 127
Copps, Victor, 52
Cory, Ehren, 267
Costa Rica, 168, 281
Cotler, Irwin, 78
Cox, Jo, 270, 271
Crosbie, John, 52
Cushing, Mary, 14
Czerny, Michael, 210

D
Davis, Victor, 46
de Chastelain, John, 75
deBrum, Tony, 164
Deese, Brian, 164
de Mestral, Armand, 238
Dewar, Paul, 127, 138, 142, 147
Didion, Joan, 112
Dion, Céline, 70
Dion, Stéphane, 121, 122, 123, 156, 284
Dolan, Mary, 11
Downer, Alexander, 92
Downie, Gord, 7
Dublin, Ireland, 11, 13, 16, 28, 33, 209
Duterte, Rodrigo, 85

E
Earth Summit 1992, 63
École Notre-Dame, Hamilton, 21, 22, 24, 25, 26
Espinosa, Patricia, 288

F
Fabius, Laurent, 162, 166, 167, 284
Fast, Ed, 185, 258
Fergus, Greg, 250
Figueres, Christiana, 168
Florida, United States, 28, 58, 103
Fontaine, Phil, 109
Ford, Doug, 278
Ford, Harrison, 200
Fort McMurray, Alberta, 174
Fox, Michael J., 192
France, 66, 67, 140, 167, 169, 262, 284, 288
Francis, Pope, 94, 210, 211, 212
Freeland, Chrystia, 156, 197

G
Galbraith, Peter, 91, 92
Garneau, Marc, 156
Gates, Melinda, 181
Germany, 198, 288
Gerwig, Greta, 202
Giffords, Gabby, 269
Gilmore, Scott, 80, 81, 84, 86, 90, 97, 101, 106, 111, 113, 126, 194, 251, 252, 253, 281
Goldenberg, Eddie, 122
Goodale, Ralph, 178
Gore, Al, 63
Guilbeault, Stephen, 234
Guterres, António, 90, 283, 288
G7 Summit Bologna Italy, 210
G7 Summit Charlevoix Quebec, 197
G7 Summit Environment Ministers Meeting Halifax, 222

H

Hajdu, Patty, 156, 273
Halliday, Fred, 75
Hamilton, Ontario, 2, 17, 30, 32, 33, 34, 42, 51, 52, 97, 122, 128, 192, 203, 237, 270, 277, 278
Harder, Peter, 153
Harper, Stephen, 119, 121, 122, 123, 136, 153, 155, 160, 161, 172, 175, 216
Hayhoe, Katharine, 235
Heyman, Bruce, 195, 280
Hollande, François, 163
Hopper, Alan, 14
Hudon, Isabelle, 262
Hulot, Nicolas, 222
Hunter, Lawson, 78

I

Ibrahim, Hindou Oumarou, 169
Ignatieff, Michael, 123
Indonesia, 2, 70, 71, 79, 80, 81, 82, 83, 84, 85, 86, 90, 91, 94
Ireland, 11, 16, 17, 28, 33, 34, 40, 50, 84, 169, 209, 277, 282
Iyer, Pico, 70

J

Jakarta, Indonesia, 78, 79, 80, 81, 82, 84, 85, 87
Jobs, Laurene Powell, 200
Jobs, Steve, 200
Johnston, David, 78

K

Kerry, John, 164, 166, 167, 191
Kianni, Sophia, 288
Kiefer, Linda, 59
Kirton, John, 67
Kissinger, Henry, 191
Kyte, Rachel, 1699

L

Lafontaine, Pierre, 186
LaForme, Harry, 108, 109, 110
Lamer, Antonio, 97, 98, 99, 108, 109

Lametti, David, 78
Laval University, Quebec, 75
LeBlanc, Dominic, 243
Leem, Selina, 169
Lévesque, René, 14
Levy, Eugene, 51
Lively, Blake, 192
London School of Economics, 73, 74, 75, 80, 104
London, United Kingdom, 13, 73, 74, 75, 284
Los Angeles, United States, 46
Lucas, Steve, 175
Lytton, British Columbia, 266

M

MacDonald, Byron, 55, 58, 59, 60, 244, 280
MacLeod, Peter, 281, 282
Mandel, Emily St. John, 112
Manitoba, Canada, 178, 230
Marin, Sanna, 261
Marshall Islands, 164, 169
Martin, Paul, 78, 121, 262
Matalin, Mary, 252
Mataram, Indonesia, 71
May, Elizabeth, 186
MC Hammer, 200
McCallum, John, 98
McCarthy, Gina, 191, 195
McDonald, Jane, 160
McGill University, 55, 76, 78, 80, 81, 104
McKenna, Dermot, 94, 199, 209, 210
McKenna, Patrick Joseph ("PJ"), 11
McKenna, Tom, 11, 13
McLaughlin, Audrey, 66
McLellan, Anne, 262
McNair, Karin, 138, 140
McNaughton, David, 242
Mena, Marcelo, 167
Mendiluce, Maria, 288
Metcalfe, Isabel, 141, 252
Mexico, 34, 194, 197, 241, 288
Michaels, Lorne, 191

Miller, Marc, 78, 243
Ministerial on Climate Action, 198
Moe, Scott, 177, 178
Mohammed, Amina, 169
Montreal Protocol, 195, 222, 223
Montreal, Quebec, 55, 119, 120, 121, 171, 222, 267
Morgan, Jennifer, 169, 288
Morneau, Bill, 156, 195, 215, 244, 273
Mulroney, Brian, 34, 52, 197, 222, 223, 224, 243
Muse, Arizona, 288
Musk, Elon, 235
Myers, Mike, 1922

N

Nakate, Vanessa, 287, 288
Naqvi, Yasir, 147
New Brunswick, Canada, 230
New York, United States, 202, 281, 282, 288
Newfoundland and Labrador, Canada, 227, 229
Nichols, Mary, 199
Nielsen, Brigitte, 76
Niroopan, Sharla, 110
North American Free Trade Agreement, 34, 195, 196, 197, 241
Northern Ireland, 11, 50, 75
Notley, Rachel, 175
Nova Scotia, Canada, 222, 242
Nunavut, Canada, 109, 226, 227, 229

O

O'Neill, Heather, 112
Obama, Barack, 142, 164, 187, 189, 190, 192, 194, 195
Obama, Michelle, 192
Obed, Natan, 227
Oh, Sandra, 192
Okalik, Maatalii, 193
Ontario, Canada, 2, 14, 109, 110, 124, 138, 153, 164, 174, 175, 177, 230, 232, 236, 267, 272, 278, 280
Ottawa, Ontario, 80, 97, 111, 133,

140, 153, 156, 157, 179, 187, 195, 210, 223, 224, 234, 242,247, 252, 253, 254, 261, 262, 269, 270, 271
Ottawa-Centre, 127, 128, 132, 138, 140, 142, 147, 153, 158, 183, 252, 253, 264, 267, 268, 278, 291
Ottenbrite, Anne, 46

P

Paola, Sister, 94
Paris, Agreement, 166, 167, 168, 169, 174, 175, 191, 195, 198, 210, 277, 284, 287
Paris, France, 155, 159, 162, 163, 167, 169, 183, 185, 187, 190, 196, 221, 284, 287
Parks Canada, 160, 208, 227, 229
Pearson, Lester B., 66
Perry, Claire, 200
Phillips, Shannon, 234, 235
Philpott, Jane, 153, 156, 241
Poilievre, Pierre, 184, 185, 216, 232
Pruitt, Scott, 196

Q

Qualtrough, Carla, 156
Quebec, Canada, 14, 16, 24, 34, 74, 75, 76, 164, 173, 175, 177, 179, 196, 197

R

Raynolds, Marlo, 160, 195, 196, 264
Reagan, Ronald, 34, 213
Redfern, Madeleine, 109
Ressa, Maria, 85
Restoule, Karen, 109
Reynolds, Ryan, 192
Rispaal, Kareen, 284
Ritz, Gerry, 202, 203, 204
Robinson, Mary, 169
Romson, Åsa, 169
Rudd, Amber, 169

S

Sabia, Michael, 267
Sajjan, Harjit, 156, 271
Sandberg, Sheryl, 113

Sarkar, Rana, 200
Saskatchewan, Canada, 174, 177, 178, 230, 236
Scheer, Andrew, 232
Schwarzenegger, Arnold, 221
Scotti, Adam, 154
Seth, Reva, 107
Shaker, Yasmin, 74, 104, 107, 108
Shapton, Leanne, 59
Short, Martin, 51
Shultz, George, 213
Skoki, 237
Sloly, Peter, 269, 270
Solomon, Evan, 236, 237
Sophie, 131, 192
Southeast Asia, 70, 85, 86
St. Mary's High School, Hamilton, 42
Stein, Janice, 67
Stern, Todd, 164, 187
Stewart, Rory, 85
Strong, Maurice, 63
Students On Ice, 226
Suharto, 80
Suzuki, David, 63, 22

T

Teixeira, Izabella, 169
Telford, Katie, 154, 242, 244, 262, 263, 264
Thailand, 70, 107
Thoenes, Sander, 90
Thomas Aquinas, St., 224
Thunberg, Greta, 287
Timor-Leste, 2, 89, 90, 91, 92, 93, 94, 104
Tokyo, Japan, 70
Toni, Ana, 288
Toronto, Ontario, 13, 33, 52, 55, 58, 59, 78, 110, 176, 223, 230, 244, 253, 278, 284
Trudeau, Justin, 123, 124, 127, 136, 142, 154, 158, 191, 192, 197, 218, 219, 222, 241, 243, 244, 248, 250
Trudeau, Pierre Elliott, 32, 33, 124, 194

Trump, Donald, 193, 194, 195, 196, 197, 198, 200, 218
Tsui, Tori, 288
Tubiana, Laurence, 169, 284, 288
Turner, John, 34

U

United Kingdom, 13, 74, 75, 111, 169, 200, 266
United States, 34, 63, 66, 74, 164, 166, 181, 187, 191, 194, 195, 196, 197, 198, 199, 200, 213, 241, 269, 280,
University of Ottawa, 140, 234
University of Toronto, 13, 14, 16, 55, 56, 57, 58, 59, 60, 230

V

Val-d'Or, Quebec, 14, 75
Victoria, British Columbia, 251, 269
Viera de Mello, Sergio, 92

W

Wainwright, Rufus, 191
Wall, Brad, 177
Washington, D.C., United States, 190, 192, 194, 195, 196, 197
The Weeknd, 192
Whitmer, Gretchen, 270, 271
Wilson-Raybould, Jody, 156, 241, 243

Z

Zhenhua, Xie, 166, 198

ABOUT THE AUTHOR

Catherine McKenna is the Founder and Chief Executive Officer of Climate and Nature Solutions. She is Canada's former minister of environment and climate change, and minister of infrastructure. She is chair of the UN Secretary General's Expert on Group Net Zero, founded Women Leading on Climate, practiced law in Canada and Indonesia, established Level Justice, a not-for-profit focused on providing justice for all, and worked for the United Nations peacekeeping mission in Timor-Leste. She has three children, is an avid open water swimmer, and lives in Ottawa. Find out more about Catherine and what she's up to at her website: www.catherinemckenna.ca.

- @cathmckenna
- @mckenna.ottawa
- @cathmckennaottcen
- @catherine-mckenna
- @cathmckenna.bsky.social